IMAGES
of America

ST. LOUIS CASA LOMA BALLROOM

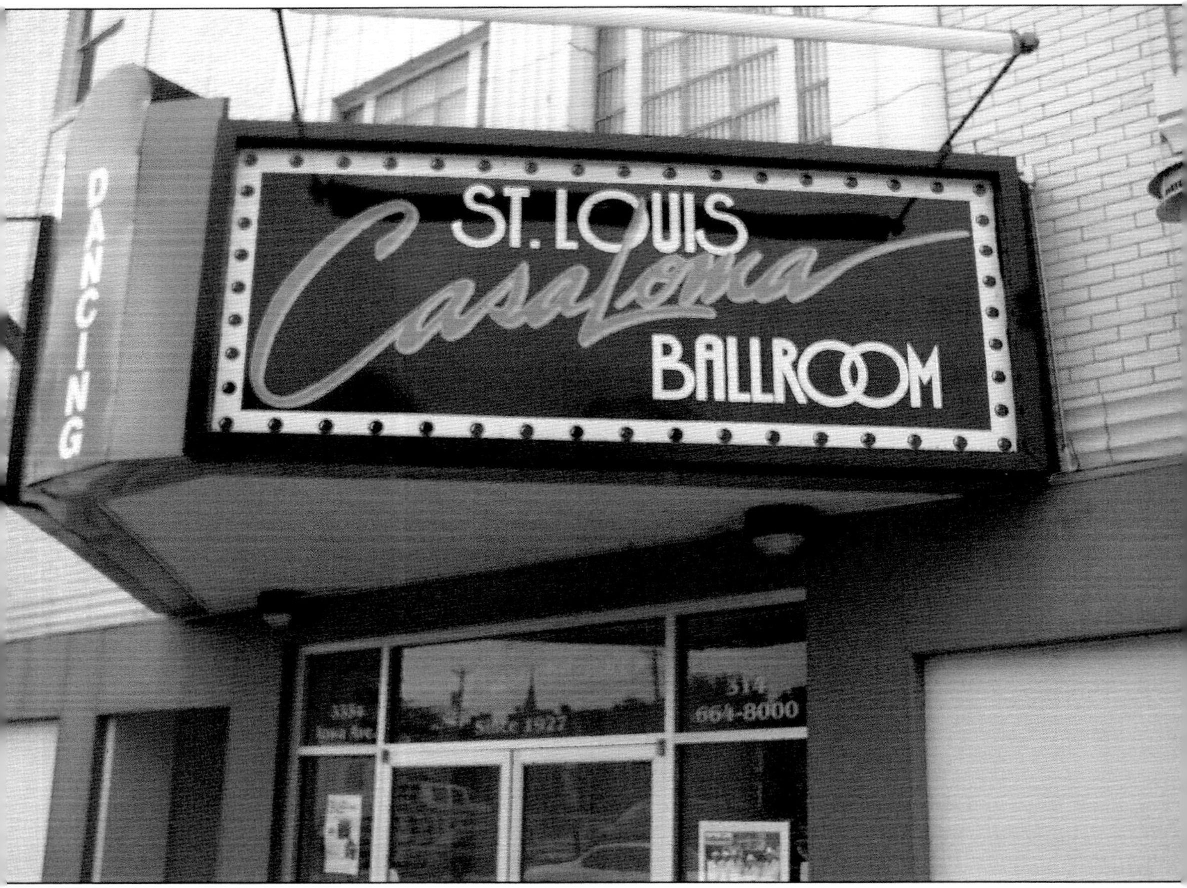

For nearly 70 years the Casa Loma Ballroom, a landmark of entertainment in St. Louis, has provided a wide range of popular music and dancing. Offering the music of such greats as Artie Shaw, Glenn Miller, Benny Goodman, Frank Sinatra, The Harry James Orchestra, the Dorseys, and Bill Haley and the Comets, this unique ballroom has served the young and the young-at-heart of St. Louis. Currently the Casa Loma Ballroom features many great touring acts in addition to the area's best top-name bands. Ballroom music and dancing, rock 'n' roll, imperial swing dancing, and many other activities ensure a full schedule of excitement at the St. Louis Casa Loma Ballroom. (Photo by Dave Lossos.)

IMAGES
of America

ST. LOUIS CASA LOMA BALLROOM

David A. Lossos

ARCADIA
PUBLISHING

ISBN 978-0-7385-3378-0

Published by Arcadia Publishing
Charleston, South Carolina

Printed in the United States of America

Library of Congress Catalog Card Number: 2004117627

For all general information contact Arcadia Publishing at:
Telephone 843-853-2070
Fax 843-853-0044
E-mail sales@arcadiapublishing.com
For customer service and orders:
Toll-Free 1-888-313-2665

Visit us on the Internet at www.arcadiapublishing.com

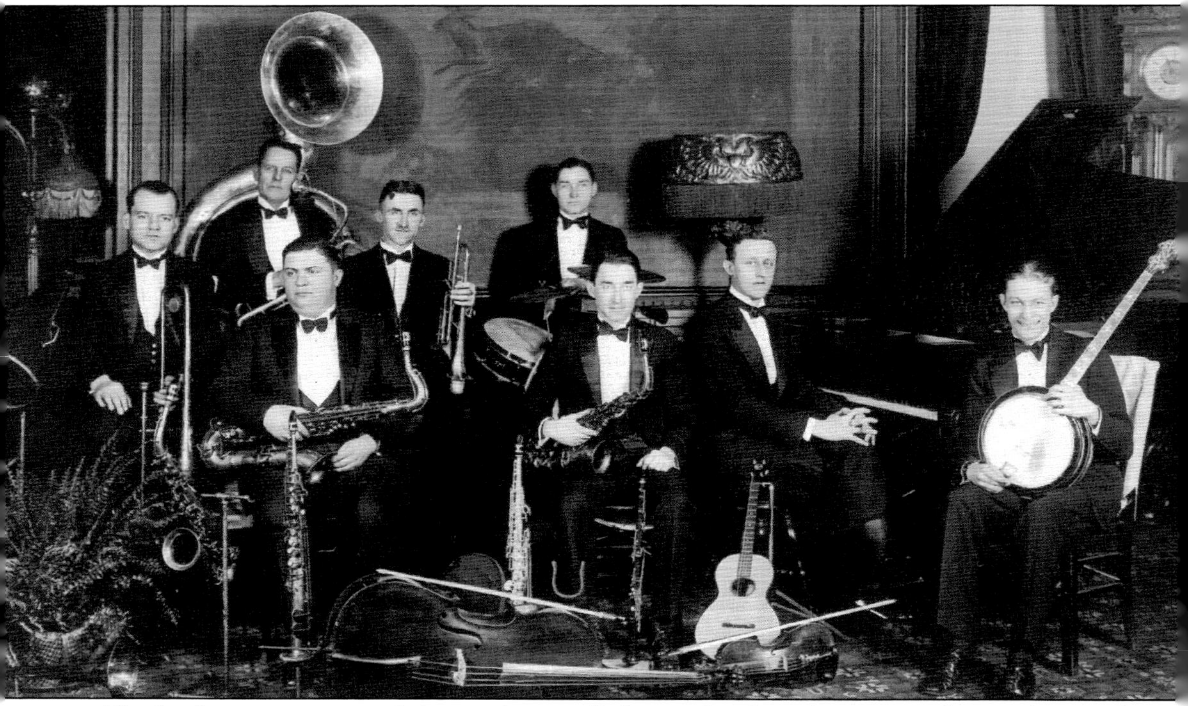

This book contains scores of photos of nationally known bands, orchestras, vocalists, and assorted celebrities who have appeared on the stage of the Casa Loma Ballroom. For each of these there are probably thousands of unnamed individuals in the background who will forever remain unnamed. The group above is my tribute to all those unknown musicians. The Ernie Collins Band, pictured here at a performance in 1926 at the Elks Club of St. Louis, was made up of local St. Louis talent. I'm sure that at one time or another time some of them played at the Casa Loma, but were never personally recognized for their contributions. The only individual I can identify is the drummer, William Ullrich. (Photo from Melissa Ullrich Peters, grand-daughter of William Ullrich.)

CONTENTS

INTRODUCTION

My main concern when I began this project was how much difficulty I would encounter in finding photos of the myriad of performers who had appeared over the years at the Casa Loma Ballroom. My fear quickly disappeared when I found Dorothy Vincent, the widow of the original manager of the Casa Loma Ballroom when it first started in 1935. She had collected over the years personally signed promo photos of nearly everybody who graced the stage over nearly three decades. My dilemma quickly went from not finding enough to choosing which ones to include in this book.

The building at Cherokee and Iowa Streets was constructed in 1927. During the first eight years there were no fewer than five different attempts to make a go of the ballroom business. All ended in financial failure. It wasn't until 1935, when partners Art Kawell and H. J. (Nap) Burian took over the reigns, that the Casa Loma Ballroom came to be. Art, an engraver by trade, and Nap, a department store clerk, had teamed up years before, and successfully managed dances at the Triangle Hall, Concordia Turners Hall, and the Alhambra Grotto prior to taking on the Casa Loma Ballroom. One of the best known trivia bits is that the name of the ballroom was chosen because Art Kawell simply liked the sound of "Casa Loma," not because of the popular group by that name. The irony is that Glen Gray's Casa Loma Orchestra never appeared on the Casa Loma Ballroom's stage. But just about everyone else did. During those early years nearly every big name, and quite a few soon-to-be big names, graced the stage at the Casa Loma.

When "Nap" Burian died in 1958 the Kawells continued to run the ballroom until they finally sold it to Joseph Roelle and Norman and Ellen Reichert in 1967. For a time, during the 1970s, the Reicherts sold their interest to the Roelles. However, in 1980, the Reicherts once again took over the operations at the Casa Loma. I was able to find very little related to that period of operation, other than the well-documented transfer that took place in 1990, when Ellen Reichert retired, and Pat and Roseann Brannon purchased the Casa Loma Ballroom.

Today you will find that much is the same as it was in the beginning. Stepping onto the dance floor is like stepping back in time. The "big bands" still play the same tunes that resonated off the walls in 1935 on most Friday evenings, and the "rock'n'roll" sounds of the 50s and 60s return on Saturdays.

Foreword

Iowa Avenue and Cherokee Street is as well known as any intersection in town because of the common thread of music that has weaved through the years and our lives. If there's a Phantom of the Casa-Loma haunting this venerable ballroom he has been made mellow by the sounds of countless bands, orchestras, combos and singers who have performed over the decades from that hall's hallowed bandstand. From his shadowy perch, probably in a corner of the balcony, he would have witnessed hundreds of thousands of dancers, doing dozens of different dances, as they glided and bounced over the smooth surface of the Casa Loma famous floating dance floor.

The Phantom would, much like his famed counterpart the Phantom of the Opera, likely while away the hours when the ballroom was dark, practicing his dance steps and music, in the dank cold caverns of the old Cherokee brewery deep beneath the building. Even though they are unseen by visitors to our mecca of music, the caves are as real as the dance hall above. These subterranean passages and the Casa Loma have something in common. They are never changing, timeless and hold a great fascination for us all.

As you turn the pages of this book you'll be turning back the hands of time to the Roaring Twenties, flappers, flivvers, and Prohibition, when this corner was first home to the New Cinderella Recreation Hall and Dance Academy, which was renamed the Showboat Ballroom, and finally, in the throes of the Great Depression, re-christened the Casa Loma. You'll relive the terrible conflagration that destroyed the original building before World War II and the construction of the new Casa Loma ballroom, which rose from the ashes like a modern day art deco Phoenix.

What a wonderful thing it would be had the sounds of all the musicians who played Casa Loma been captured there on recordings. Tommy Dorsey, Frankie Yankovic, Stan Kenton, Ralph Marterie, Benny Goodman, Bill Haley & The Comets, Russ Morgan, Jimmy Dorsey, the Glenn Miller orchestra, Ralph Flanagan, the De Castro Sisters, Donald O'Connor, Bobby Darin, Artie Shaw—the list seems endless. Many radio and TV shows such as KSD-TV's St. Louis Hop with Russ Carter originated from the Casa Loma, as well as big band network broadcasts over the Mutual Broadcasting System and the Columbia Broadcasting System. Most every DJ worked that great hall, including: Rush Hughes, Ed Bonner, and yours truly from KXOK; Ed Wilson and King Richard from KWK; Gil Newsome of KSD; Chuck Norman and Dick Clayton from WIL; and many dozens more.

If you're ever in the ballroom before a dance when the long shadows of dusk filter through the windows and no one's around, sit quietly and you'll almost hear the sounds of the players and performers softly playing from the past. And if you half close your eyes you can clearly imagine the dance floor filled with all those people who through the years came for the music, the dancing, and the romance of the Casa Loma.

As home to the Cinderella, Showboat, and Casa Loma, this corner of Cherokee Street has remained a constant in the swirl of commercial change over the decades. Gone are the Cinderella theatre, S. S. Kresge, Kroger, Barney's Army Goods, F. W. Woolworth, Salle Ann shop, Schenberg's market, Switzerland Creamery, Walgreen's, J. C. Penney, Morris Variety, the streetcars, Proper Shoe, 9-0-5, Universal Sandwich Shop, Roy Dixson's jewelry, White Castle,

Schady's barber shop, Park Drug, Libson's, Boxer's, Star Square Auto Supply, Mode-O-Day frock shop, Thom McAn shoes, Neumode hosiery, Dau Home Furnishing, Charlie Houska's grocery, Neisner Bros., and literally hundreds more. These names and businesses, and the people and their dreams have all vanished now, but magically, through music and the efforts of its owners, such as today's Pat Brannon, the Casa Loma legend and future dreams continue as timeless as the cave below.

Long live the Casa Loma!

Ron (Johnny Rabbitt) Elz

One

THE EARLY YEARS

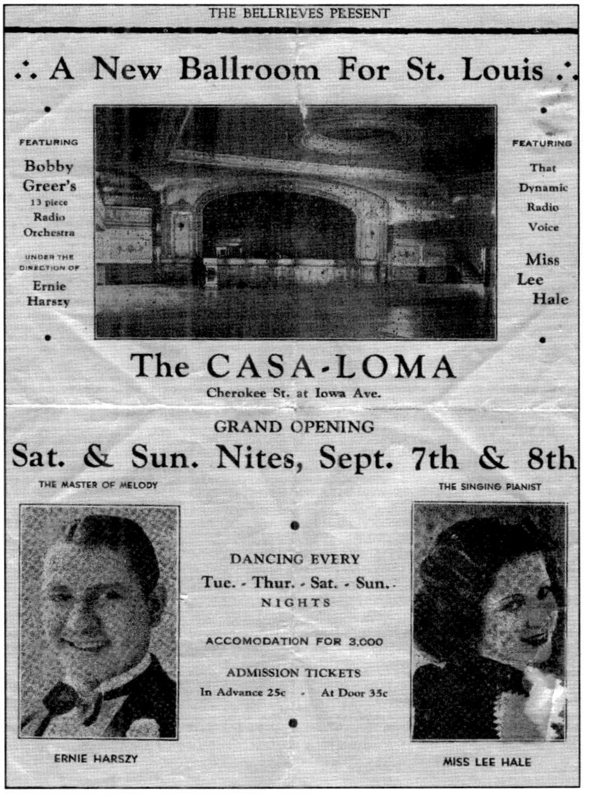

With this advertisement that appeared in the St. Louis Post-Dispatch, a new era in entertainment in St. Louis began on Saturday night, September 7, 1935. A beautiful ballroom known as the Casa Loma began its long and distinguished tradition, bringing the best music in the country through its doors. Opening night boasted the Bobby Greer Orchestra under the direction of Ernie Harzy, with Lee Hale as the featured vocalist. Under the pseudonym of the "Bellrieves," Art Kawell and his partner, H. J. "Nap" Burian, built a St. Louis landmark that still proudly continues the legacy that started nearly 70 years ago. (Ad from Carol Kawell Ellis, daughter of Art Kawell.)

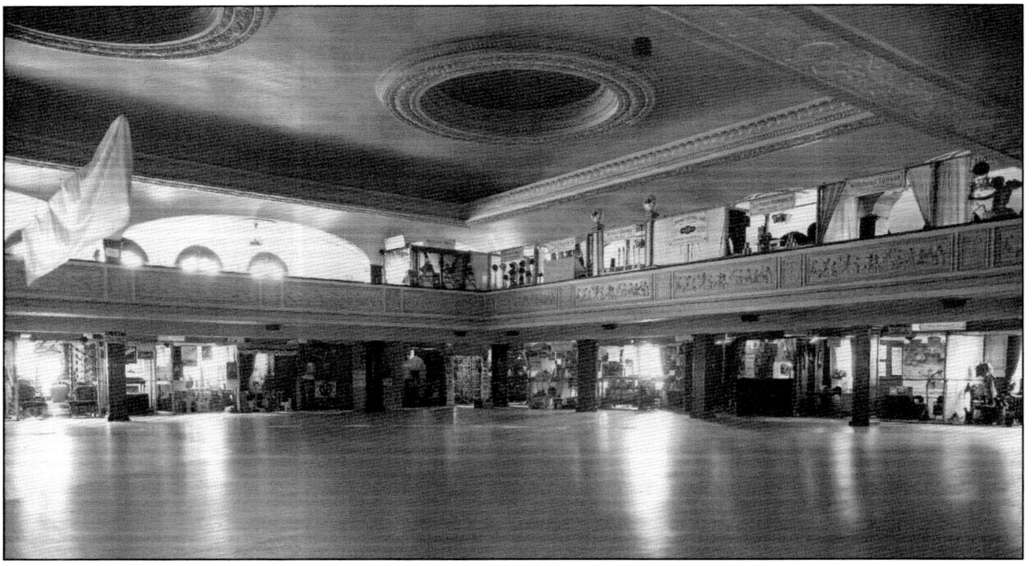

One of the rare photos of the Casa Loma Ballroom as it appeared when first built in 1927. Note the ornate ceiling and balcony railings, along with the various "advertising booths" around the perimeter of both floors. The booths represented local businesses, including Kriwanek Brothers, The Hat Mart, Dilg Schuesser Co., Wessel's Texaco, Cherokee National Bank, A. G. Maass Plumbing, Wilshire I-on-A Co., the new Cherokee Tom-Boy Market, and Schonberg's Markets. (Photo from Carol Kawell Ellis.)

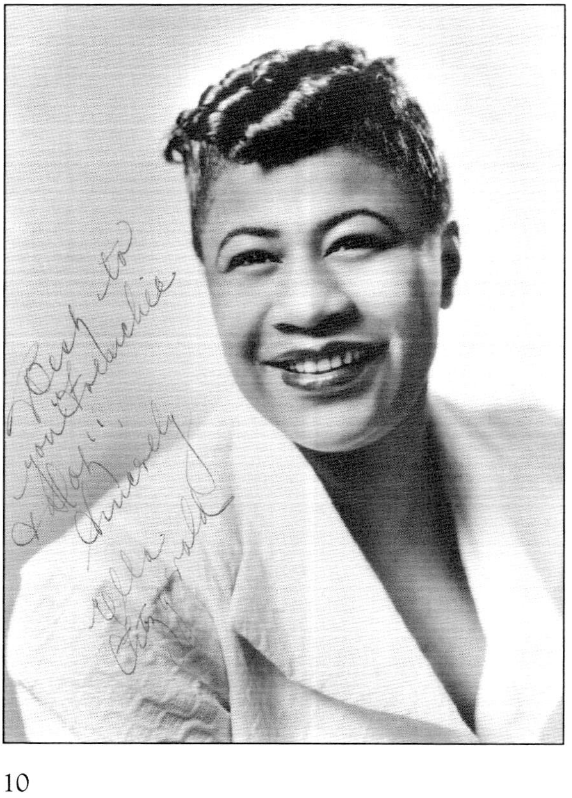

In 1931, Chick Webb formed his own orchestra and it quickly became the house band for the Savoy in Harlem. In 1935, he hired 17-year-old Ella Fitzgerald as vocalist, recognizing her awesome talent at a young age, and made her the vocal soloist of his band. Since she was officially too young to tour, he adopted her and helped to guide her to greatness. Together, they formed a powerful partnership and recorded over 60 songs in the next 3 years, including *A Tisket, A Tasket*, which remained at the top of the charts for 17 weeks. After Webb died in June of 1939, Ella Fitzgerald took over the orchestra for two years, before the group finally broke up in 1942. This photo was given to "Frenchie & Dot" Vincent on the occasion of Ella's Casa Loma Ballroom appearance, with the Chick Webb Orchestra that she then led, on Sunday, November 19, 1939, just a few short months after the death of her mentor and adopted father. (Photo from Dorothy Vincent.)

From the beginning, in 1935, Frenchy Vincent was the manager of the Casa Loma Ballroom. He and his wife Dorothy are pictured here about the time of his retirement in the early 1960s. When I spoke to Dorothy the first time she was quick to point out that, although not employed at the Casa Loma, she was with Frenchy four nights a week. That explains why she has in her possession personalized inscriptions from about 150 performers who played at the Casa Loma during the 1930s, 40s, and 50s. When I asked for a photo of she and her husband in the early years she couldn't find one. I gladly settled for this photo that she carries in her wallet. (Photo from Dorothy Vincent.)

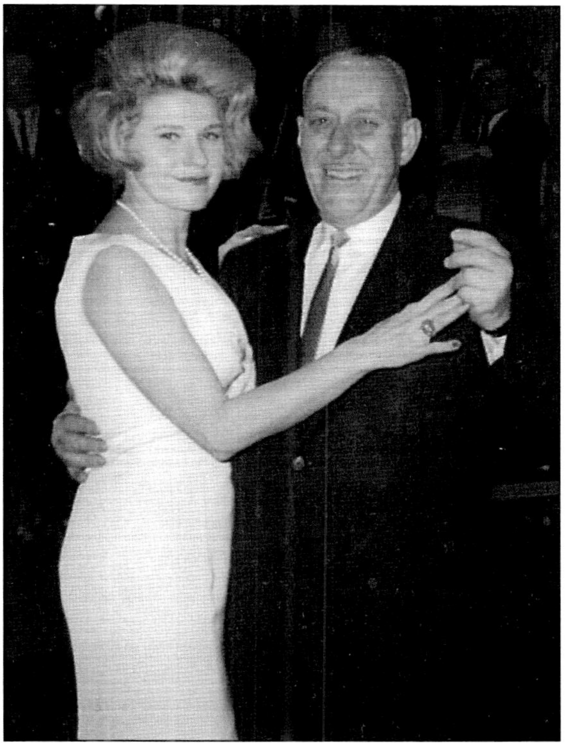

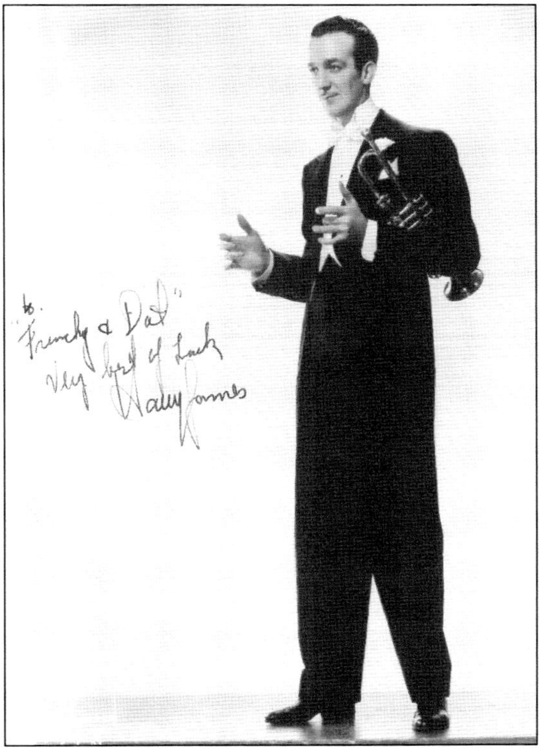

Harry James is best remembered today for his colorful trumpet playing and as the husband of pin-up girl Betty Grable. In 1935, he joined Ben Pollack's orchestra, leaving in December 1936 for the Benny Goodman band. During his time with Goodman, James became very popular with the jazz crowd for his colorful, ear-shattering trumpet playing. He became so popular that when he decided to leave Goodman in December 1938 to form his own band, Goodman himself financed the outfit. The Harry James Orchestra debuted in February 1939. In June of that year, James hired the inexperienced Frank Sinatra as his male vocalist. It was on November 5, 1939, that the relatively unknown Sinatra made his debut at the Casa Loma Ballroom, just barely mentioned at the bottom of the nightly bill. (Photo from Dorothy Vincent. Inscription reads "To Frenchy & Dot, Very best of luck, Harry James.")

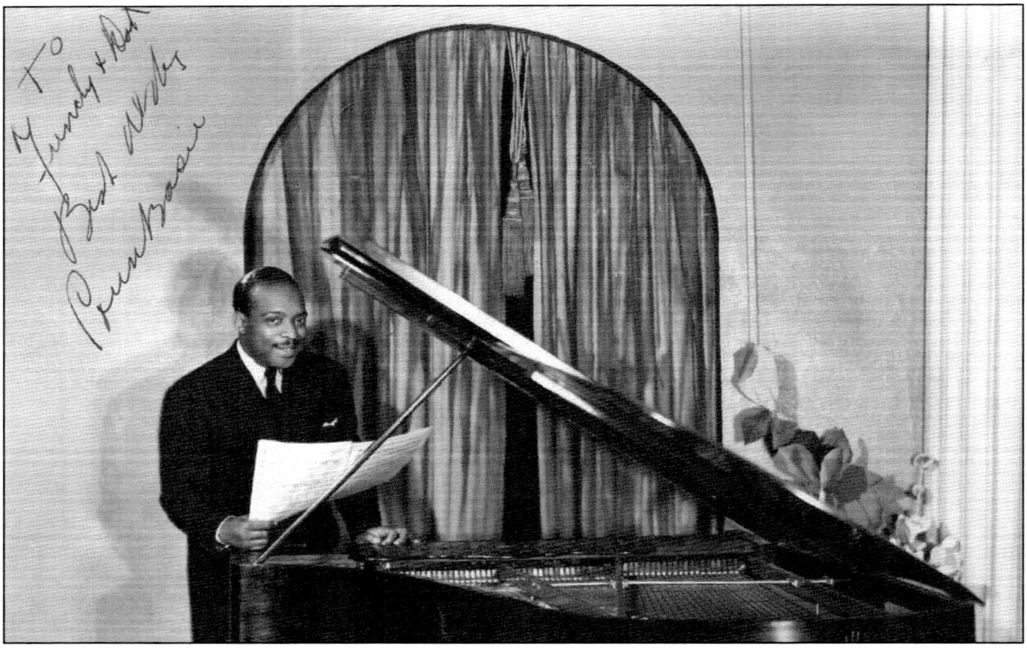

Just a year after their first Carnegie Hall concert, the Count Basie band played at the Casa Loma Ballroom on Saturday, December 2, 1939. Not counting the vocalists, it had grown from thirteen to fifteen members, but just seven of the original thirteen remained. The band still had years of legendary greatness yet to come. (Photo from Dorothy Vincent. Inscription reads "To Frenchy & Dot, Best Wishes, Count Basie.")

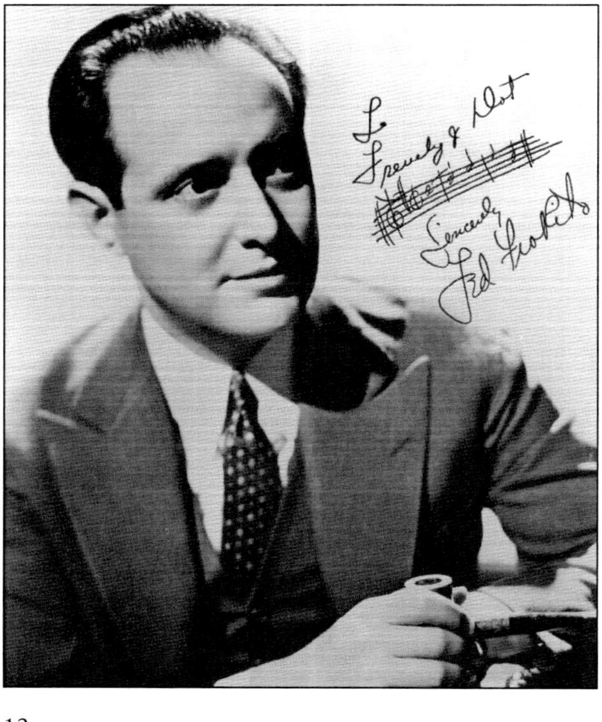

Bandleader and keyboardist Ted FioRito was known for using trick rhythms, temple blocks, musical triplets, and a Hammond organ in his arrangements. Betty Grable was a featured vocalist in the early thirties. Future actor Leif Ericson also sang at one time. In the late thirties, Fio Rito stopped using tricks and modernized his orchestra. On the night of December 10, 1939, the featured vocalist at the Casa Loma Ballroom was Pat Travers. (Photo from Dorothy Vincent. Inscription reads "To Frenchy & Dot, Sincerely, Ted FioRito.")

In 1932, influenced by Guy Lombardo, Jan Garber decided to switch musical styles and began playing dance music. The new group became quite successful, touring the country and appearing on the Burns and Allen radio program. (Photo from Dorothy Vincent. Inscription reads "Cheerios, Jan Garber '39.")

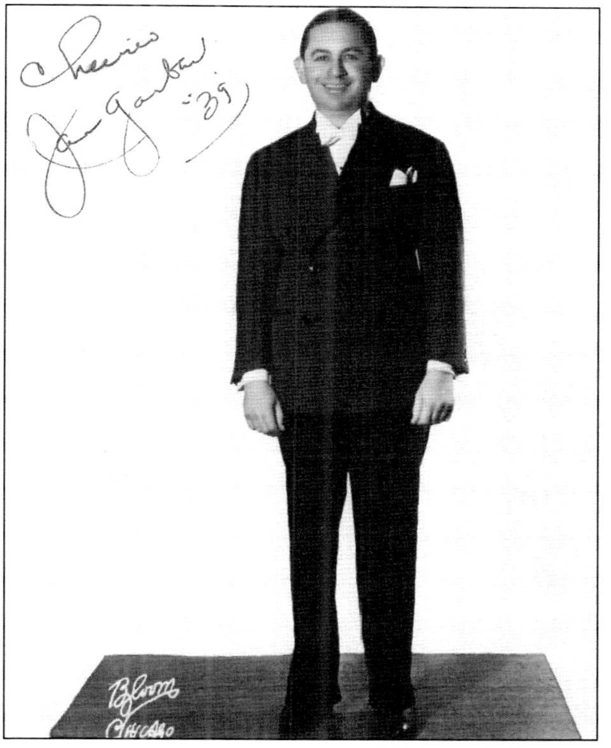

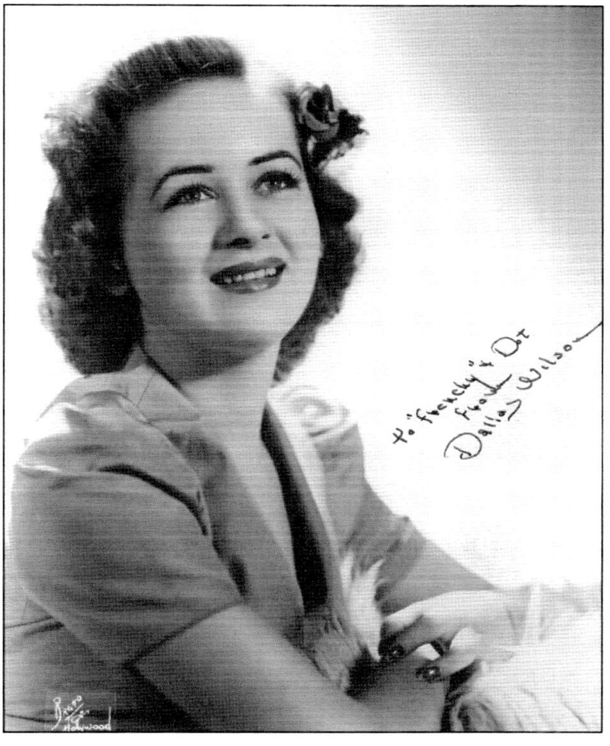

On September 12, 1939, Dallas Wilson was the featured vocalist with the Jan Garber Orchestra when they entertained the crowd at the Casa Loma Ballroom. (Photo from Dorothy Vincent. Inscription reads "To 'Frenchy' & Dot from Dallas Wilson.")

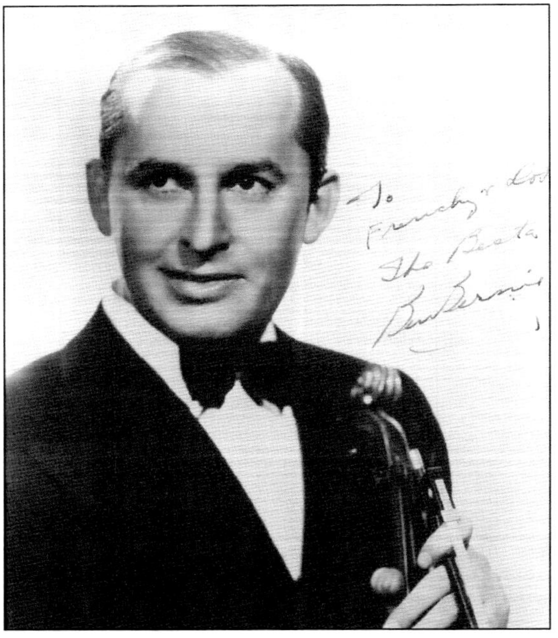

The Roosevelt Hotel in New York was built just in time for Ben Bernie and the 'lads'; they were the first group to play there. Originally scheduled for only a short engagement, the orchestra became the Roosevelt's exclusively from 1923 to 1929. Ben Bernie and his Orchestra remained popular into 1940s, yet they never quite caught the swing bug. He loved cigars and when not holding a violin, he always had one, which perhaps contributed to his sudden illness and death in 1943. This promo photo pictures him as he would have appeared during his Sunday afternoon performance at the Casa Loma Ballroom on October 1, 1939. (Photo from Dorothy Vincent. Inscription reads "To Frenchy & Dot, The Best, Ben Bernie.")

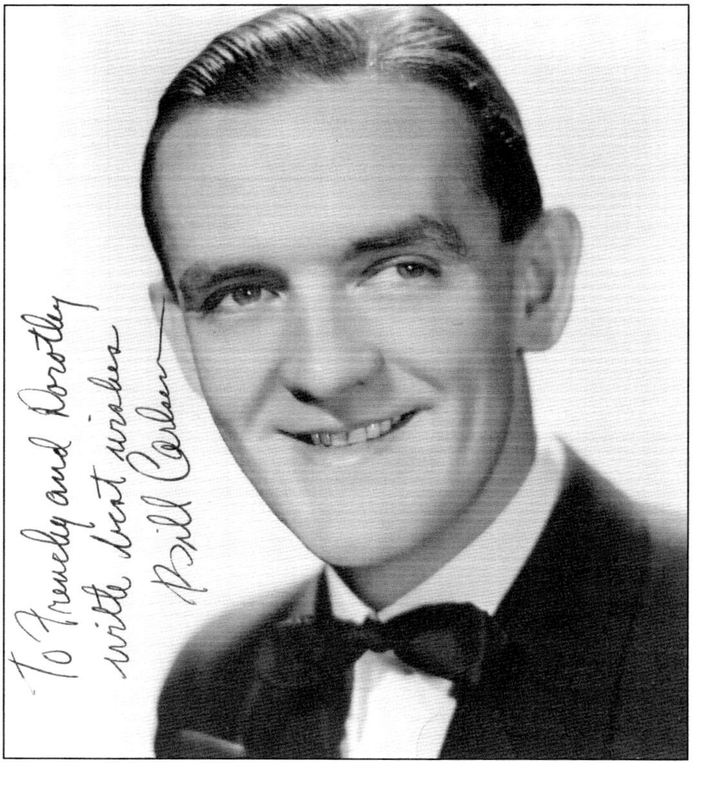

Bill Carlsen, Milwaukee's waltz king, and his twelve piece band played the Casa Loma Ballroom on October 29, 1939. Bill Carlsen was a reed player who directed the house band for a restaurant called The Wisconsin Roof. The band, known as both The Wisconsin Roof Orchestra and the Bill Carlsen Orchestra, was big in the Midwest, especially Chicago. (Photo from Dorothy Vincent. Inscription reads "To Frenchy and Dorothy with best wishes, Bill Carlsen.")

During the 1920s The Jimmy Joy Orchestra toured the Southwest, and cut some sides for the old Okey Record company. In the 1930s, he switched over to a "sweet music" style of band, and became a popular attraction in the Midwest area. He is still remembered for his ability to play two clarinets at the same time. His theme song was "Shine On Harvest Moon." His orchestra performed at the Casa Loma Ballroom on October 8, 1939. (Photo from Dorothy Vincent. Inscription reads "Very best wishes to Frenchy and 'Dot,' Jimmy Joy.")

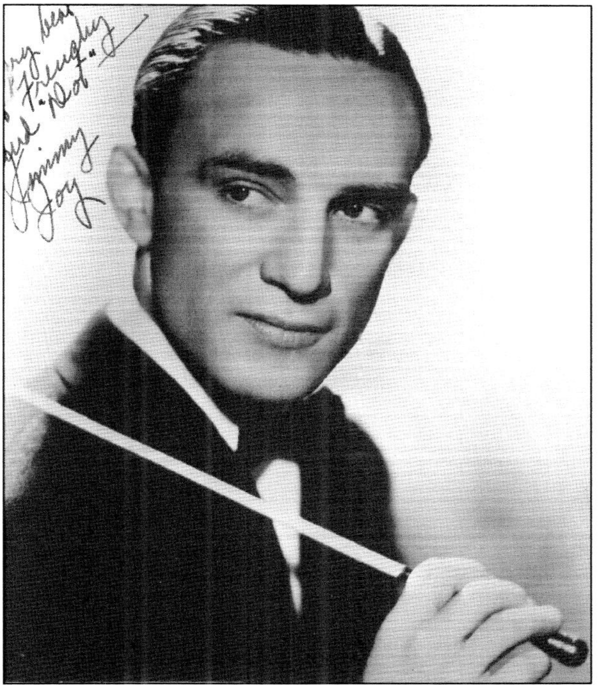

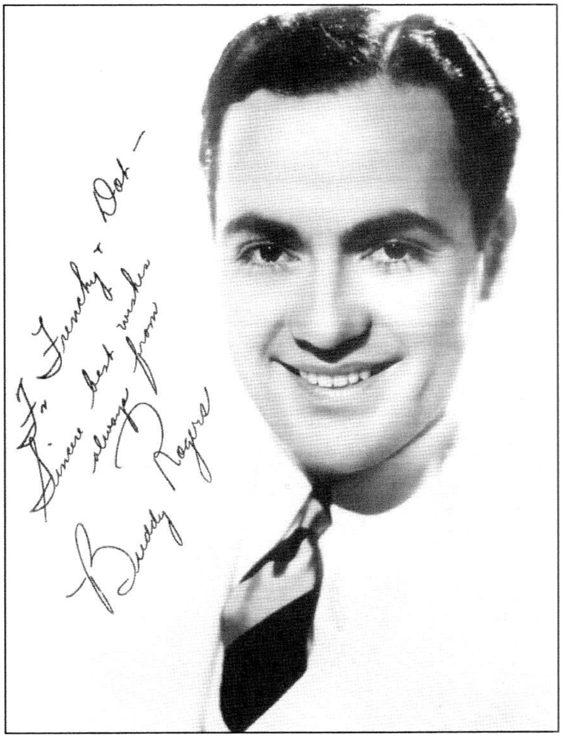

Charles (Buddy) Rogers was as much a movie star as he was a recording artist. He started in silent movies, including *Wings* in 1927, the first movie to win an Academy Award for best picture. His vocal expression helped him survive the transition to talkies, and he continued to appear in movies. In 1932 he toured with a band managed by Richard Himber. Rogers was an instrumentalist as well as a singer, and could play piano, accordion, drums, trumpet, trombone, saxophone, and clarinet. In 1936 he married Mary Pickford, one of the early stars of silent movies and a co-founder of United Artists. He led a band on a radio show in 1937, and in 1938 formed his own dance band. On November 26, 1939, the Buddy Rogers Orchestra entertained the audience at the Casa Loma Ballroom. (Photo from Dorothy Vincent. Inscription reads "To Frenchy & Dot—Sincere best wishes always from Buddy Rogers.")

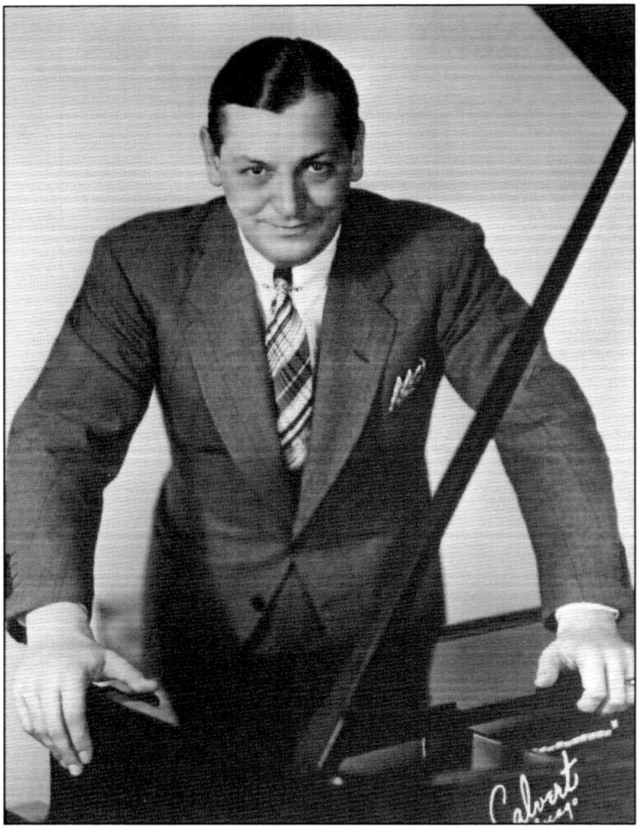

Joe Sanders loved baseball and music. As a young man he sang in local quartets, and in the Kansas City Oratorio Society. Along the way, he also became a well-trained pianist. A chance meeting with Carleton Coon proved fruitful—the two men hit it off right away, and soon formed their own orchestra. When Coon died in May 1932, Joe Sanders started a band of his own which became known as Joe Sanders and His Orchestra. While it was an excellent orchestra, the Joe Sanders Band never achieved the fame of the Coon-Sanders aggregation, and lasted only briefly. Sanders was also a composer. He penned such songs as "Blue Moonlight," "Little Orphan Annie" (a minor hit), "She Loves Me Just The Same," and "Beloved." Joe Sanders and his Orchestra appeared at the Casa Loma Ballroom on September 19, 1939. (Photo from Dorothy Vincent.)

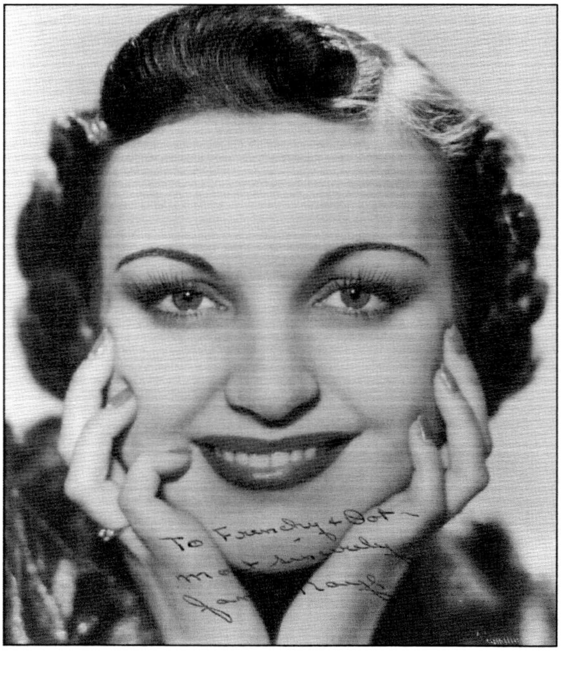

Jane Kaye appeared in 1939 as the featured singer of the Joe Sanders Orchestra. (Photo from Dorothy Vincent. Inscription reads "To Frenchy & Dot—Most sincerely, Jane Kaye.")

The Mitchell Ayres Orchestra was formed in the mid 1930s. The new outfit elected violinist Ayres as its front man. The orchestra appeared in three movies in the early forties before disbanding. (Photo from Dorothy Vincent. Inscription reads "For Frenchy & Dorothy, My very best wishes, Sincerely, Mitchell Ayres.")

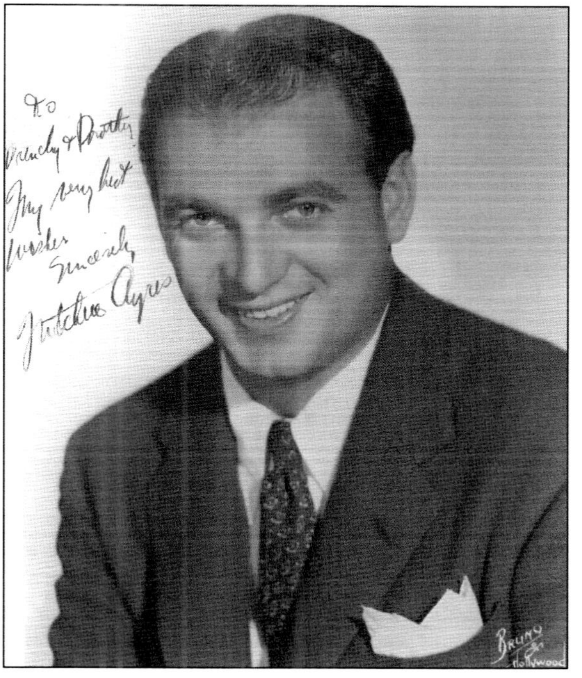

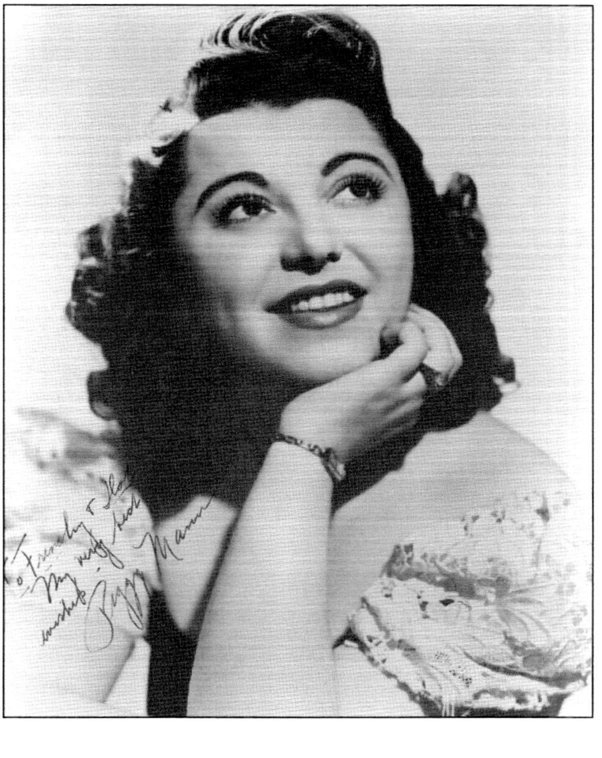

The Mitchell Ayres Orchestra's featured soloist the night they appeared at the Casa Loma Ballroom was Peggy Mann. (Photo from Dorothy Vincent. Inscription reads "For Frenchy & Dot, my very best wishes, Peggy Mann.")

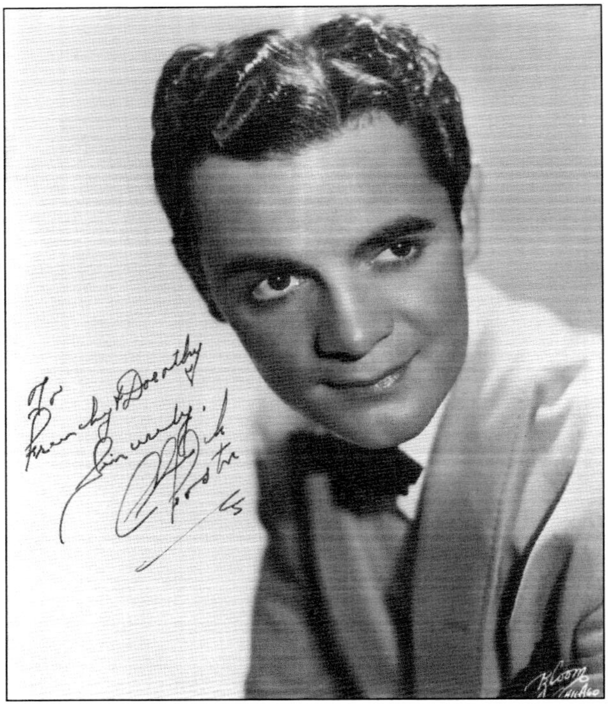

The Chuck Foster orchestra was formed in the mid-1930s. The theme song of the orchestra was "Oh! You Beautiful Doll," which was always vocalized by Chuck. He would look out into the audience, pick out one of the female patrons, and sing the words of his theme just to her. (Photo from Dorothy Vincent. Inscription reads: "To Frenchy & Dorothy, Sincerely, Chuck Foster.")

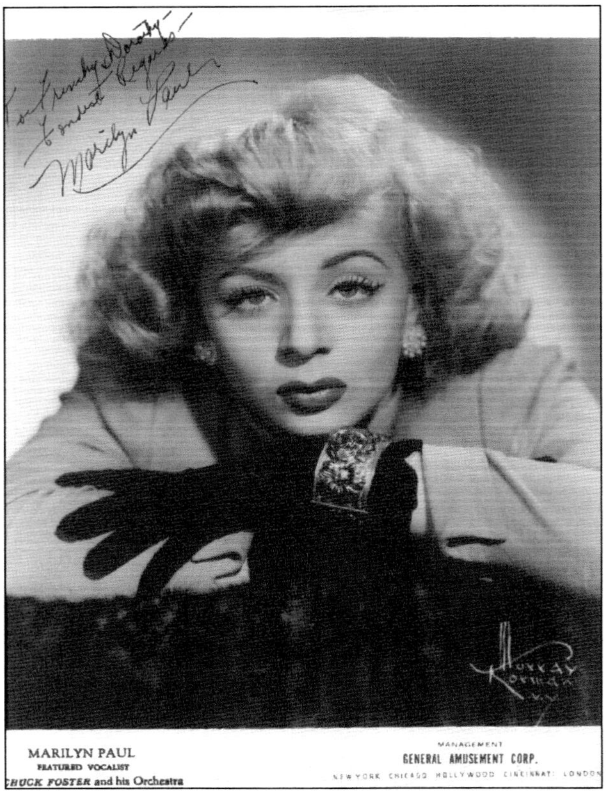

Singing lead vocal that night was Marilyn Paul. (Photo from Dorothy Vincent. Inscription reads: "To Frenchy & Dorothy, Fondest Regards, Marilyn Paul.")

Johnny "Scat" Davis joined Fred Waring in the mid-thirties. With Waring, he became a featured performer and vocalist. Hollywood brought him more opportunities. Starting in 1937, he made 15 films over the next seven years. His most famous role was in *Hollywood Hotel*, in which he introduced the song "Hooray for Hollywood." In 1939 Davis formed his own orchestra. (Photo from Dorothy Vincent.)

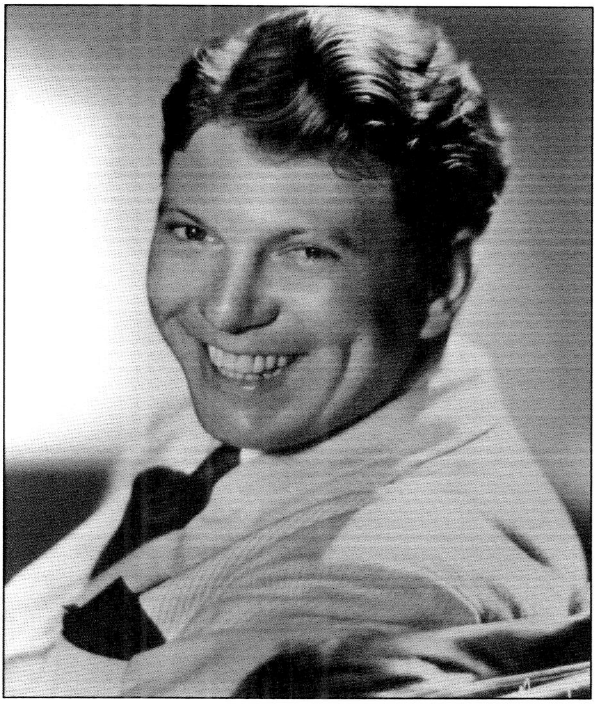

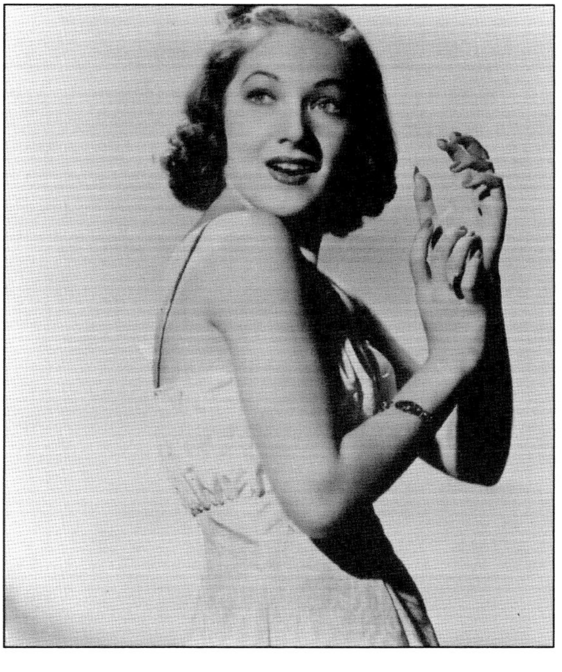

Appearing with the Scat Davis Orchestra the night they played at the Casa Loma Ballroom was Julie Sherwin. (Photo from Dorothy Vincent.)

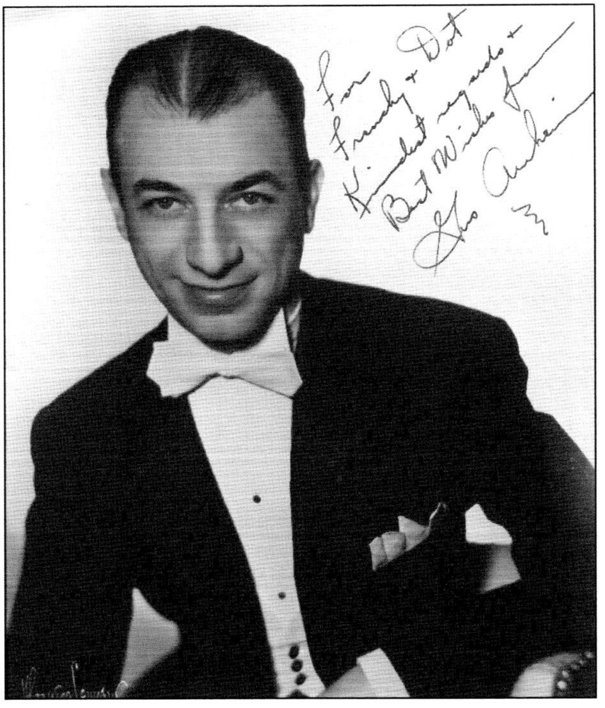

Gus Arnheim's orchestra was formed in 1927 at the Cocoanut Grove in Los Angeles. The most popular band on the West coast, it featured several good singers, including, for a time, Bing Crosby. As a matter of fact, Bing Crosby recorded his first solo hit, "I Surrender Dear," with Arnheim. In the late thirties, Arnheim revamped and updated his group, scoring big at the Congress Casino in Chicago with his new swinging sound. Arnheim alumni include Stan Kenton, Jimmie Grier, Shirley Ross, Russ Columbo, Charlie Spivak, Woody Herman, actor Fred McMurray (sax), and game show host Art Fleming (drums). Arnheim retired from the band business after the war. (Photo from Dorothy Vincent. Inscription reads "For Frenchy & Dot, Kindest regards & Best Wishes, Gus Arnheim.")

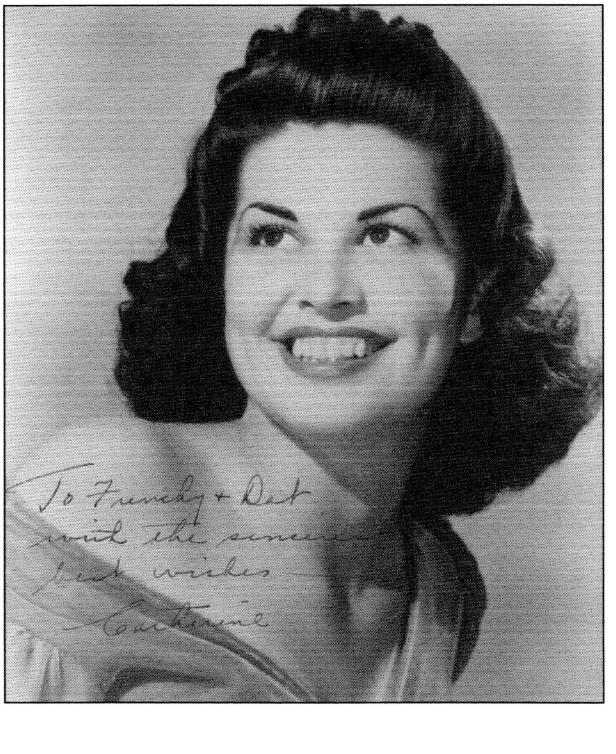

The featured singer with Gus Arnheim's orchestra the night they played the Casa Loma Ballroom was Catherine Joyce. (Photo from Dorothy Vincent. Inscription reads "To Frenchy & Dot, with the sincerest best wishes, Catherine.")

Most of us probably remember Skitch Henderson from the *Tonight Show* with Steve Allen and then Johnny Carson. But his remarkable career started back in 1937 when he filled in for an ailing accompanist for an MGM promotional tour featuring Judy Garland and Mickey Rooney. He then went on to work with Bob Hope, Bing Crosby, and Frank Sinatra (Skitch played the piano on Sinatra's first record). Although this photo is undated, I'd assume it was taken early in his career, based on his youthful appearance. (Photo from Dorothy Vincent. Inscription reads: "To Dorothy and Frenchy, Thanks for the help when I needed it! Skitch.")

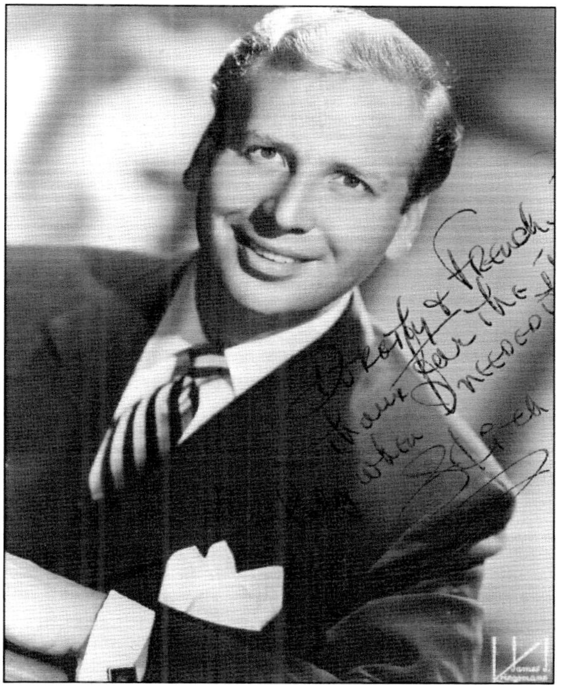

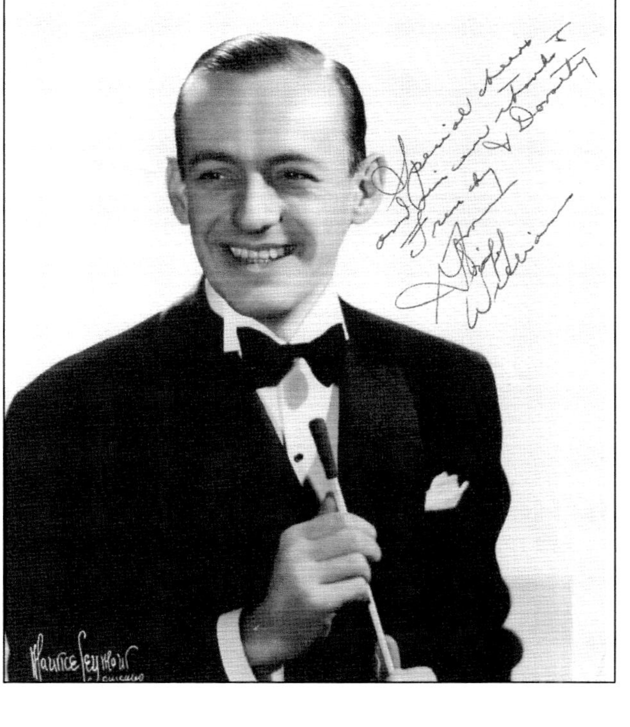

I'm sure the audience at the Casa Loma was agreeing with Griff Williams and his Orchestra's rendition of "We Could Have Danced All Night" played during their appearance on stage. (Photo from Dorothy Vincent.)

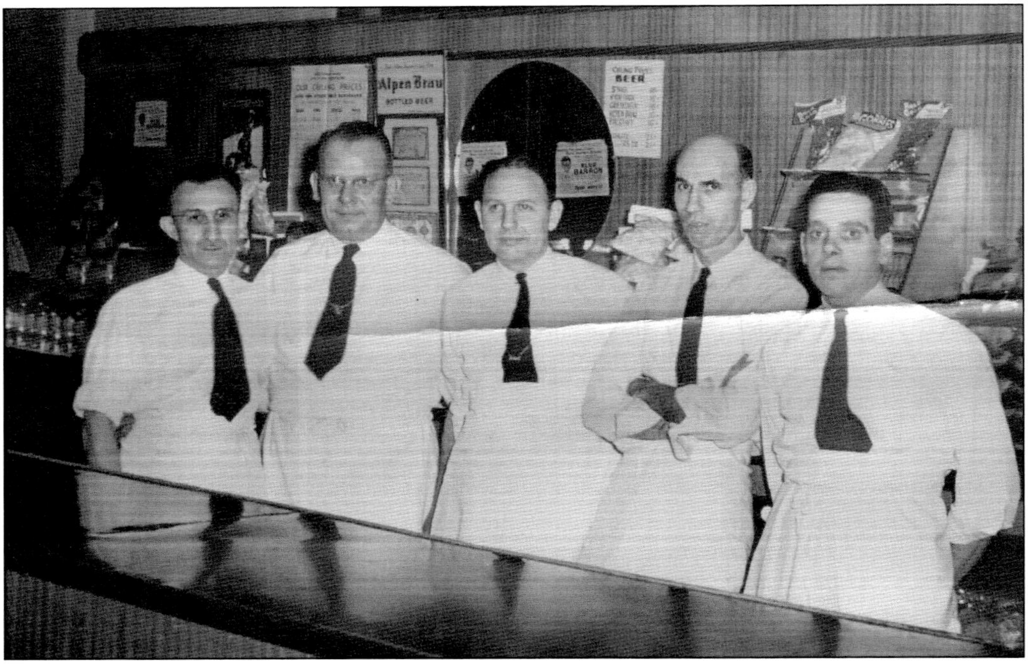

Only sixteen cents for a Stag, Falstaff, or a Griesedieck, but it cost a nickel more for a Schlitz. That's John Buckmueller second from the right. (Photo from Carol Kawell Ellis.)

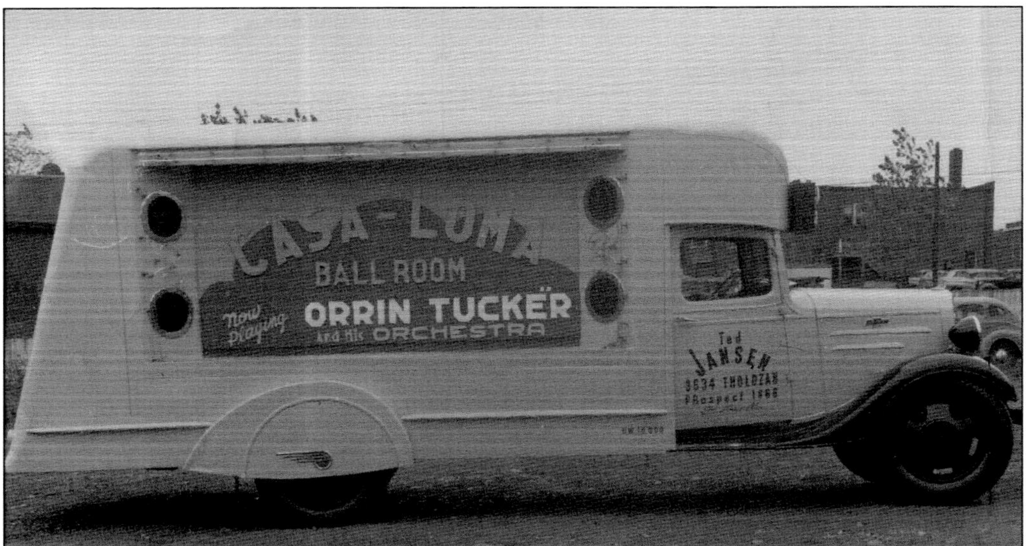

It pays to advertise. This "billboard on a truck" let everyone in St. Louis know that the Orrin Tucker Orchestra was playing at the Casa-Loma Ballroom. A native of St. Louis, Orrin studied to be a doctor, but ended up as a singer and a bandleader. He was leading a successful, though not well-known, orchestra in 1939 when his female vocalist, Wee Bonnie Baker, recorded an old World War I tune called "Oh, Johnny, Oh, Johnny, Oh!" With the help of her sexy sighs and coos, Tucker found himself with a hit record and one of the hottest bands in the country. (Photo from Carol Kawell Ellis.)

Two

The Fire and Rebuilding

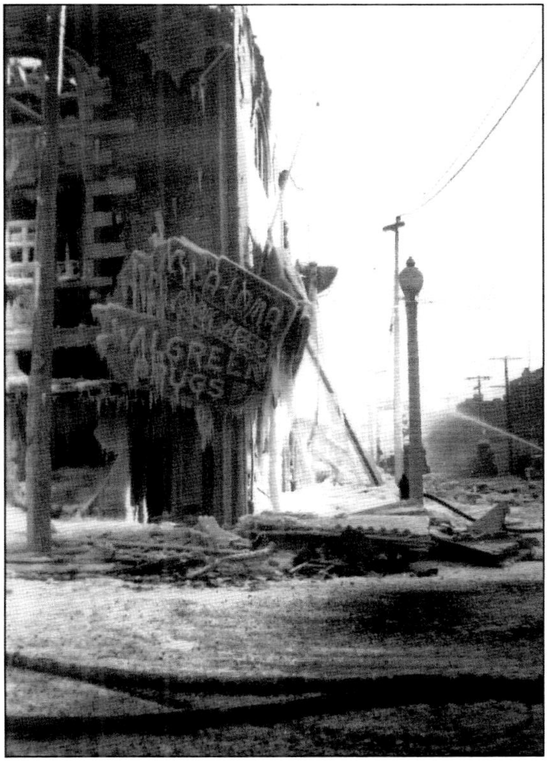

On the evening of January 19, 1940 disaster struck the Casa Loma Ballroom. Subzero temperatures made for some amazing pictures, as shown on the next few pages. By the end of the year, the shell that previously housed the Casa Loma was rebuilt into a new dance hall, very similar to the old one. This photo is taken looking east down Cherokee Street. (Photo from Jeanne Provaznik, taken by her father Edward Provaznik.)

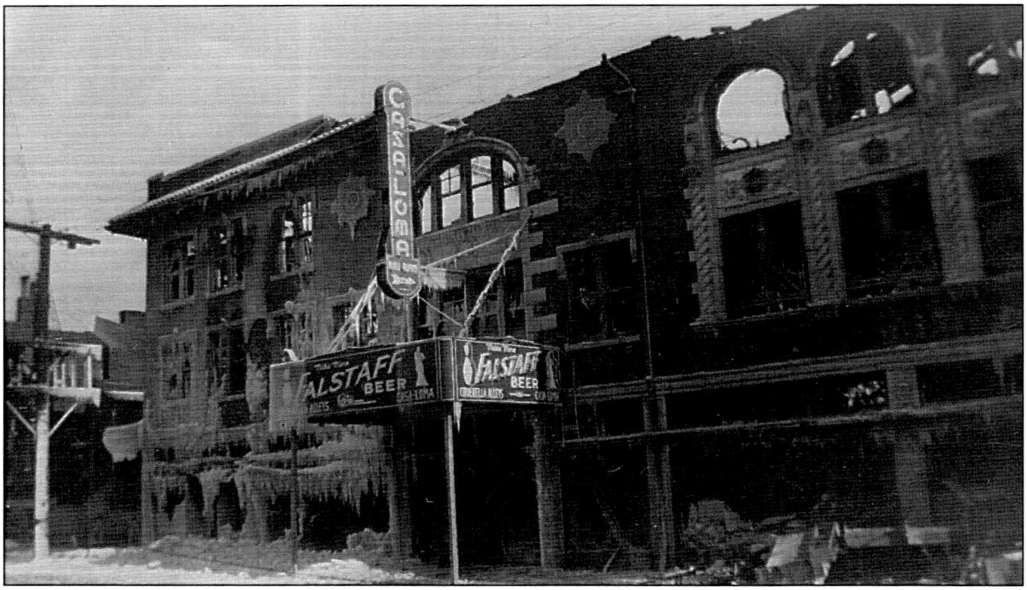

It's hard to believe that this shell was rebuilt into the Casa Loma Ballroom that still stands on the corner of Iowa and Cherokee. (Photo from Carol Kawell Ellis.)

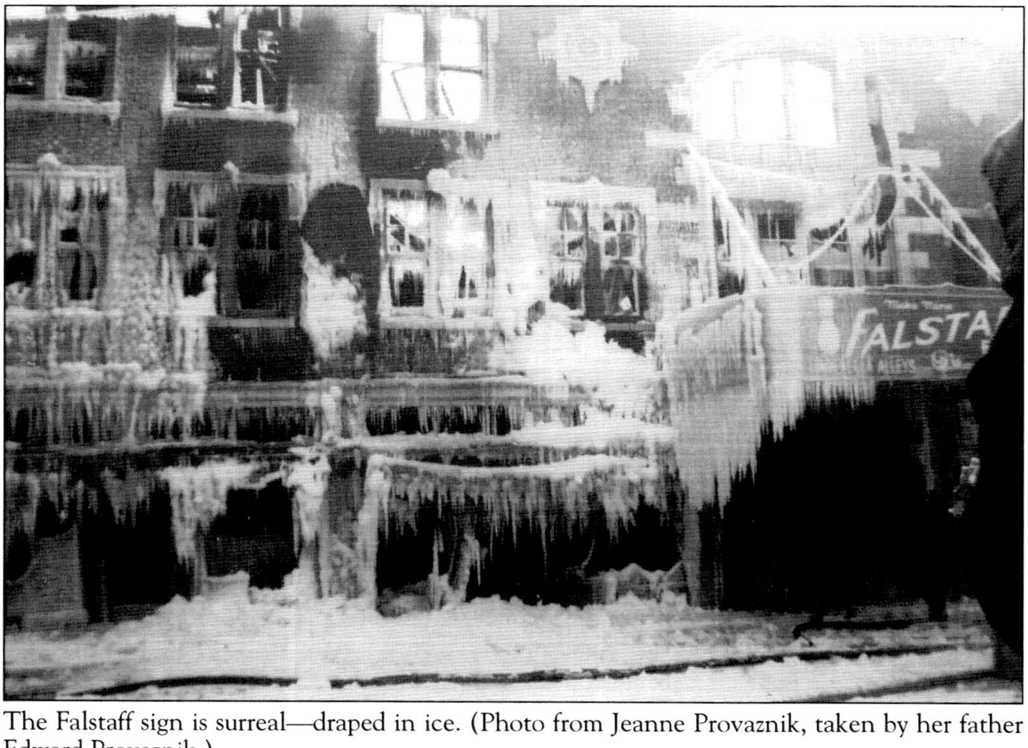

The Falstaff sign is surreal—draped in ice. (Photo from Jeanne Provaznik, taken by her father Edward Provaznik.)

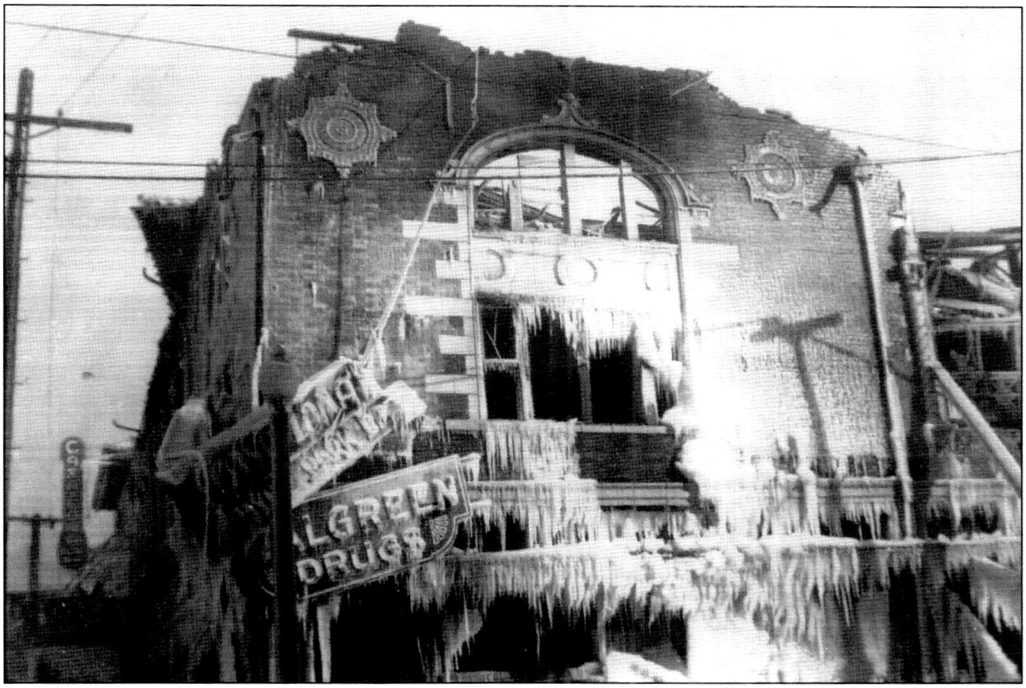

A Walgreen Drugs sign hangs below a remnant of the Casa Loma sign. (Photo from Jeanne Provaznik, taken by her father Edward Provaznik.)

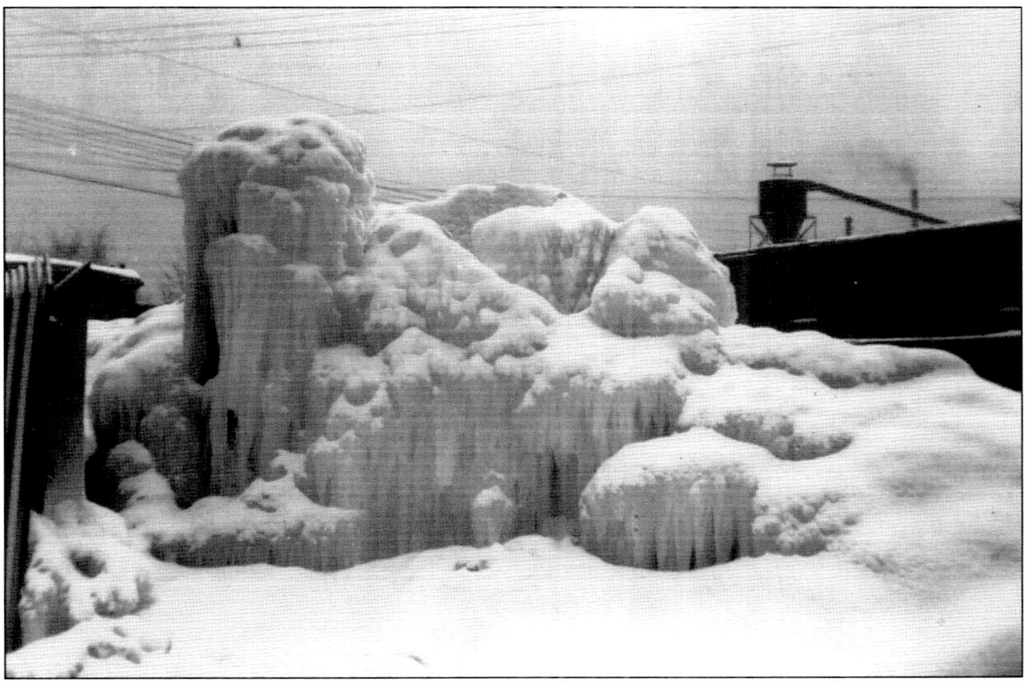

This "ice sculpture" hides the Casa Loma's remains. (Photo from Jeanne Provaznik, taken by her father Edward Provaznik.)

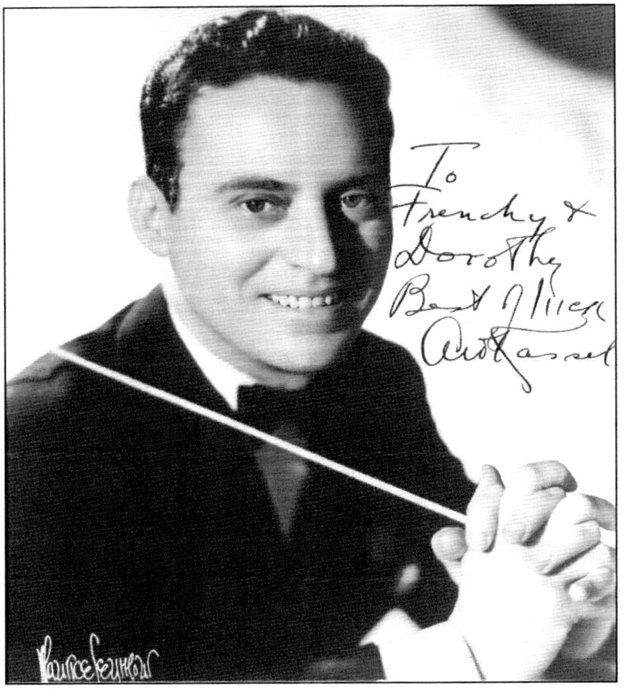

Art Kassel and his "Kassels in the Air" were a staple on the Chicago music scene for more than 30 years. He and his orchestra appeared at the Alhambra Grotto on February 25, 1940, less than a month after the disastrous fire at the Casa Loma. The Alhambra Grotto was used by the Casa Loma management on a number of occasions while the Casa Loma Ballroom was being rebuilt. Art Kassel's theme song was "Doodle Doo Doo." (Photo courtesy of Dorothy Vincent. Inscription reads "To Frenchy and Dorothy, Best of Luck, Art Kassel.")

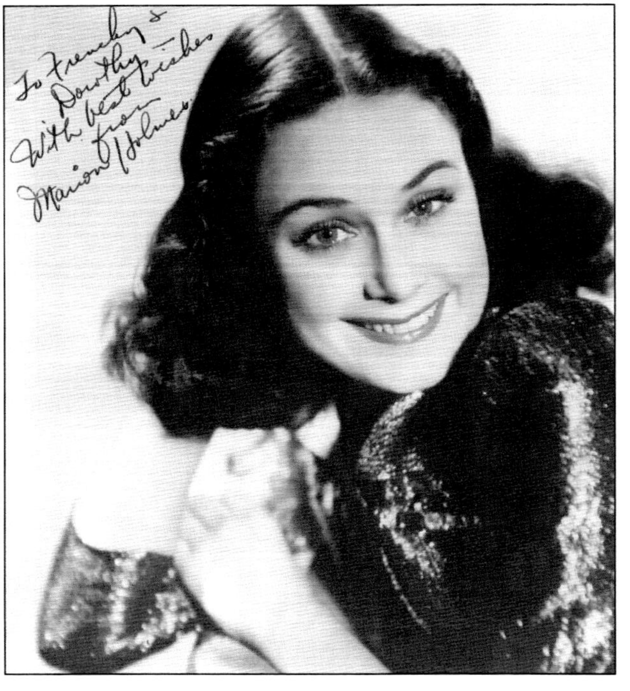

Marion Holmes was the featured vocalist with the Art Kassel and his "Kassels in the Air" Orchestra. (Photo courtesy of Dorothy Vincent. Inscription reads "To Frenchy & Dorothy, with best wishes from Marion Holmes.")

Ironically, it was during an engagement at the Hotel Chase in St. Louis, that Jerome Rohkar legally changed his name to Gray Gordon. This photo shows Gray Gordon with Tic/Toc as part of his signature. He developed the "Tic Toc Rhythm" style in late 1937 while playing in Chicago. He had the drummer, Frank Adams, tapping out a 'tick-tock rhythm' on the Temple Blocks which established the tempo of the song and also identified the band to radio listeners. Gray Gordon and his Orchestra played the Casa Loma Ballroom on a few dates in 1939 and 1940. (Photo from Dorothy Vincent. Inscription reads "Frenchy and Dot—best of luck always, Gray Gordon Tic/Toc.")

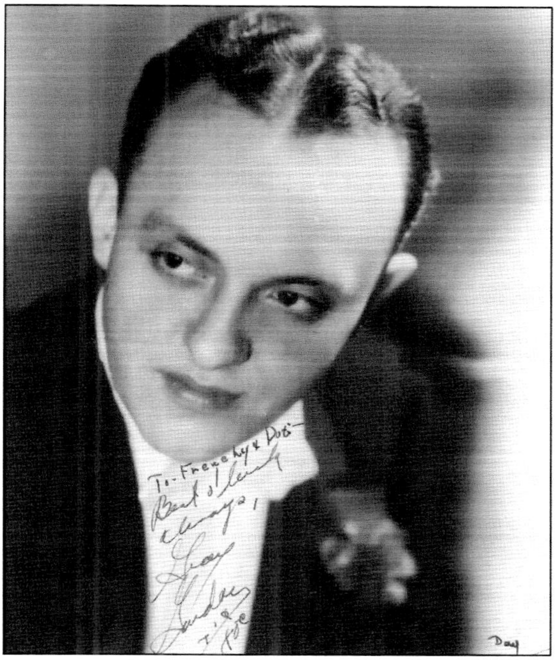

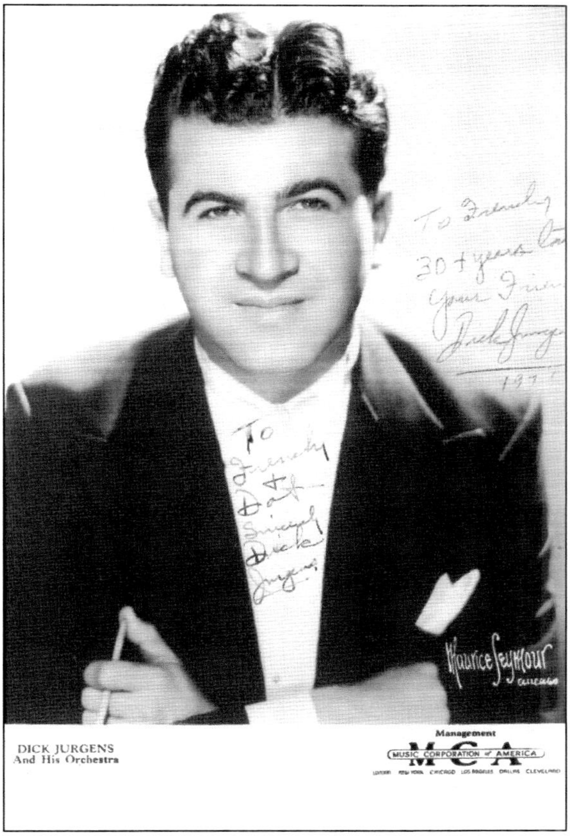

Dick Jurgens had already become an accomplished trumpeter by age 14. Dick and his brother Will formed their first band together. Over time the band developed into a polished ensemble, with a sound that was ideal for ballrooms. Eddy Howard was the orchestra's first singer. In World War II, Dick saw service with the U. S. Marine Corps, where he and brother Will toured the South Pacific war areas with an entertainment unit they had formed. When the war ended, Dick returned to Chicago, where he worked until 1956 when they disbanded. In 1969, 13 years after disbanding, he was asked to form a unit for a club in a suburb of Chicago. The band played there until 1976, when Jurgens retired. The Casa Loma Ballroom had the distinct honor of hosting the Dick Jurgens Orchestra in both the early years and at the end of Jurgens' fine career. This photo was originally signed by Dick Jurgens on the occasion of his performance on December 4, 1939. He signed the same photo nearly 32 years later when he returned with his last group. (Photo from Dorothy Vincent.)

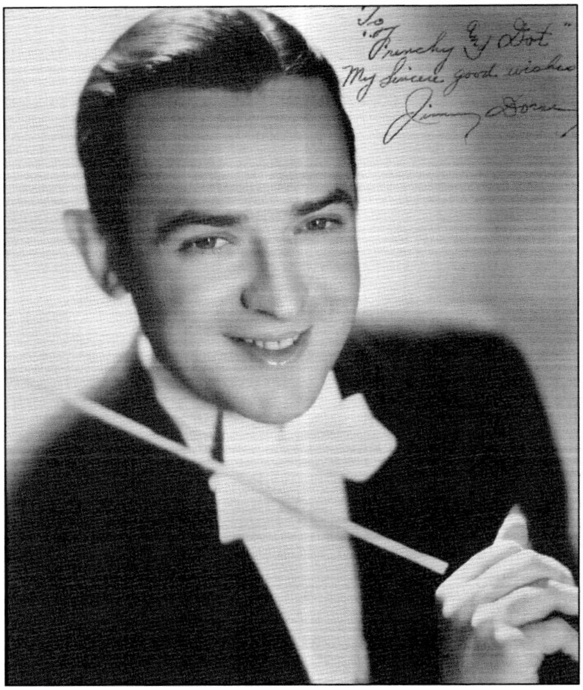

Jimmy Dorsey and his orchestra played at the Alhambra Grotto in February 1940 while the Casa Loma was being rebuilt. (Photo from Dorothy Vincent. Inscription reads "To Frenchy and Dot, My sincere good wishes—Jimmy Dorsey.")

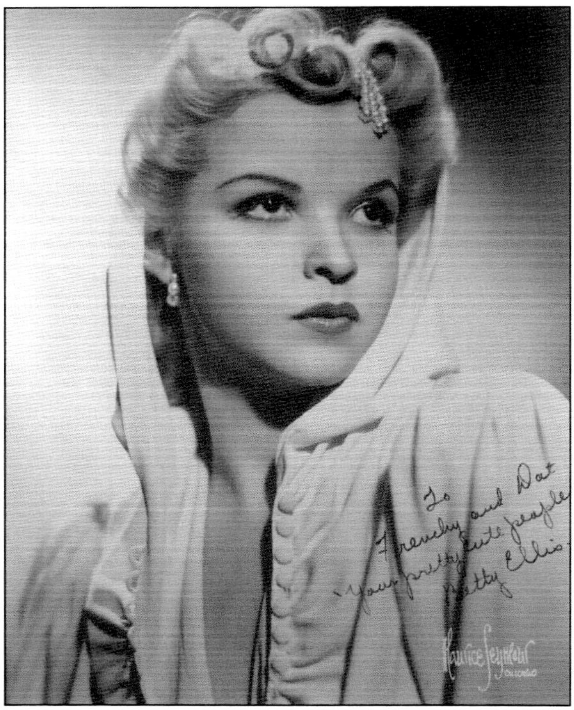

Another venue used by Casa Loma management during the reconstruction of the ballroom was the Hotel Jefferson. Pictured here is Betty Ellis as she appeared at the benefit dance there in February 1940. She was the female vocalist with the Tony Di Pardo Orchestra. (Photo from Dorothy Vincent. Inscription reads "To Frenchy and Dorothy, 'Your (sp) pretty cute peoples'—Betty Ellis.")

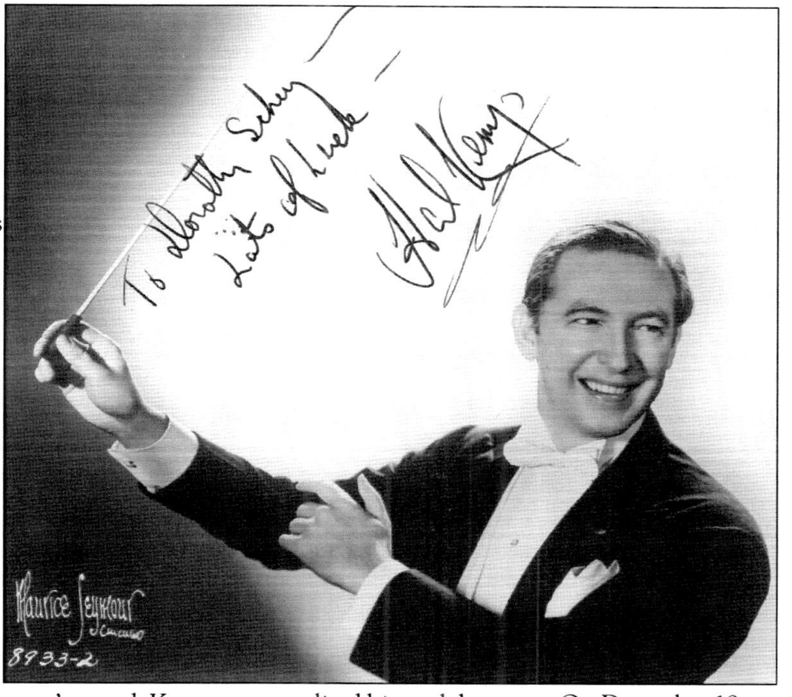

Hal Kemp led the most popular and most musical sweet band of the mid-1930s. Kemp studied piano, trumpet, alto sax, and clarinet as a youth. The Kemp band of the late thirties couldn't seem to make up its mind about whether to be a swing band or a sweet band. Its popularity began to slip. Future actress Janet Blair was one of the female vocalists. She appeared at the Alhambra Grotto on March 13, 1940. By late 1940, Blair and two key musicians had departed the band and Kemp, realizing the need for a change, decided to revamp the group's sound. Kemp never realized his goal, however. On December 19, 1940, just about eight months after his St. Louis engagement, while driving from Los Angeles to a booking in San Francisco, his car hit another head on. He died two days later. (Photo from Dorothy Vincent. Inscription reads "To Dorothy Schey, Lots of luck, Hal Kemp.")

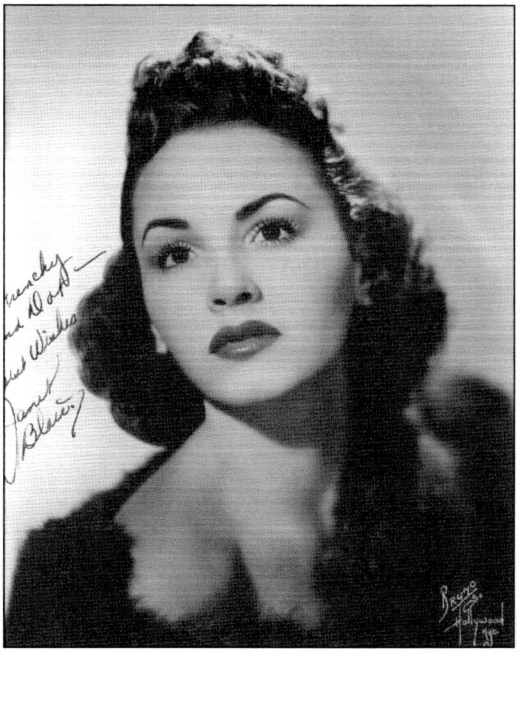

Janet Blair was the lead vocalist with the Hal Kemp Orchestra when it played in St. Louis in 1940. After leaving Kemp Janet Blair would move to Hollywood and become a starring actress. (Photo from Dorothy Vincent. Inscription reads "To Frenchy and Dot, Best Wishes, Janet Blair.")

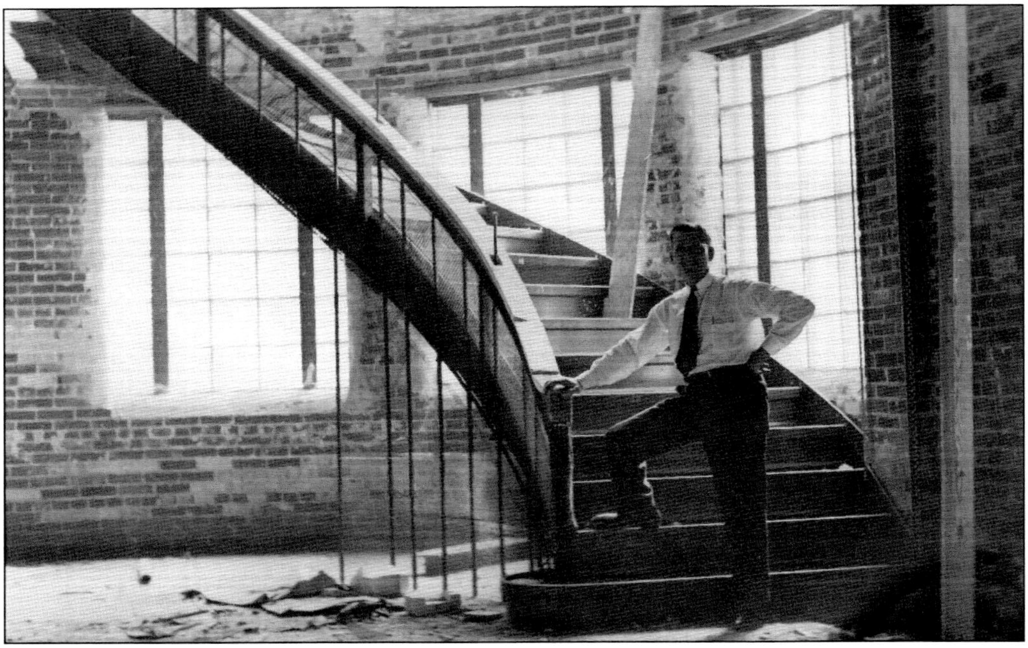

The rebuilding began almost immediately. Here the spiral staircase that many current patrons of the Casa Loma can readily recognize is in the final stage of construction. "Nap" Burien, co-owner, inspects the progress. (Photo from Carol Kawell Ellis.)

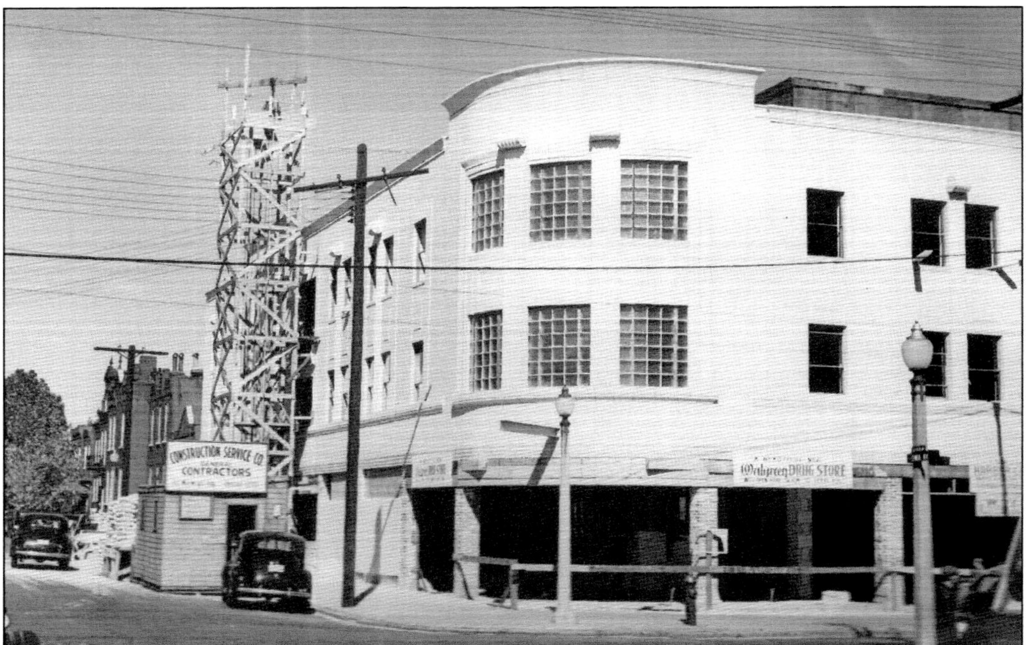

Scaffolding provided easy access to the ballroom level for the workers. (Photo from Carol Kawell Ellis.)

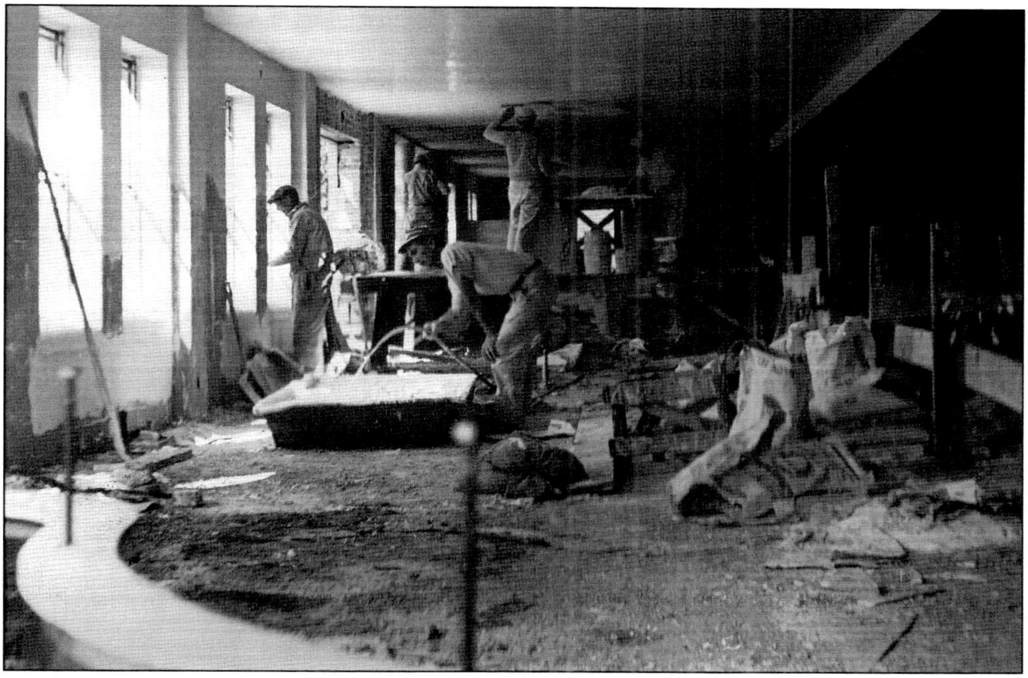

Workers put the finishing touches on the walls and ceilings. (Photo from Carol Kawell Ellis.)

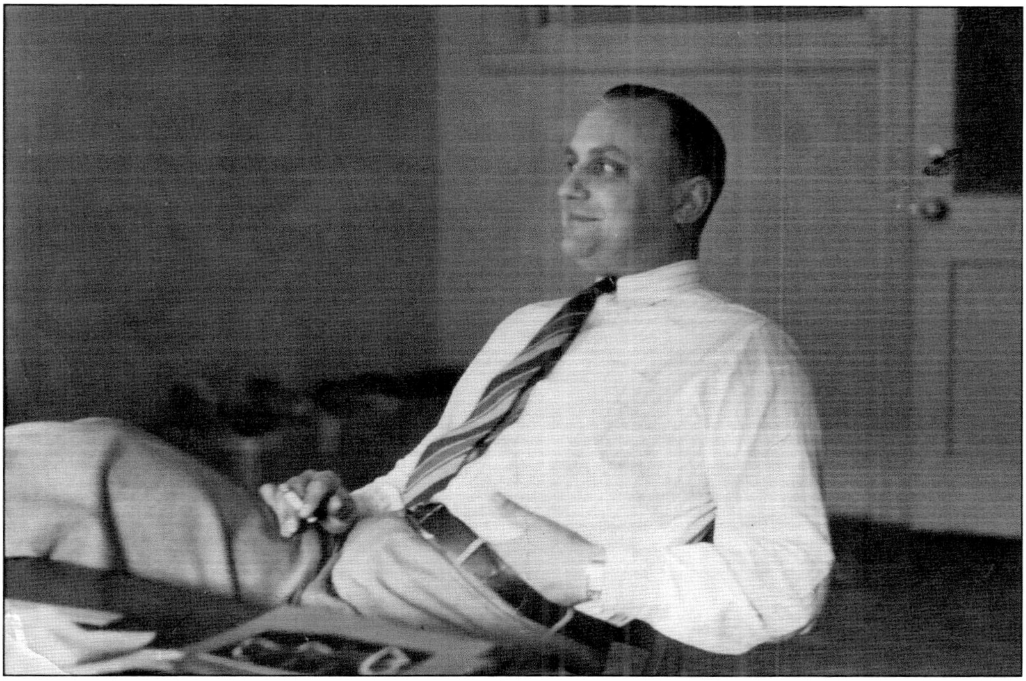

Art Kawell sits back in his newly constructed office at the Casa Loma Ballroom. This photo was taken on October 9, 1940, less than ten months after the devastating fire destroyed the building. (Photo from Carol Kawell Ellis.)

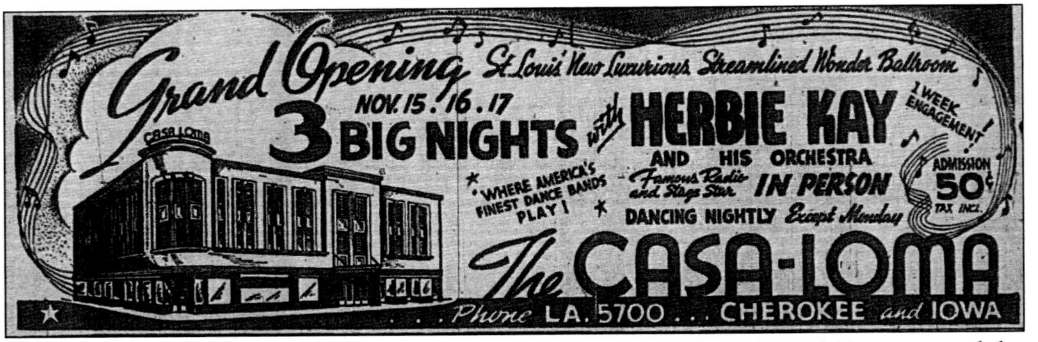

This small ad appeared in the St. Louis Post Dispatch on November 15, 1940. It announced the opening of the newly rebuilt Casa-Loma. (Image taken from microfilm records of the *St. Louis Post-Dispatch* by Dave Lossos.)

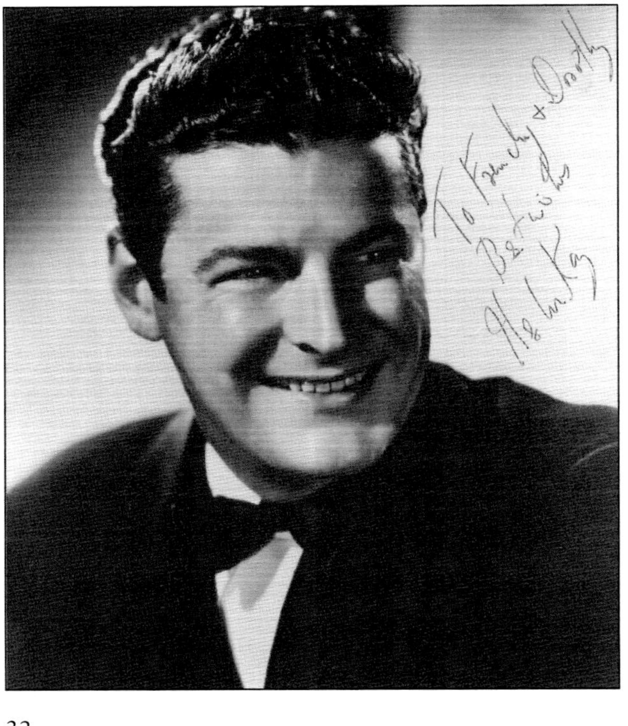

For more than ten months, while the Casa Loma Ballroom was being rebuilt, the music and dancing continued unabated at various alternative locations. But on November 15, 1940, the doors opened again at Iowa and Cherokee. Performing that opening night was Herbie Kay and His Orchestra. Eleven hundred people showed up that night, and the word spread fast. The following night over 2000 patrons jammed the brand new Casa Loma Ballroom dance floor. (Photo from Dorothy Vincent. Inscription reads: " To Frenchy & Dorothy, Best Wishes, Herbie Kay.")

Herbie Kay and his Orchestra attracted a large following during the 1930s and 1940s, featuring a sweet dance tempo. Though the group was initially based in the Chicago area it later toured nationally. Vocalists were Wynne Fair, Ellen Conner, and future screen legend Dorothy Lamour, Kay's wife. The couple was married in 1935, Dorothy left for a Hollywood career in 1937, and they divorced in 1939. The Herbie Kay Orchestra played the Casa Loma Ballroom in both the 1930s and the 1940s. (Photo from Dorothy Vincent. Inscription reads "To Frenchy Vincent and Dot Schey, Best wishes, Herbie Kay.")

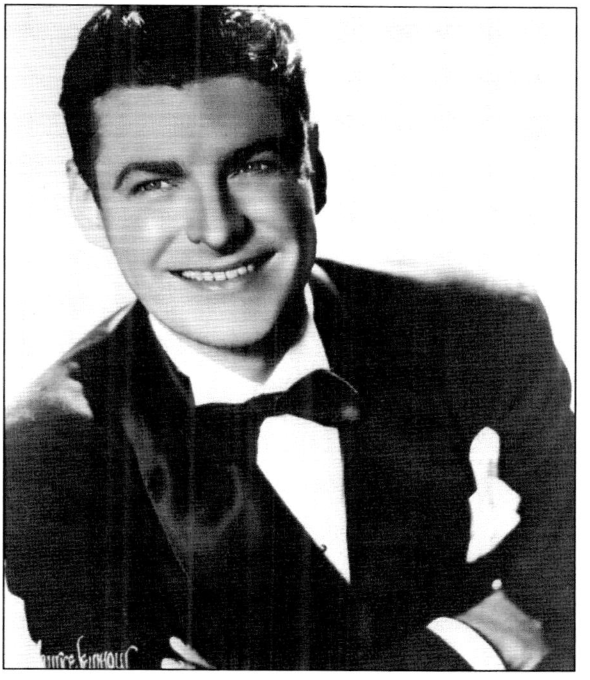

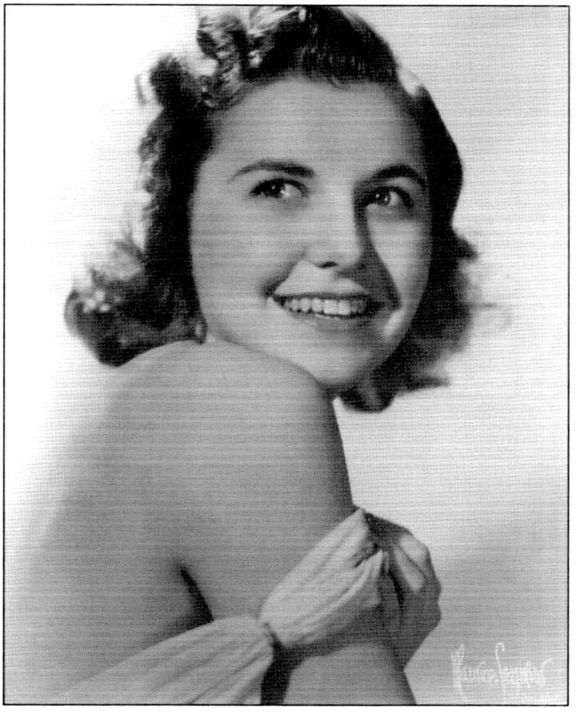

During an engagement at the Casa Loma Ballroom in November of 1940, the lead singer with the Herbie Kay Orchestra was Ellen Conner. (Photo from Dorothy Vincent.)

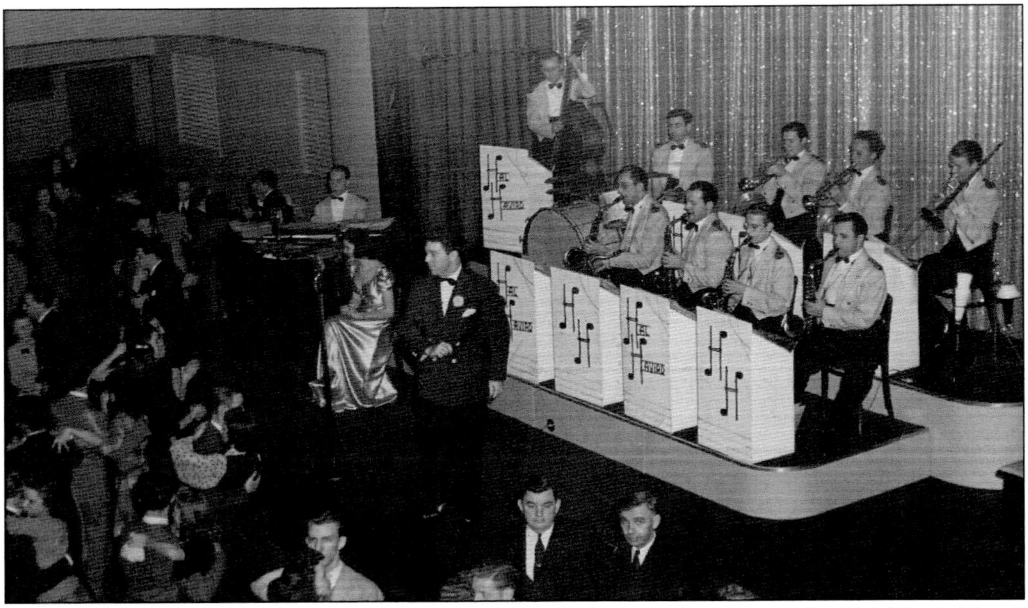

A rare photo from 1941 that shows the Casa Loma Ballroom. On stage is the Hal Havird band with the following individuals: Hal Havird (bandleader), Dorothy Hesse (vocalist), Virgil Smith (piano), Art Fay (drummer), Joe Sahaida (trumpet, 3rd from right, back row), Alex Hauptman (trumpet, 2nd from right, back row), Gene Babbitt (tenor sax, far right, front row). Gene was the brother of the late Harry Babbitt, longtime vocalist with Kay Kaiser. The Babbitts were both from St. Louis. (Photo from Leona Sahaida, wife of the late Joe Sahaida, stage name Joe Sherwood—via son-in-law Ed Kotowski.)

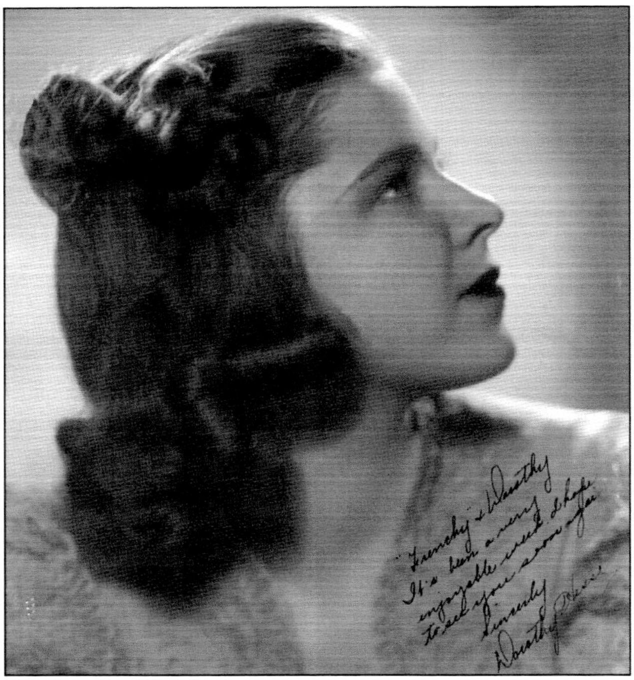

The featured vocalist pictured onstage above and to the left is Dorothy Hesse. (Photo from Dorothy Vincent. Inscription reads "Frenchy and Dorothy, It's been a very enjoyable week. I hope to see you soon again. Sincerely, Dorothy Hesse.")

Three

THE WAR YEARS AND BEYOND

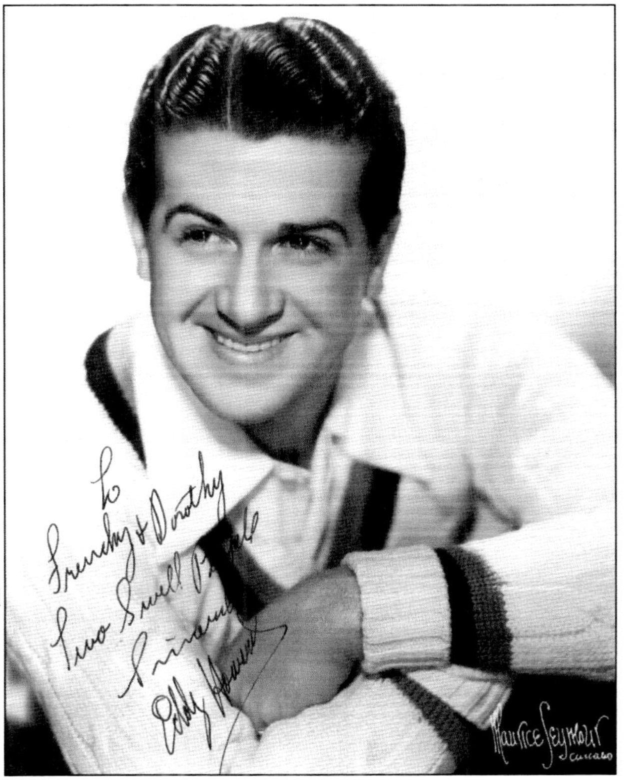

The Casa Loma flourished during the depression, and continued to draw huge crowds into the war years. Servicemen home on leave, or getting ready to ship out, packed the ballroom. Many individuals met their spouses at the Casa Loma Ballroom during this period of turmoil in the world.

One performer who saw his share of uniforms on the dance floor was Eddy Howard. A native Californian, Howard attended medical school, but in 1934 at age 20 he became the resident crooner with the Dick Jurgens Orchestra. In 1941 he formed his own band, which played the Casa Loma Ballroom that year. (Photo from Dorothy Vincent. Inscription reads "To Frenchy & Dorothy, Two Swell People, Sincerely, Eddy Howard.")

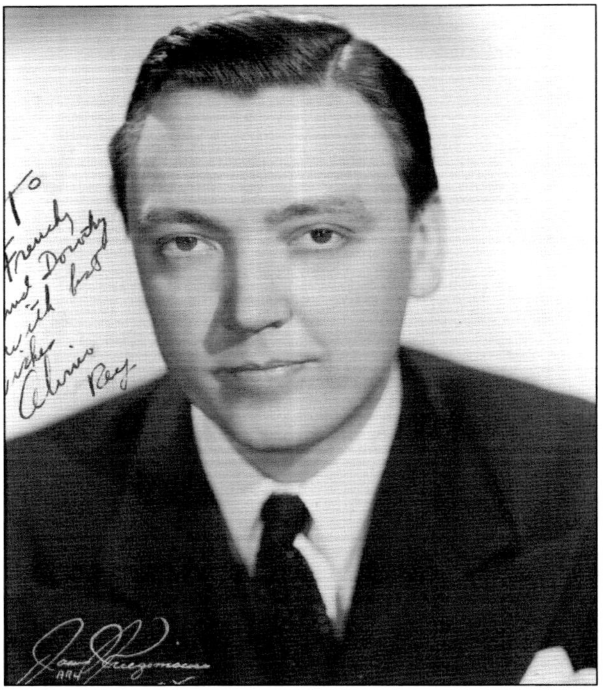

In 1939 guitarist Alvino Rey decided to form his own band. Having just married Louise King a few years earlier, he was easily able to the convince the singing King Sisters (see below) to join him. Prior to entering the Navy in 1944, Alvino Rey played with his Orchestra at the Casa Loma Ballroom. (Photo from Dorothy Vincent. Inscription reads "To Frenchy & Dorothy with best wishes, Alvino Rey.)

One of the big band era's most popular and enduring vocal groups, the King Sisters—Donna, Yvonne, Louise, and Alyce—were born and raised in Salt Lake City, Utah. Taking their stage name from their father, vocal trainer Daddy King Driggs, the siblings first attracted attention while appearing with the Horace Heidt Band in 1935 and enjoying a three-year tenure on Heidt's radio series. In 1939 the King Sisters joined a new band formed by Louise's husband, the legendary guitarist Alvino Rey. In addition to appearing on Rey's hits "Nighty Night" and "I Said No," the sisters also scored a series of smashes issued under their own name, among them "I Understand," "I'll Get By," and "In the Mood." At the peak of their success, in the early 1940s, the King Sisters also appeared in a number of Hollywood features. By this time they were no longer working with Rey, who had dissolved his band upon entering the armed forces; throughout 1944 the siblings were regulars on Kay Kyser's radio series, but during the postwar years their popularity declined. In 1965, however, the King Sisters—as well as members of their extended family, including Rey—were tapped by the ABC television network to host their own weekly variety show. (Photo from Dorothy Vincent. Inscription reads "To Frenchie & Dot, Best Wishes, The 4 King Sisters." Then each of the King sisters signed it.)

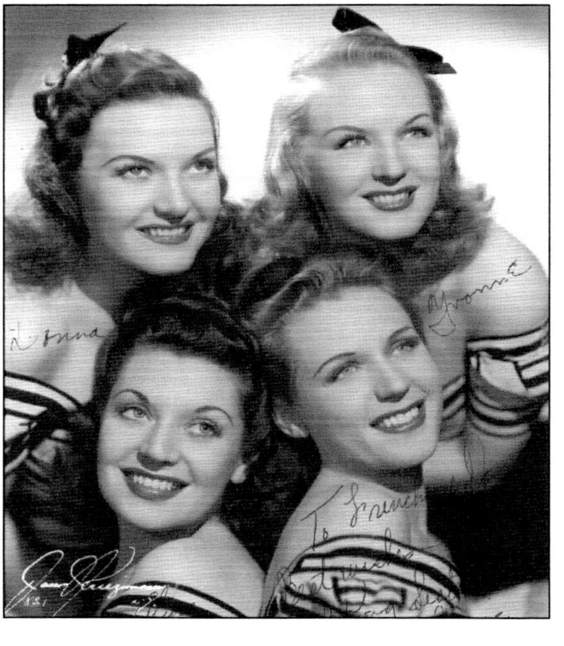

Bob Crosby and his orchestra played the Casa Loma Ballroom in 1941. Bing's youngest sibling, Bob, followed in Bing's footsteps, first as a singer, then as a bandleader. Bob had his own 15-minute radio show called *Club 15* from 1946 through 1952 and a half-hour daytime show from 1953 to 1955 titled *The Bob Crosby Show*, both on CBS. Bob's recordings topped the charts with "In a Little Gypsy Tea Room" in 1935, "Whispers in the Dark" in 1937, and "Day In, Day Out" in 1939. (Photo courtesy of Dorothy Vincent. Inscription reads "Frenchy and Dorothy, Regards, Bob Crosby, Casa Loma '41.")

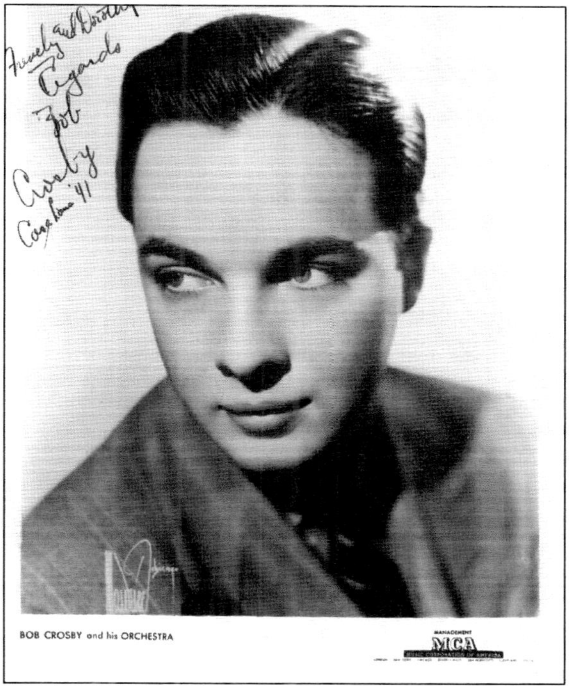

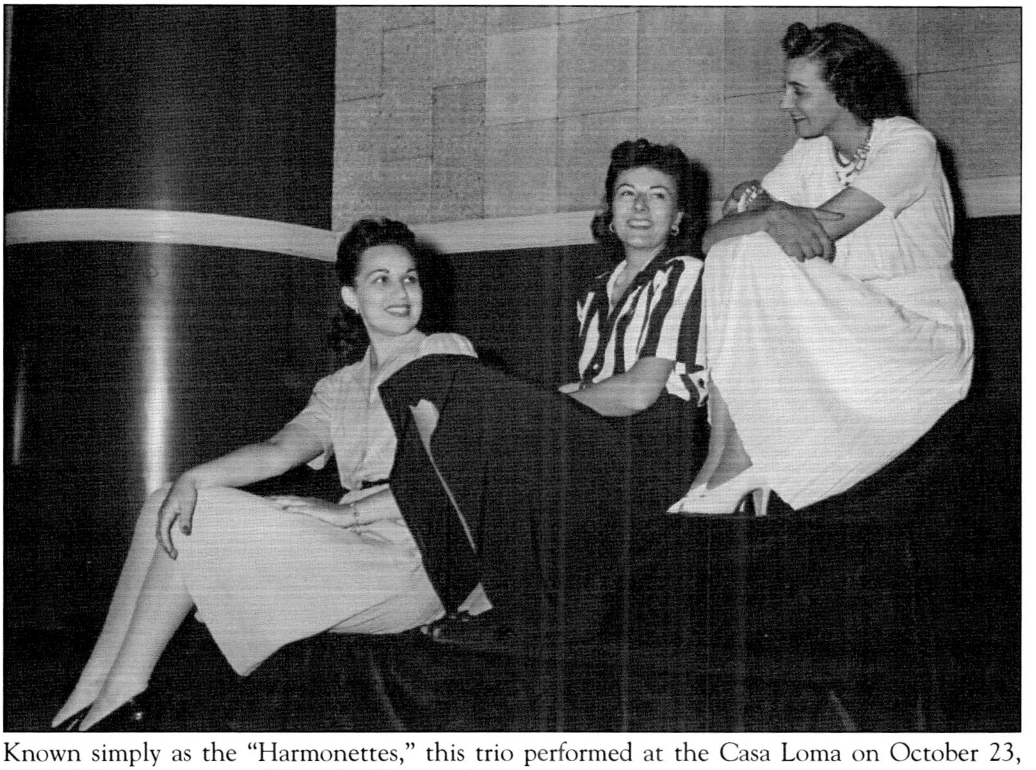

Known simply as the "Harmonettes," this trio performed at the Casa Loma on October 23, 1941. (Photo courtesy of Dorothy Vincent.)

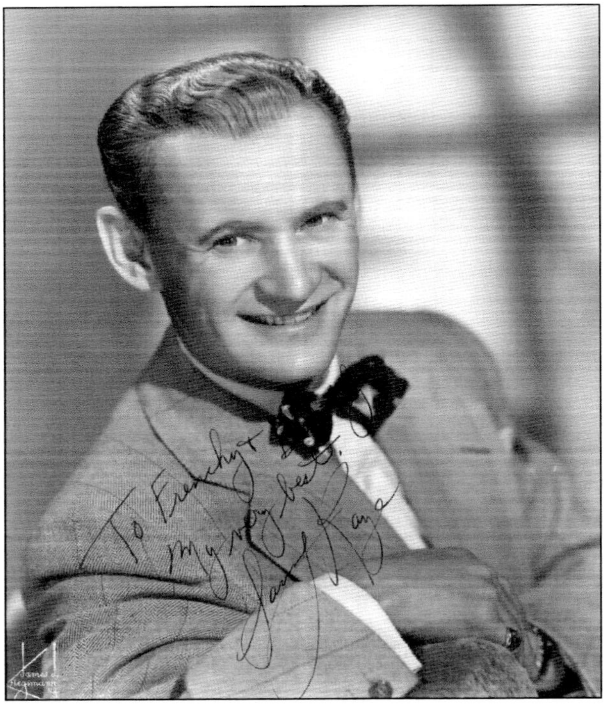

Sammy Kaye was a famous big band musician, songwriter, and band leader. He was known for an audience participation gimmick called "So you want to lead a band?" Audience members would be called onto stage in an attempt to conduct the orchestra, with the possibility of winning batons. (Photo from Dorothy Vincent. Inscription reads "To Frenchy & Dorothy, My very best, Sammy Kaye.")

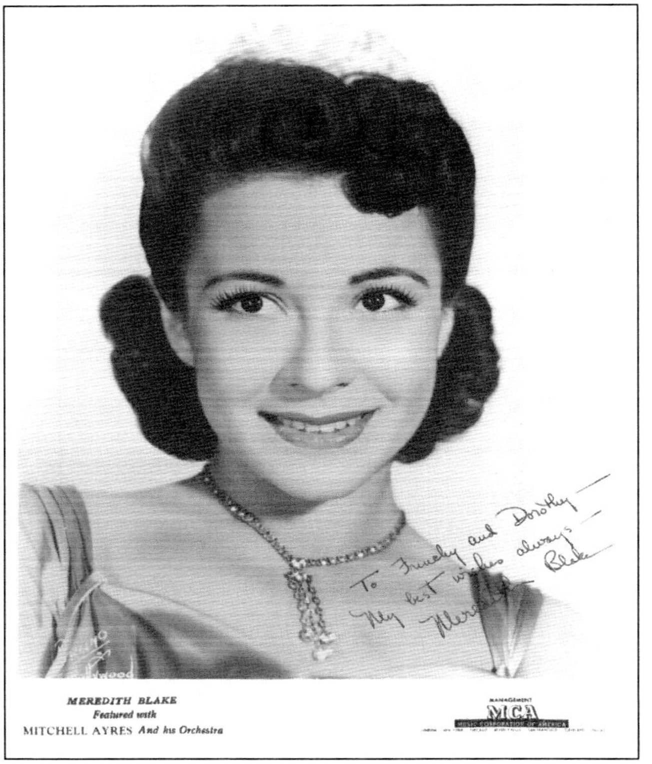

Meredith Blake was the featured vocalist the night the Mitchell Ayres Orchestra played at the Casa Loma Ballroom. The orchestra, whose catch phrase was "Fashions in Music," was one of the more musical ballroom bands. The orchestra appeared in three movies in the early forties before disbanding. (Photo from Dorothy Vincent. Inscription reads "To Frenchy and Dorothy, My best wishes always, Meredith Blake.")

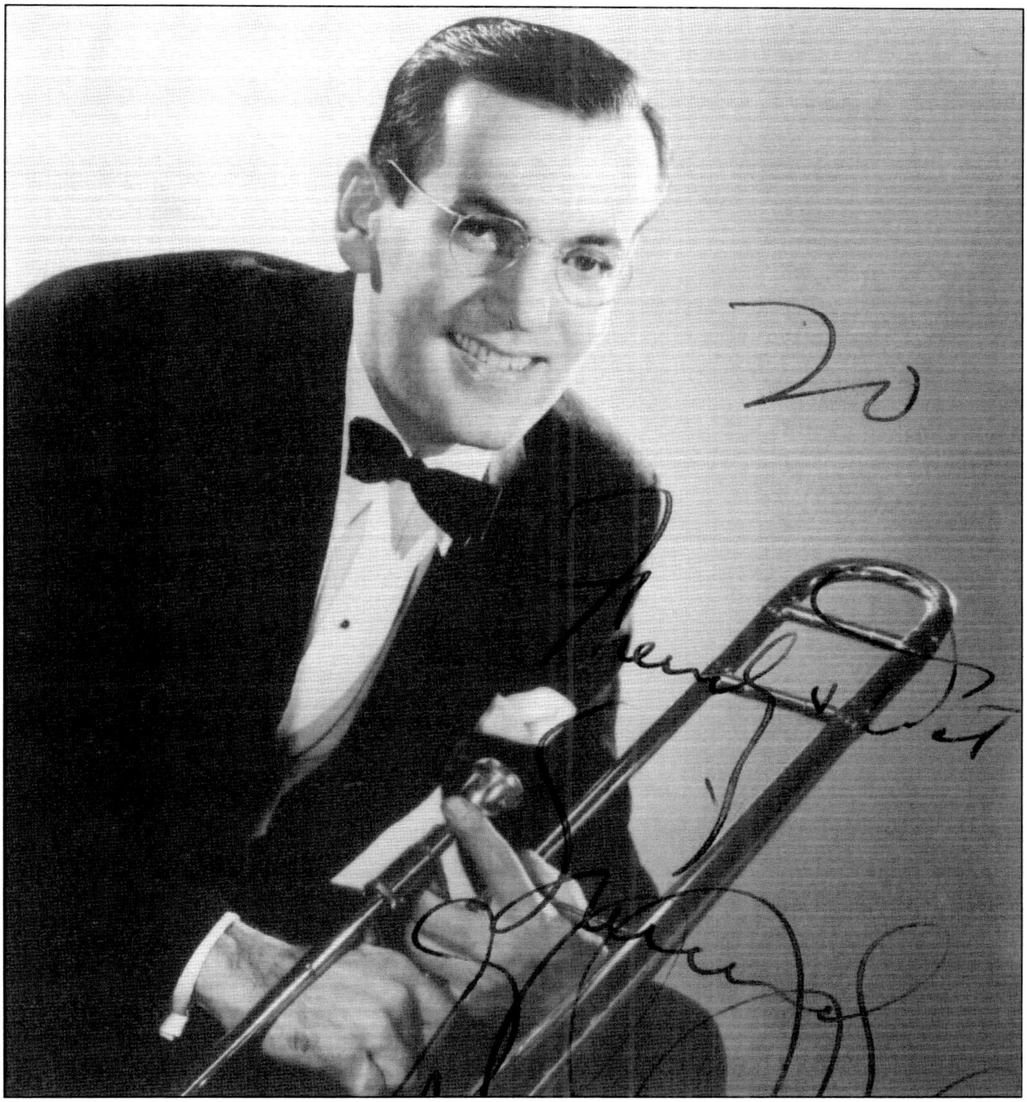

In 1937, Glenn Miller formed his first band, but was unsuccessful. Just a year later he formed an orchestra that was soon breaking attendance records all up and down the east coast. There were record-breaking recordings as well, such as "Tuxedo Junction," which sold 115,000 copies in the first week, "In the Mood," and "Pennsylvania 6-5000," all appearing on the RCA Victor Bluebird label. In early 1940, Glenn Miller's *Moonlight Serenade* radio series aired three times a week over CBS. In 1941, it was off to Hollywood where the band worked on its first movie, which featured the million-selling record "Chattanooga Choo Choo." During the war the Glenn Miller Army Air Force Band performed over 800 times. Of these, 500 were broadcasts heard by millions. In fall of 1944, the band was scheduled to go on a six-week tour of Europe and planned to station in Paris during that time. Miller decided to travel ahead, to make the proper arrangements for the group's arrival. And so, on December 15th, Glenn Miller boarded a transport plane to Paris, never to be seen again. The Casa Loma Ballroom was indeed fortunate to be a part of the legacy left behind by this artist. (Photo from Dorothy Vincent. Inscription reads "To Frenchy & Dot, Sincerely, Glenn Miller.")

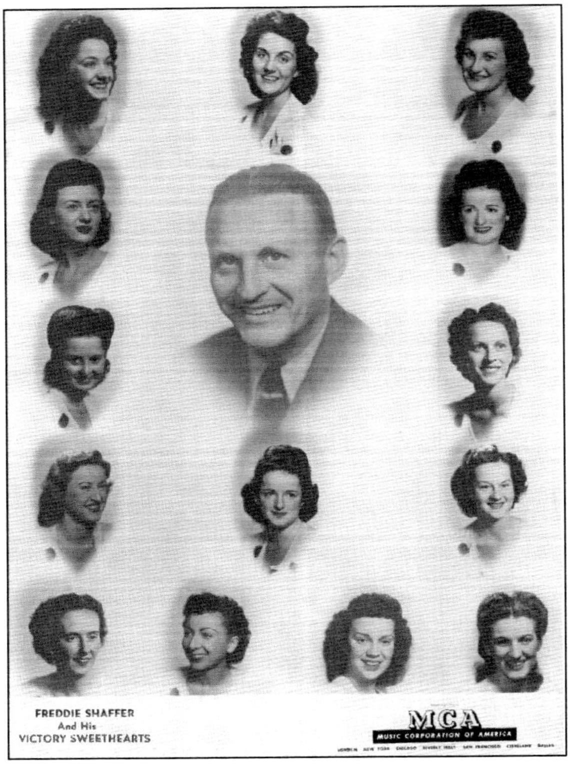

In 1942, Freddie Shaffer and his all-female orchestra band were offered a job to play for a week at Geneva On The Lake, Ohio. The "girls" were so well received they stayed the summer. The band was then booked for the USO and toured the eastern part of the United States, as well as military bases during World War II. The group was known as Freddie Shaffer and the "Victory Sweethearts." (Photo from Dorothy Vincent.)

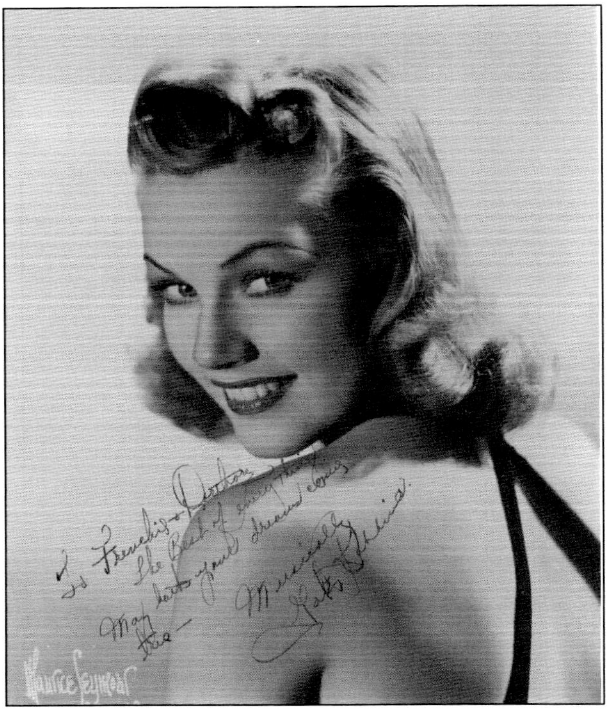

Statuesque brunette actress Gale Robbins was a model and singer before entering films in 1944. Gale Robbins was the featured soloist with the Phil Levant Orchestra when they played the Casa Loma Ballroom. (Photo from Dorothy Vincent. Inscription reads "To Frenchy & Dorothy, The Best of everything, May both your dreams come true—Musically, Gale Robbins.)

Barbara Carroll was the soloist who performed the night the Freddy Nagel Orchestra played the Casa Loma Ballroom in the early 1940s. (Photo from Dorothy Vincent. Inscription reads "To Frenchy and Dorothy, It was grand being here—knowing you and Best Wishes, Always, Barbara Carroll.")

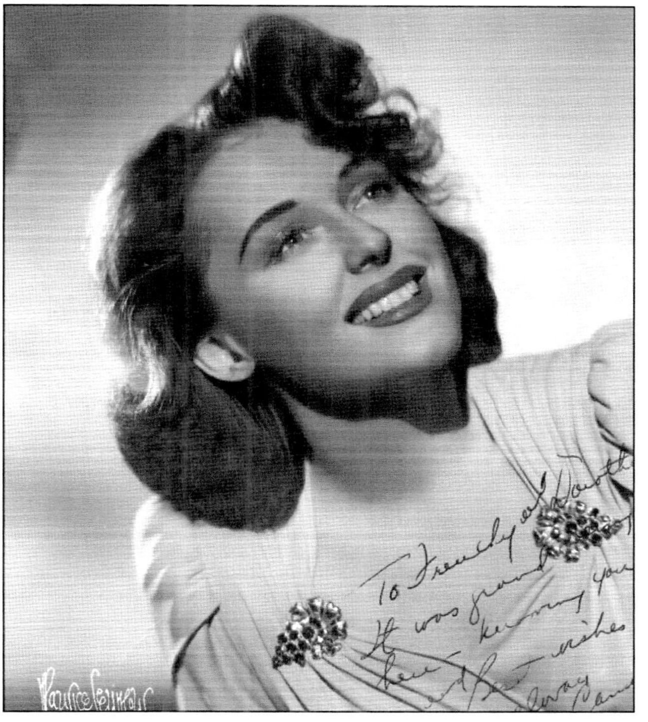

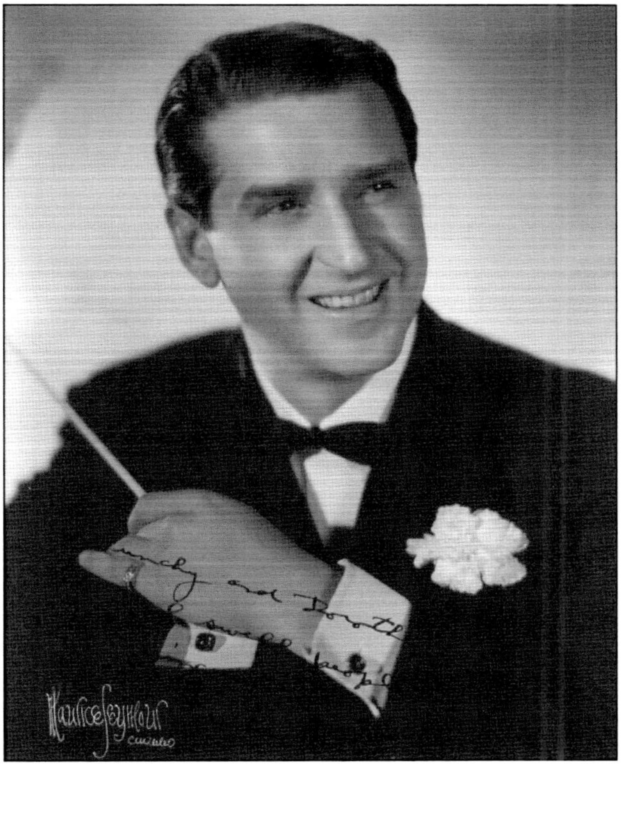

By the time he played the Casa Loma Ballroom in the early 1940s, Freddy Nagel's Orchestra had changed into a much more solid swing and dance band. (Photo from Dorothy Vincent. Inscription reads "To Frenchy and Dorothy, Two swell people, Sincerely, Freddy Nagel.")

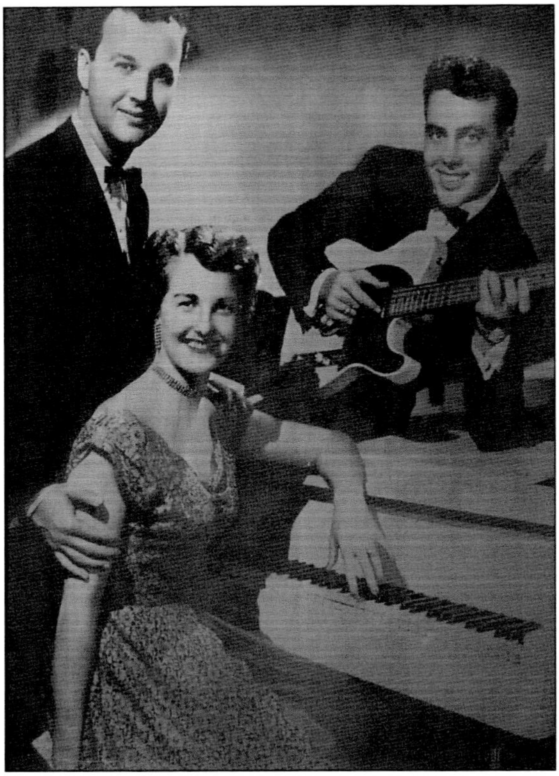

Regrettably, very few of the large photos of past performers at the Casa Loma Ballroom grace its walls today. As a matter of fact, there are only two left. The picture to the left has stumped countless patrons trying to remember their names. Do you know who they are? (Photo by Dave Lossos, taken directly of the wall hanging at the Casa Loma Ballroom.)

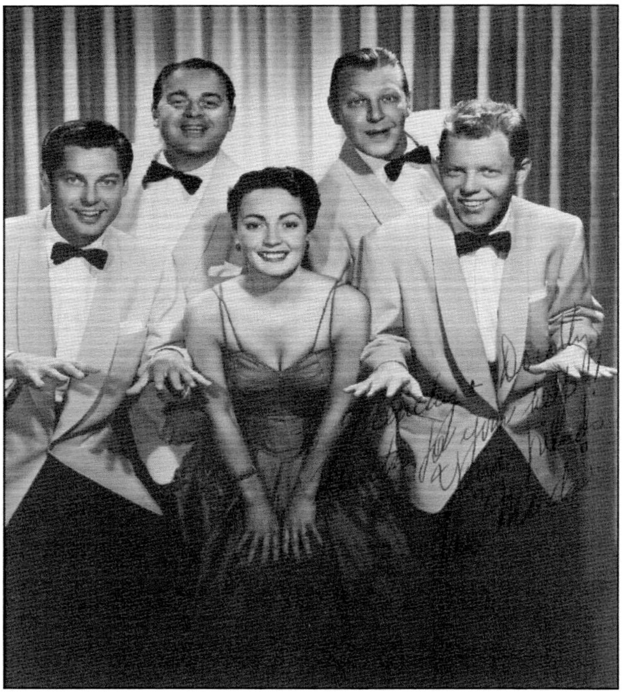

The other picture that remains hanging is of the Modernaires. They made their first professional appearance as a male quartet with Charlie Barnet at the Glen Island Casino in 1936. They signed with Glenn Miller in early 1941. When singer Paula Kelly joined Miller later that year, she became the fifth member of the group. Member Hal Tennyson, who also played tenor sax, often filled in for sick or absent Miller musicians. (Photo from Dorothy Vincent. Inscription reads "To Frenchy and Dorothy, Thanks for all your help! Your friends, the 'Mods.'")

Dick Haymes, probably best known as Rita Hayworth's second husband, was the featured vocalist with the Harry James band when they played the Casa Loma Ballroom. (Photo from Dorothy Vincent. Inscription reads: "To Frenchy and Dot, Best Wishes, Sincerely, Dick Haymes.")

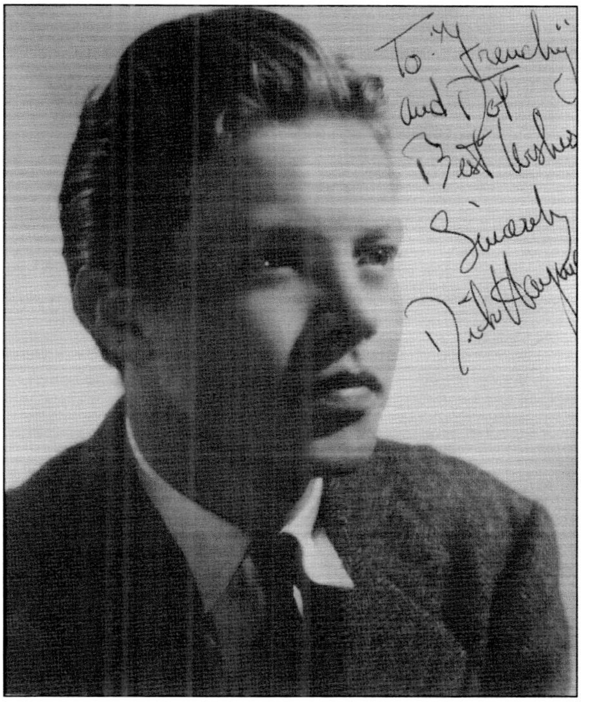

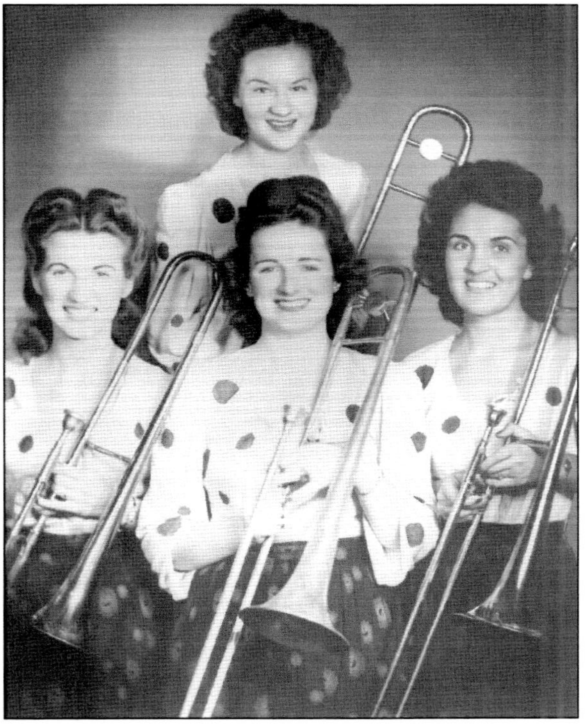

During the war years some women found employment in traditionally male oriented jobs. Here is the Freddie Shaffer Trombone Quartette that played at the Casa Loma Ballroom. (Photo from Dorothy Vincent.)

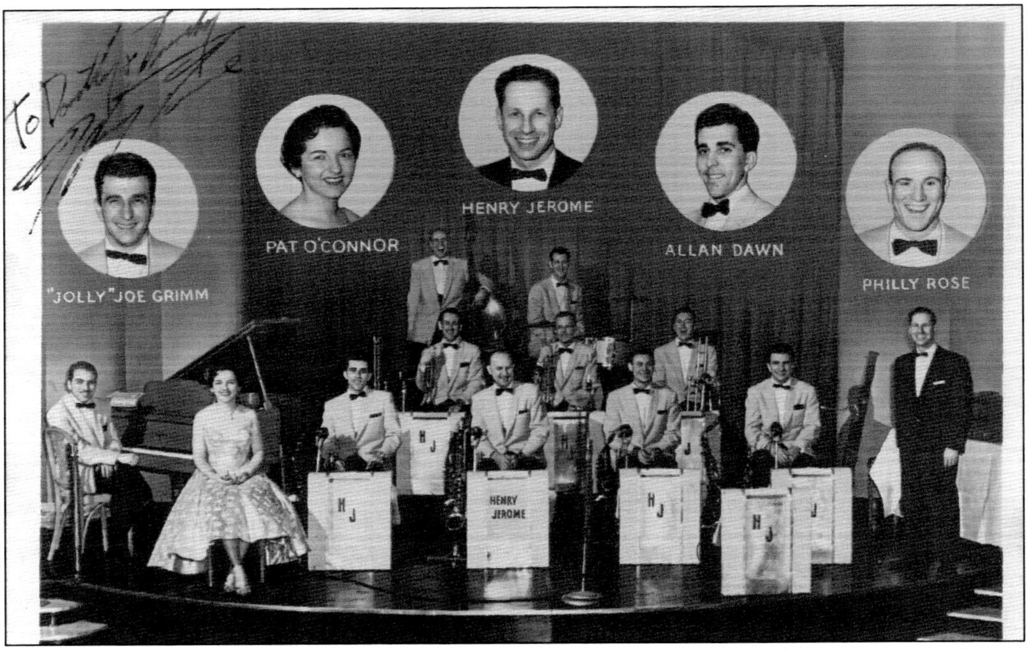

In 1932, Henry Jerome formed his first dance band orchestra in Norwich, Connecticut. It was a 10 piece band, plus vocalists Frank Warren and David Allen. From the mid 1930s on through the end of the 1940s, Jerome's orchestra worked continuously playing on steamships and in hotels, and ballrooms, including the Casa Loma. In 1945 members of the band included two saxophonists, Leonard Garment, and Alan Greenspan (yes, THAT Alan Greenspan), and Al Haig (no, not THAT Al Haig) on piano. Eventually Leonard Garment became Richard Nixon's personal attorney, and recommended his old band partner turned economist, Alan Greenspan, to President Nixon for a position in his administration. (Photo from Dorothy Vincent. Inscription reads "To Frenchy & Dorothy, Henry Jerome.)

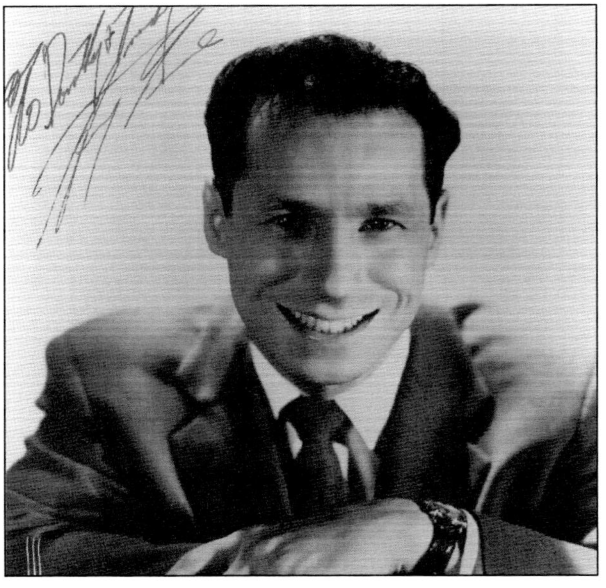

Here's another photo of Henry Jerome, given to Frenchy and Dorothy the night his orchestra played at the Casa Loma Ballroom. (Photo from Dorothy Vincent.)

Saxophone and clarinet player Shep Fields led one of America's most successful "sweet" bands of the 30s, best remembered for its "rippling rhythm" sound, introduced by blowing through a straw into a glass of water. The band enjoyed 38 hits between 1936 and 1943, including seven number ones. (Photo from Dorothy Vincent. Inscription reads "To Frenchy & Dorothy, Shep Fields.")

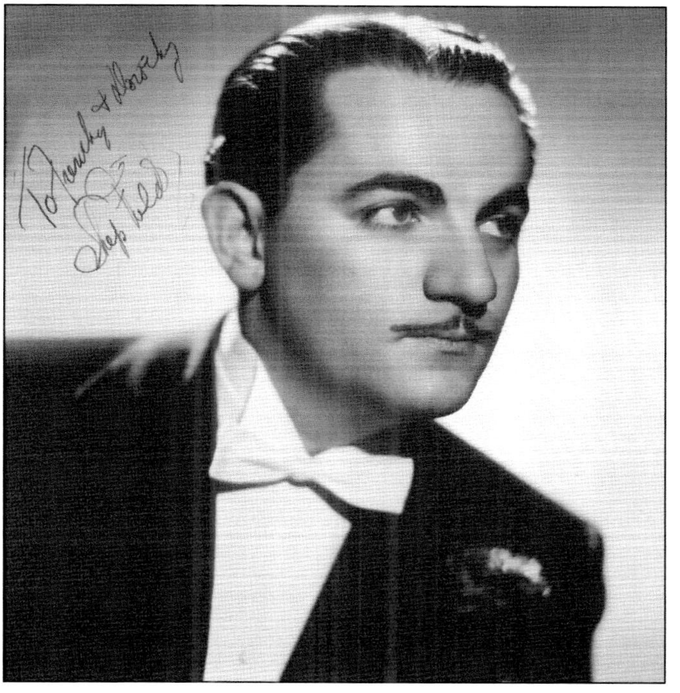

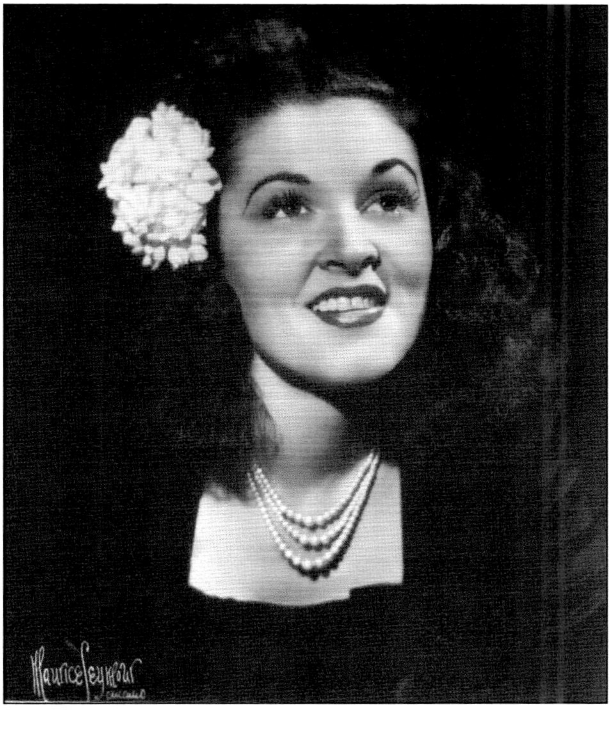

Dorothy Allen was the featured singer the night the Shep Fields Orchestra played at the Casa Loma Ballroom. (Photo from Dorothy Vincent. Inscription reads "To Frenchy & "Dotte", Best Wishes, Dorothy Allen.")

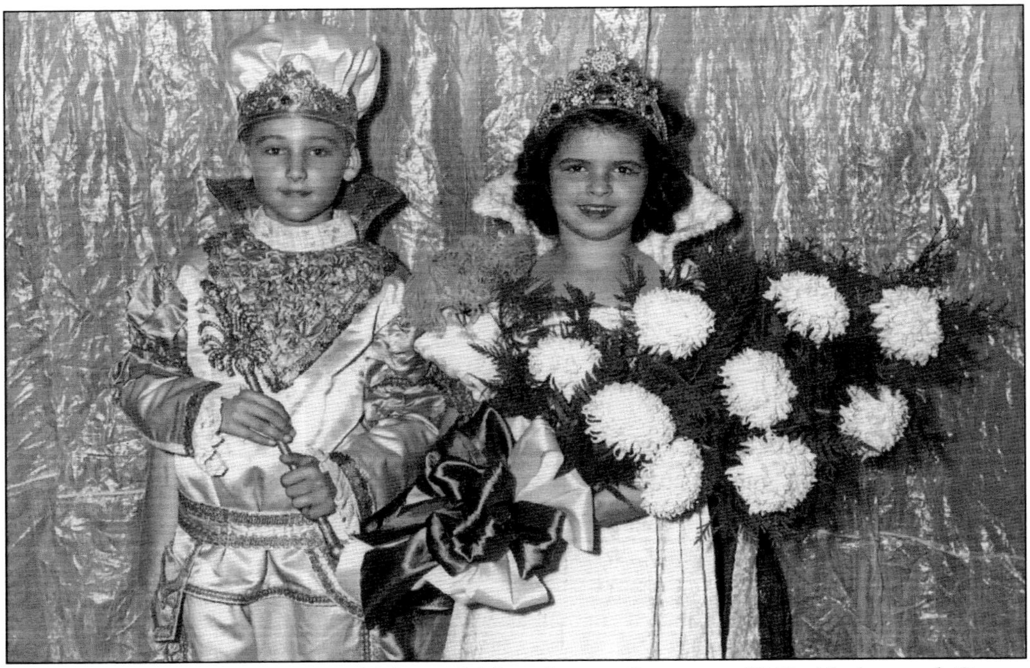

King Kenneth Siepman, son of Mr. and Mrs. August Siepman, 5043 Alaska, and Queen Marlene Meier, daughter of Mr. and Mrs. Thomas Meier, 3316A Cherokee St., following their coronation on the night of October 28, 1946, at the Casa Loma ballroom, chosen to rule over the Cherokee Business Association Court of Youth and Happiness for the year 1946-1947. (Photo from Gerry and Marlene Strait.)

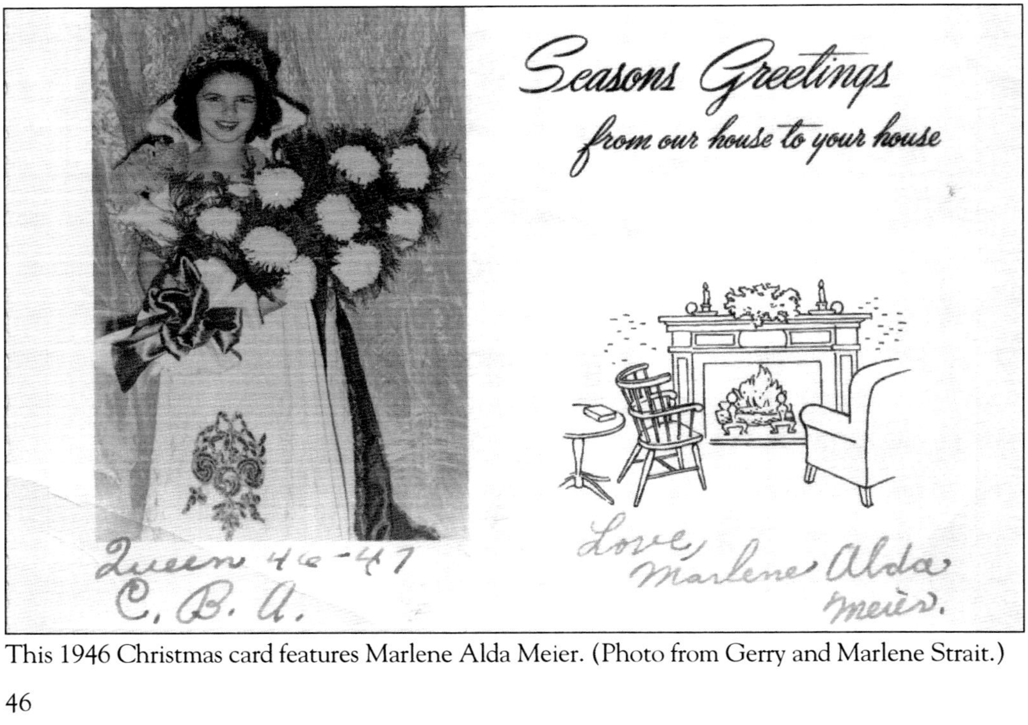

This 1946 Christmas card features Marlene Alda Meier. (Photo from Gerry and Marlene Strait.)

The Nick Stuart Orchestra played the Casa Loma Ballroom a number of times in the 1940s and 50s. (Photo from Dorothy Vincent. Inscription reads "To Frenchy and Dorothy, It was a real pleasure being back in St. Louis and most of all with you folks. Hope it won't be to (sp) long before we're together again. Nick Stuart 12/4/1947.")

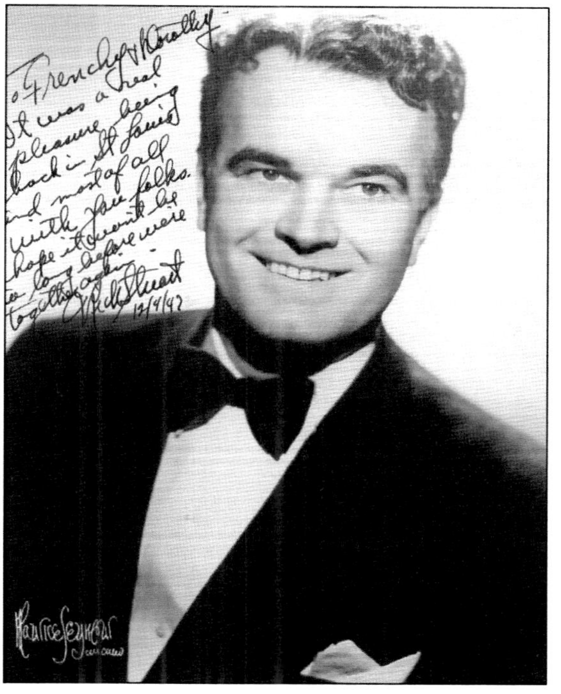

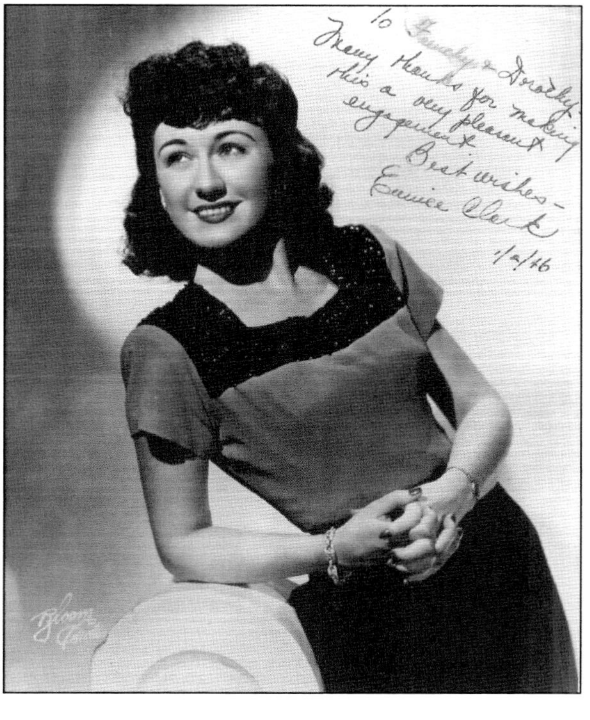

Eunice Clark was the featured vocalist when Will Back and His Orchestra played the Casa Loma Ballroom on New Years Eve of 1945. (Photo from Dorothy Vincent. Inscription reads "To Frenchy and Dorothy, Many thanks for making this a very pleasant engagement. Best Wishes, Eunice Clark.")

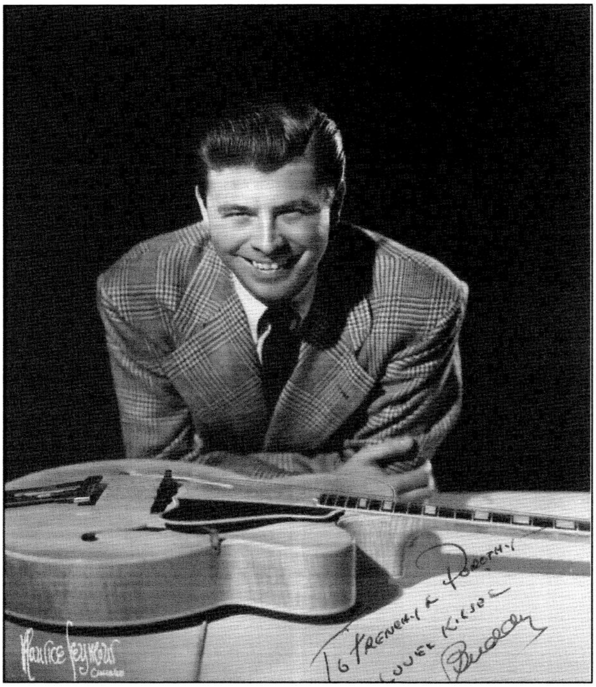

Bandleader Buddy Moreno was a featured singer and guitarist with the Griff Williams, Dick Jurgens, and Harry James orchestras before heading up his own group in the late 1940s. The band, patterned after the Jurgens orchestra, debuted at the Casa Loma Ballroom in St. Louis in the fall of 1947. Buddy has called the St. Louis area home since 1957. (Photo from Dorothy Vincent. Inscription reads: "To Frenchy & Dorothy, Love & Kisses, Buddy.")

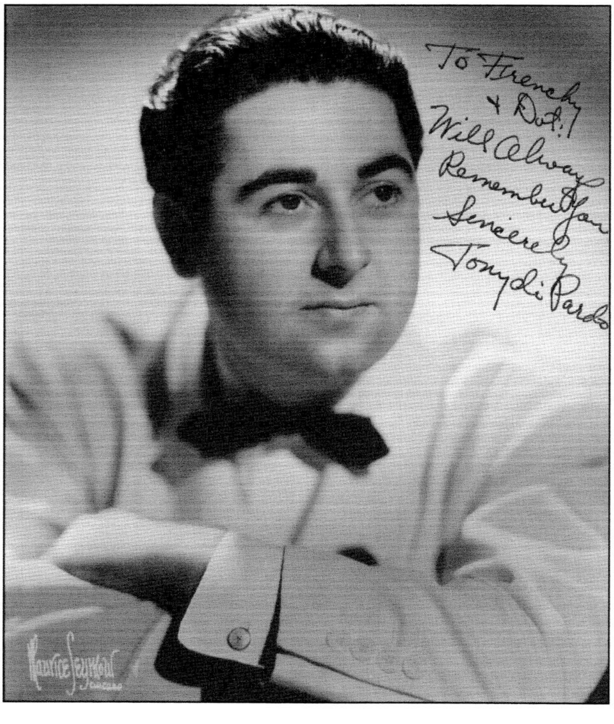

Tony DiPardo, a St. Louis native, got his start in music in his hometown. He quickly found success with his orchestra. Today Tony DiPardo is an icon in Kansas City where he is the longtime bandleader of the Kansas City Chiefs. As Tony is fond of saying ""Not bad, for a poor little Italian boy from St. Louis." (Photo from Dorothy Vincent. Inscription reads: "To Frenchy & Dot: Will Always Remember You, Sincerely, Tony di Pardo.")

Blue Barron's specialty was sweet orchestras, such as those of Guy Lombardo, Kay Kyser, and Sammy Kaye, whom he managed. In 1936, he decided to form his own orchestra along those same lines. Barron's biggest success came in 1949, with the hit song "Cruisin' Down the River," which held the number one spot for seven weeks. (Photo from Dorothy Vincent. Inscription reads "To Frenchy & Dot—Most cordially, Blue Barron.")

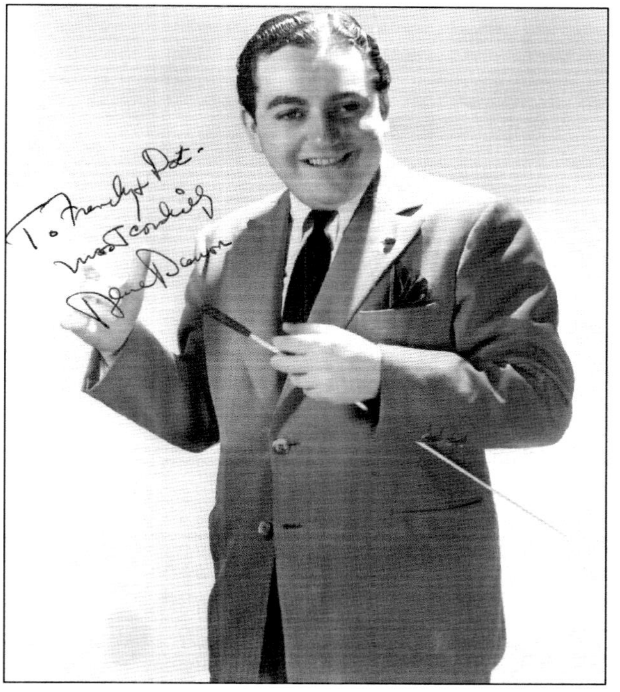

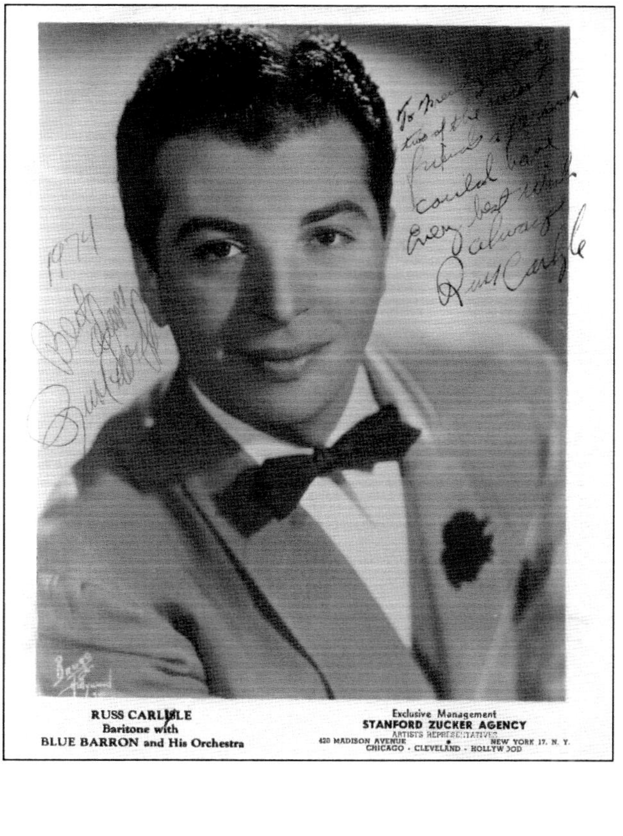

Russ Carlyle was the featured vocalist for several years with the Blue Barron Orchestra. At his first appearance at the Casa Loma Ballroom in the 1940s he signed this photo "To Frenchy and Dot, Two of the nicest friends a person could have, Every best wishes always, Russ Carlyle." In a return in 1974 he re-signed the same photo. (Photo from Dorothy Vincent.)

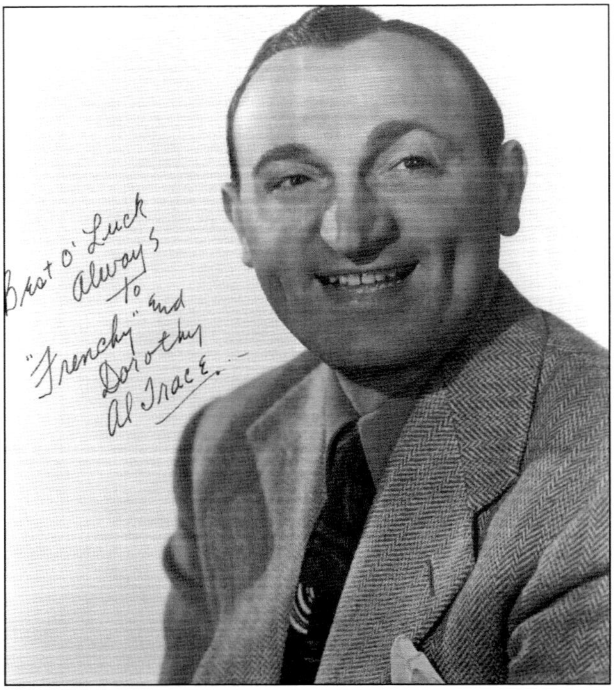

The Al Trace Orchestra's theme songs included "Sweet Words and Music," then, "Mairzy Doats". Al was one of that select group of men who have achieved fame as both bandleaders and composers. Initially a drummer, Al Trace formed his first band for an engagement at the 1933 Chicago World's Fair. Later, the band had their own radio show, *It Pays To Be Ignorant*. Among the approximately 300 songs that Trace wrote was "If I'd Known You Were Comin' I'd Have Baked a Cake." Many of Al's recordings featured his own compositions, and were big hits, that sold well in the 1940s and the 1950s. (Photo from Dorothy Vincent.)

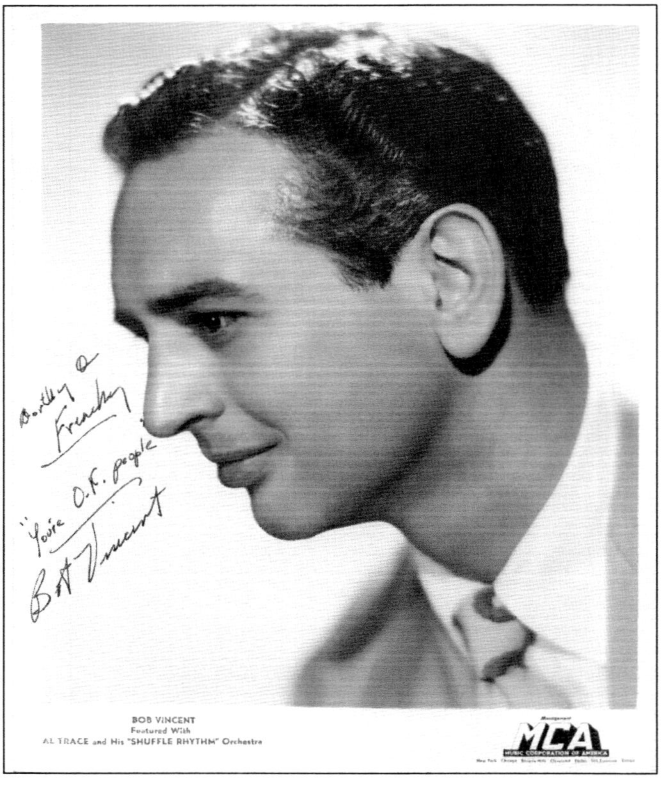

The vocalist at the time the Al Trace Orchestra played the Casa Loma Ballroom was Bob Vincent. His tune "You Call Everybody Darlin'" hit the top of the charts on September 22, 1948. (Photo from Dorothy Vincent.)

Artie Shaw's recording of "Begin the Beguine" catapulted him into the ranks of top band leaders and he was immediately dubbed the new "King of Swing." Superstardom was not Artie's thing, though, and over the course of his fabulous career he took numerous respites from both recording and performing. Later he formed a touring band with a large string section with which he recorded several more smash hits, among them "Star Dust," "Moonglow," "Dancing in the Dark," and many others. (Photo from Dorothy Vincent. Inscription reads: "To Frenchy a& Dorothy, Best Wishes, Artie Shaw.")

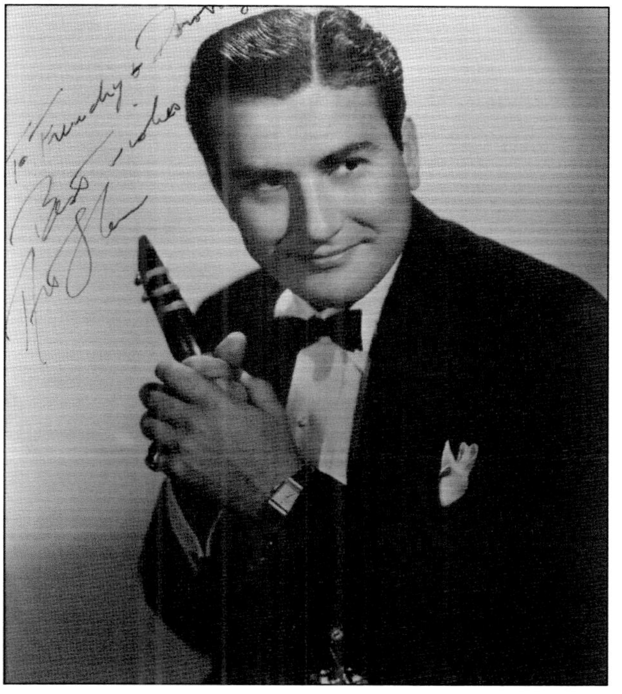

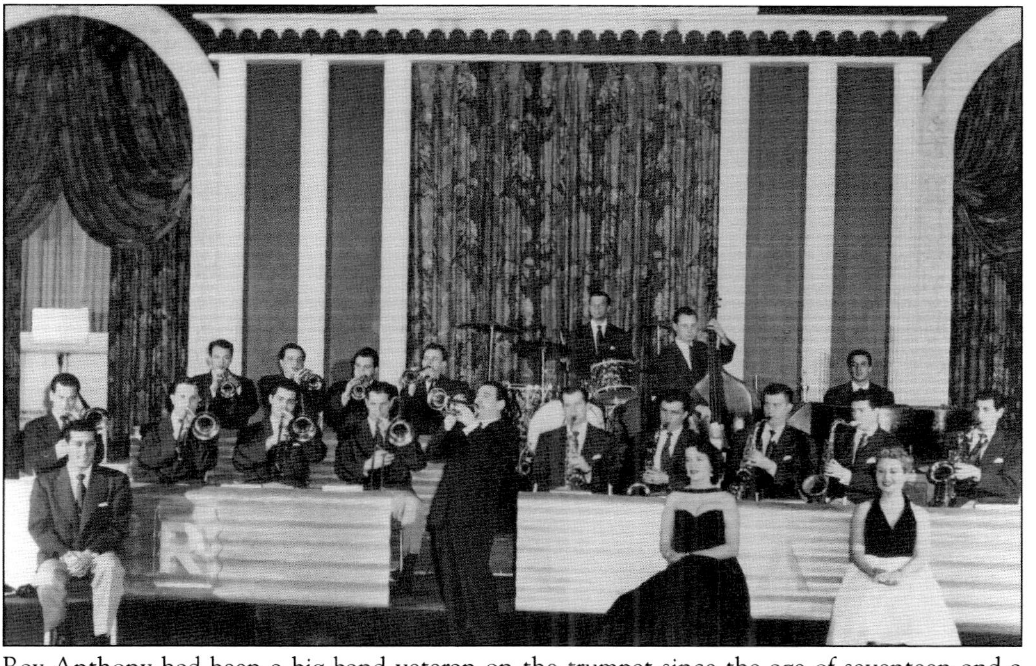

Ray Anthony had been a big band veteran on the trumpet since the age of seventeen and a member of the Glenn Miller orchestra in 1941. After the war he organized his first band in his hometown of Cleveland. His first hit record for Capitol was in late 1949, an instrumental version of "A Dreamer's Holiday," which just barely missed the top ten listing. (Photo from Carol Kawell Ellis.)

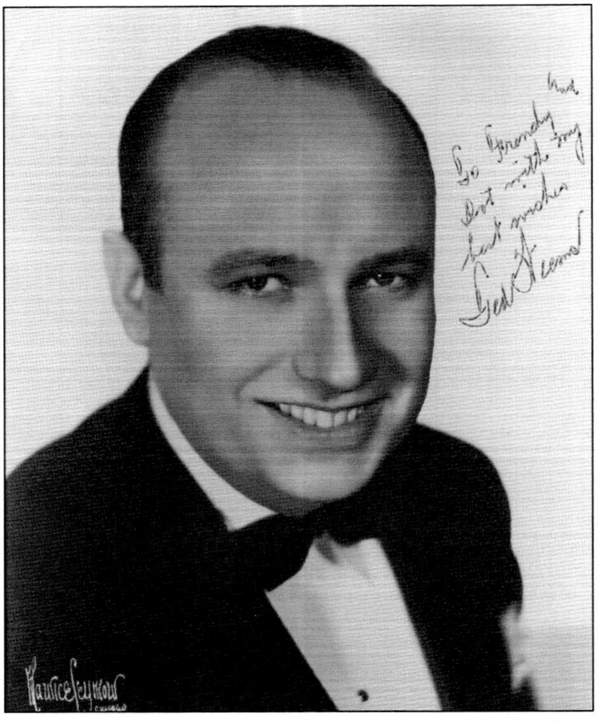

Ted Weems was a popular midwestern bandleader who started his band in 1923. Around 1925 he moved his band to Chicago where he played in hotels and ballrooms around the city while also touring the Midwest. In 1932 the Ted Weems Orchestra started appearing regularly on a sponsored nationwide radio program with Jack Benny. He could regularly be heard on radio during the 1930s and 1940s on such shows as *The Fibber McGee* and *Molly* and *Beat The Band*. In 1936 vocalist Perry Como joined the band. In 1942 the Weems Orchestra disbanded, but after World War II, Weems put together another band that continued until the early 1950s. (Photo from Dorothy Vincent. Inscription reads "To Frenchy and Dot with my best wishes, Ted Weems.")

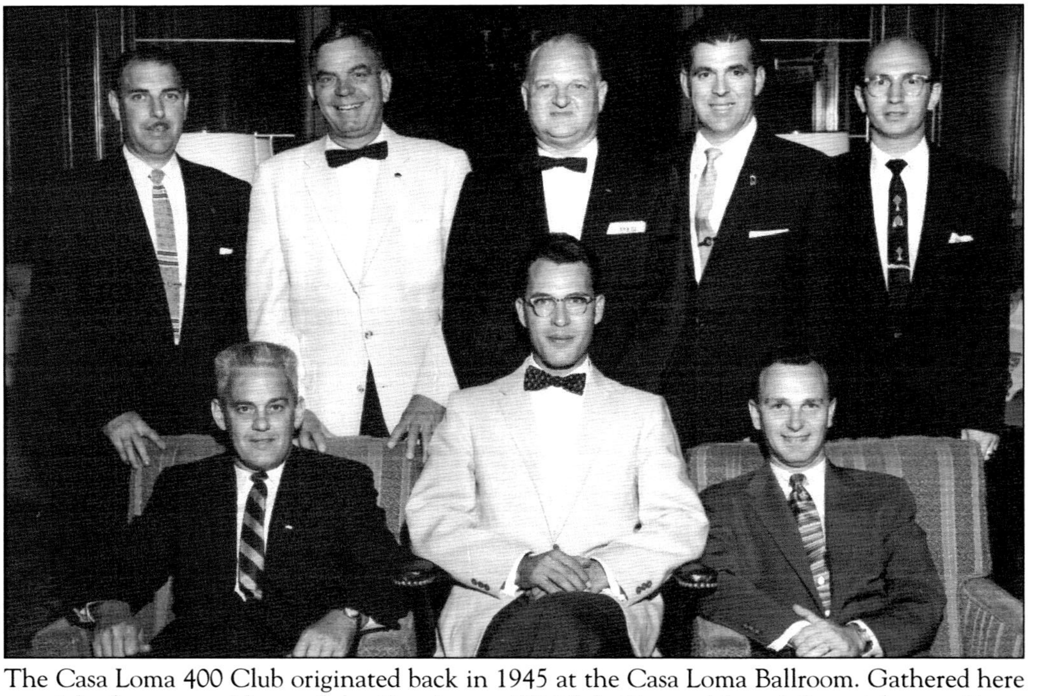

The Casa Loma 400 Club originated back in 1945 at the Casa Loma Ballroom. Gathered here are eight former presidents of the Casa Loma 400 Club. Pictured from left to right are: (front row) Walt Champ, unknown, and Paul Terwesten; (back row) Bill Gorey, Juke Box, Vic Koenig, Al Ciolek, and Vernon Wagner. (Photo from John and Marian Hargis.)

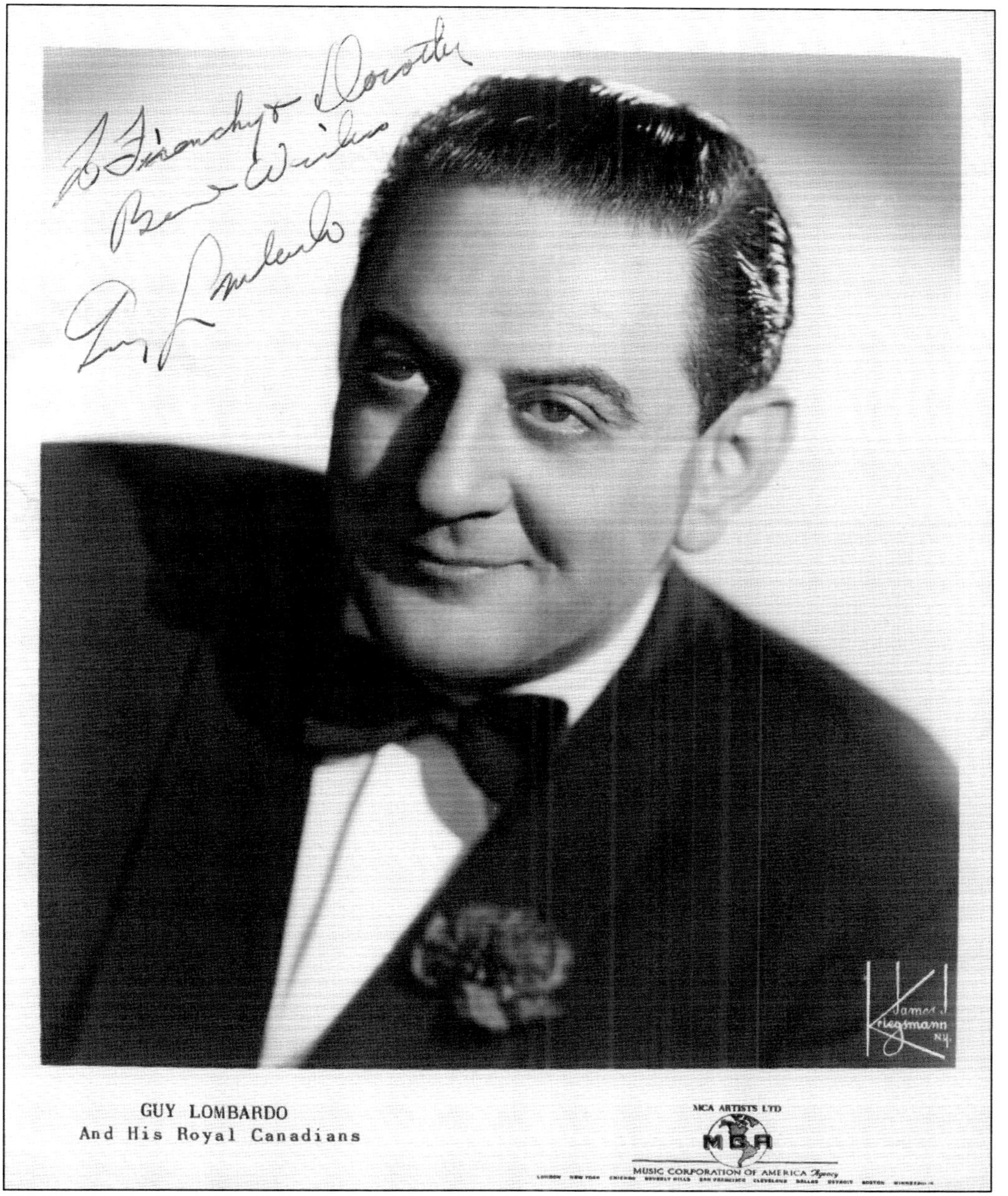

Born in London, Ontario, Canada on June 19, 1902, Guy Lombardo went on to become the most popular band leader on the American music scene. His orchestra, The Royal Canadians, sold over 100 million records. Between 1929 and 1952 there wasn't a year that a Lombardo record didn't make the chart, and 21 of them hit number one. (Photo from Dorothy Vincent. Inscription reads "To Frenchy & Dorothy, Best Wishes, Guy Lombardo.")

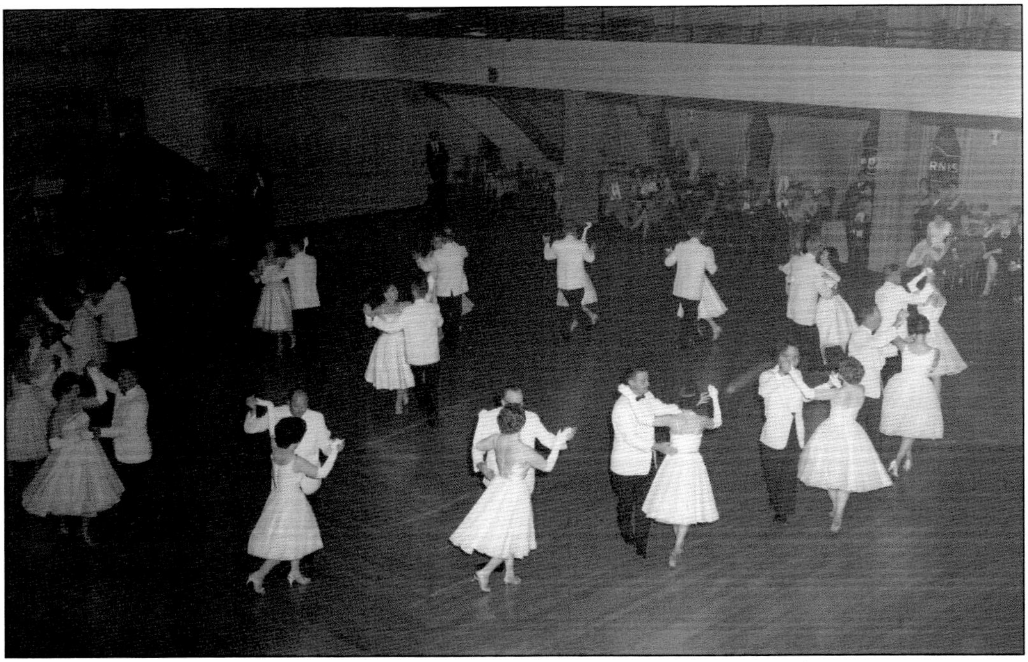

The Plaza Dance Club puts on a show at the Casa Loma Ballroom—truly poetry in motion. (Photo from Carol Kawell Ellis.)

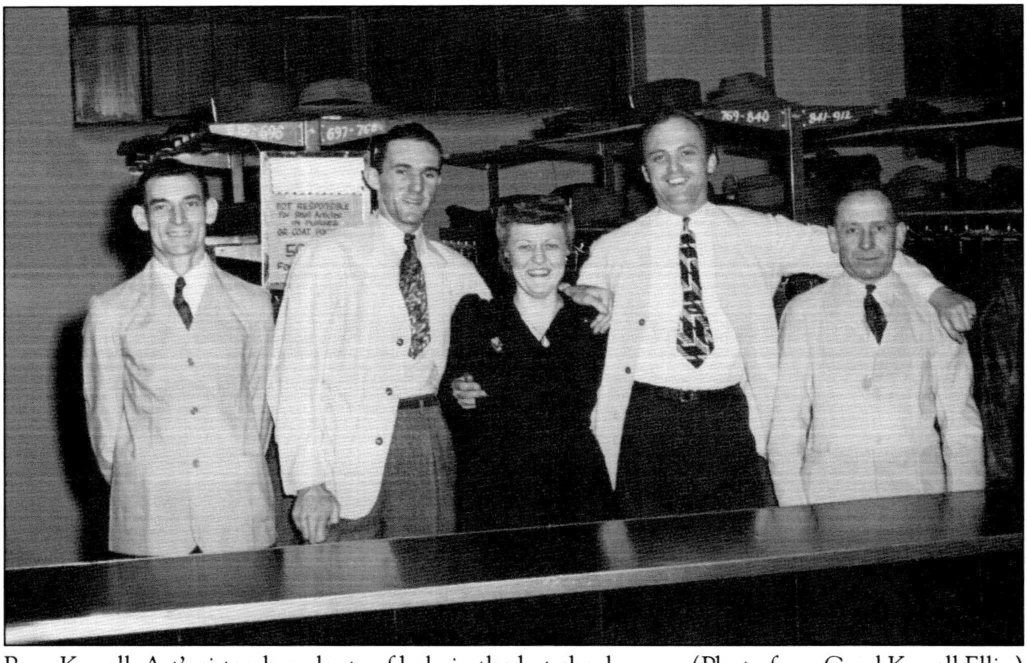

Rose Kawell, Art's sister, has plenty of help in the hat check room. (Photo from Carol Kawell Ellis.)

Four

Transition to the 1950s

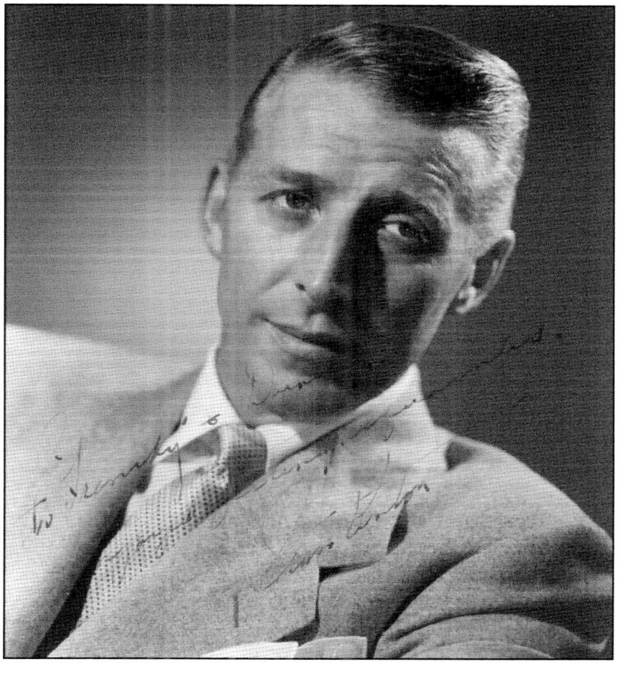

In the late 1940s, with the big band era coming to an end, and with many of the best orchestras disbanding, Stan Kenton was able to keep and even to increase his following, immune to the declining fortunes of other bands. His theme song was "Artistry in Rhythm." Kenton is remembered today as a leader who brought unbridled enthusiasm to jazz performance. (Photo from Dorothy Vincent.)

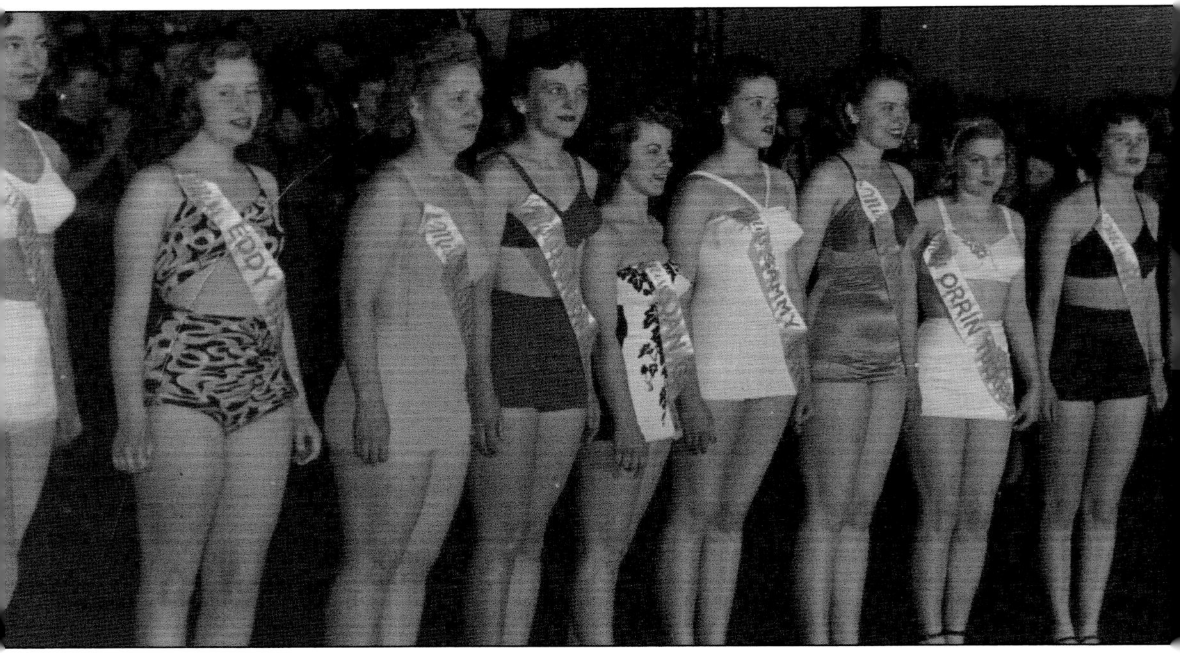

The contestants in this Miss Casa Loma contest line up one last time for the panel of judges.

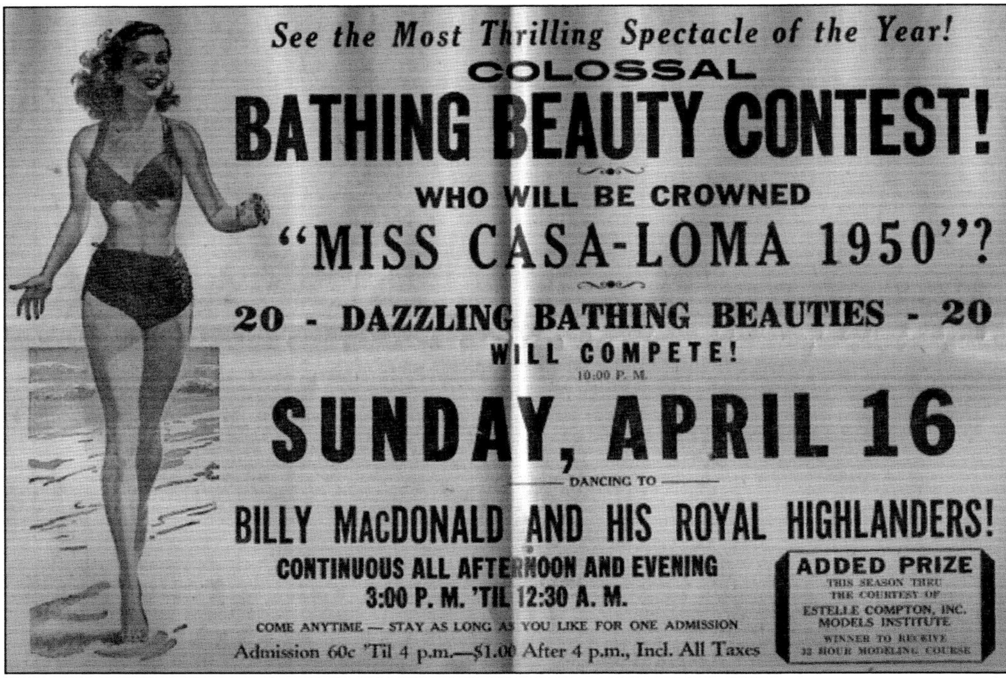

This 1950 newspaper advertisement possibly goes a little overboard in its claim for spectators to "See the Most Thrilling Spectacle of the Year!" However, in the late 1940s and through the 1950s the annual Miss Casa-Loma Bathing Beauty Contest was a much anticipated event in St. Louis. (Advertisement copy from Carol Kawell Ellis.)

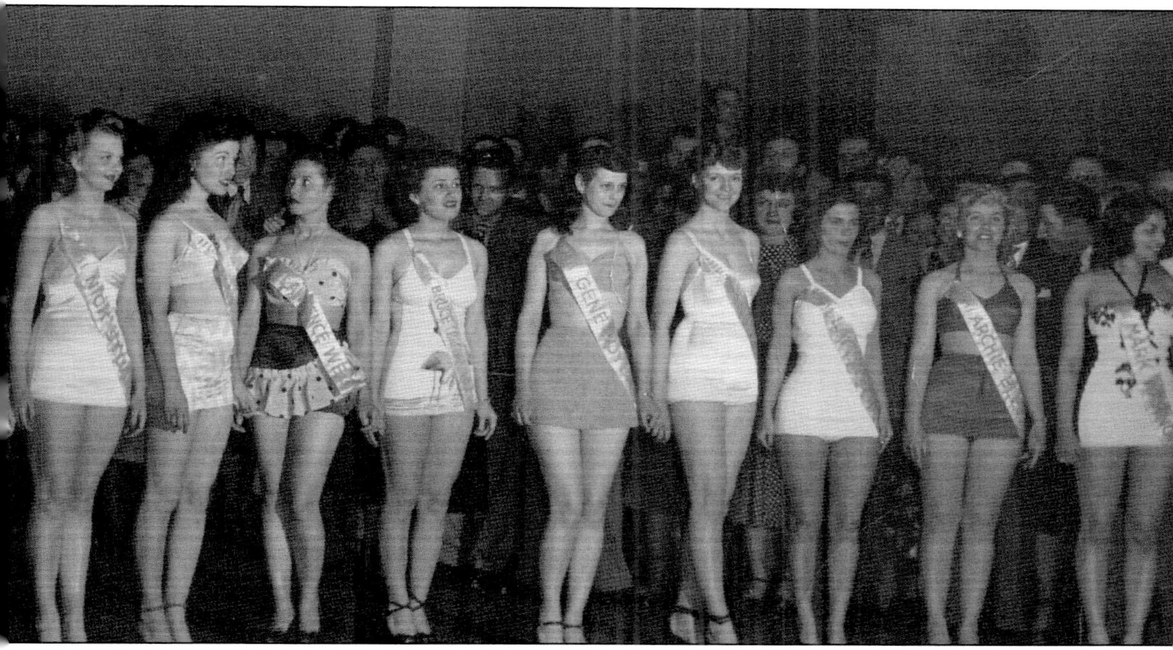

(Photo from Carol Kawell Ellis.)

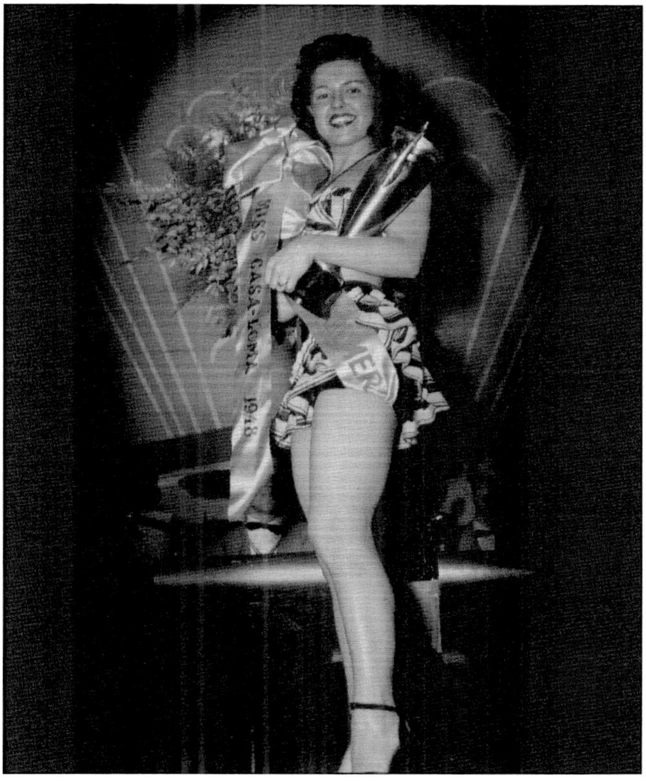

The winner of the title of "Miss Casa-Loma 1948" was Susan Smith (as Miss Jimmy Palmer). (Photo from Carol Kawell Ellis.)

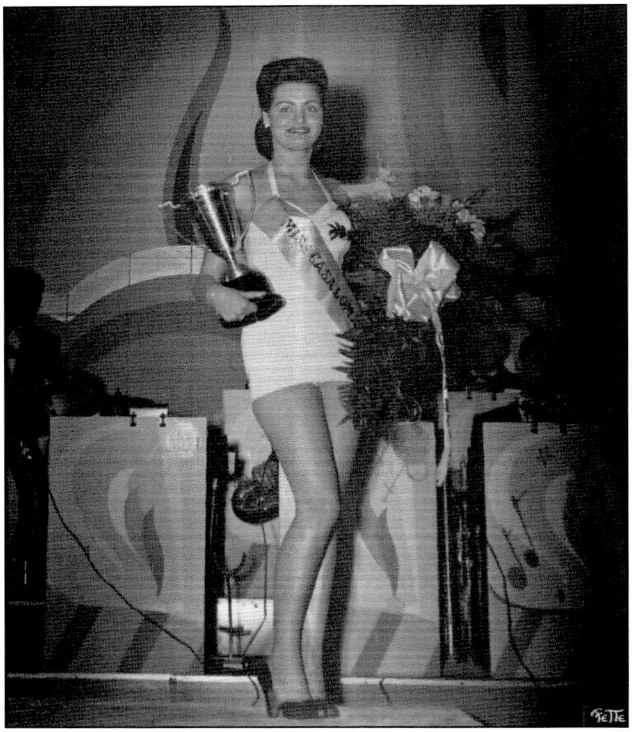

Miss Vickie Ossana was the winner of the 1949 contest. (Photo from Carol Kawell Ellis.)

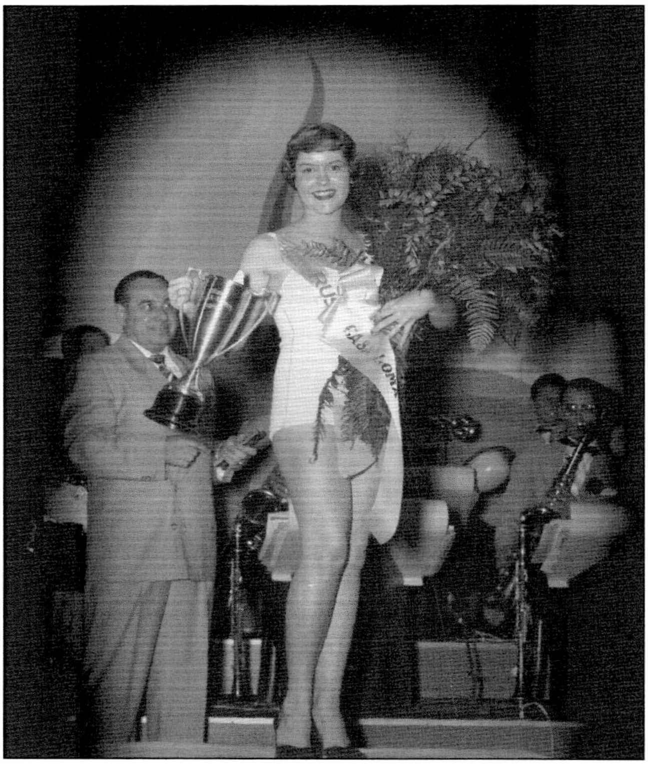

Miss Judy Hellerude (as Miss Russ Carlyle) was crowned Miss Casa-Loma in 1950. (Photo from Carol Kawell Ellis.)

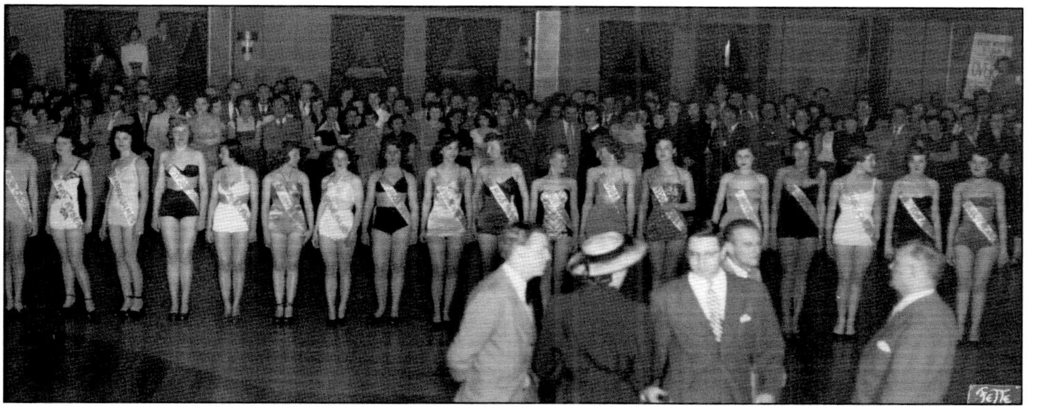

It's not difficult to see why the judges had a tough decision to make with all these lovely "Miss Casa-Loma" hopefuls vying for the crown. Some additional winners in the 1950s included Dorothy Bowen ('51), Lilly Mae Bruno ('52), and Rita Burnett ('53). (Photo from Carol Kawell Ellis.)

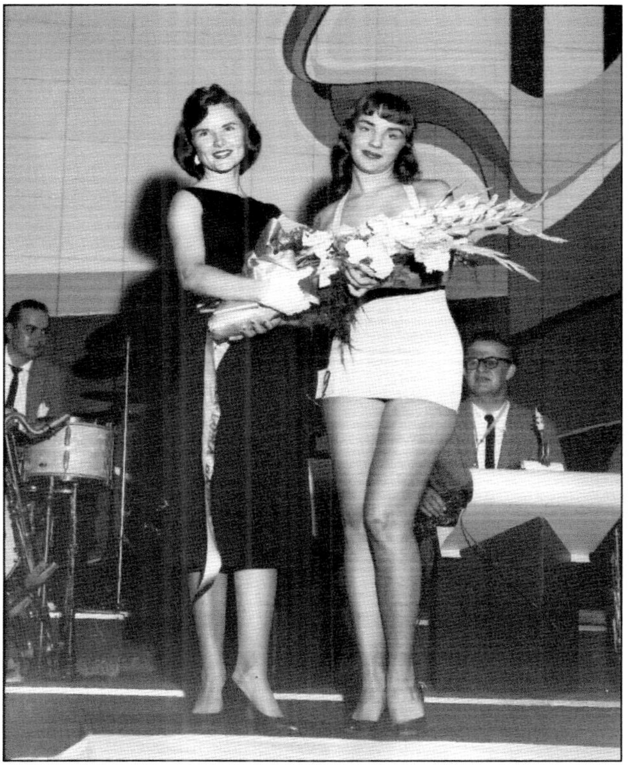

This photo shows Miss Casa-Loma 1956, Bennie Pritchard, turning over the reign to newly crowned 1957 winner, Peggy Tuhro, in one of the last occasions of this annual event. In the 1980s, Peggy Tuhro Goetz presented the owners of the Casa Loma Ballroom with the trophy that she was awarded back in 1957. Sadly that trophy is nowhere to be found at the Casa Loma Ballroom today. (Photo from Carol Kawell Ellis.)

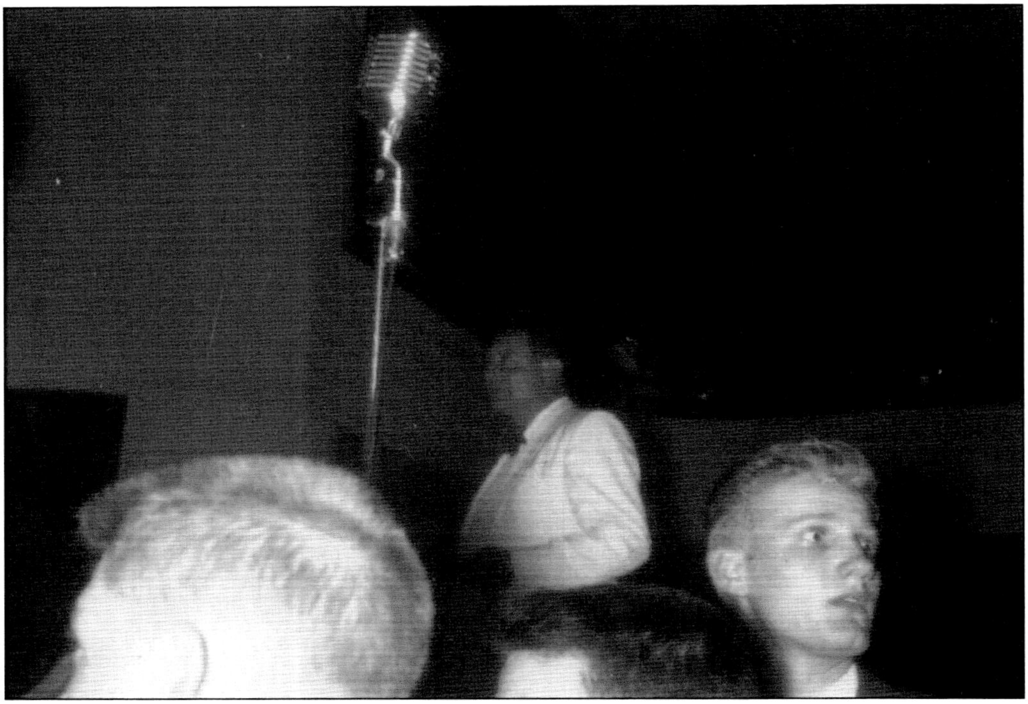

The next few pages contain a number of rare photographs that were taken in the early 1950s during live performances at the Casa Loma Ballroom. In this one we see Guy Lombardo on stage in 1952 with a number of audience members getting a close-up look at the famous orchestra. (Photo from Al Williams.)

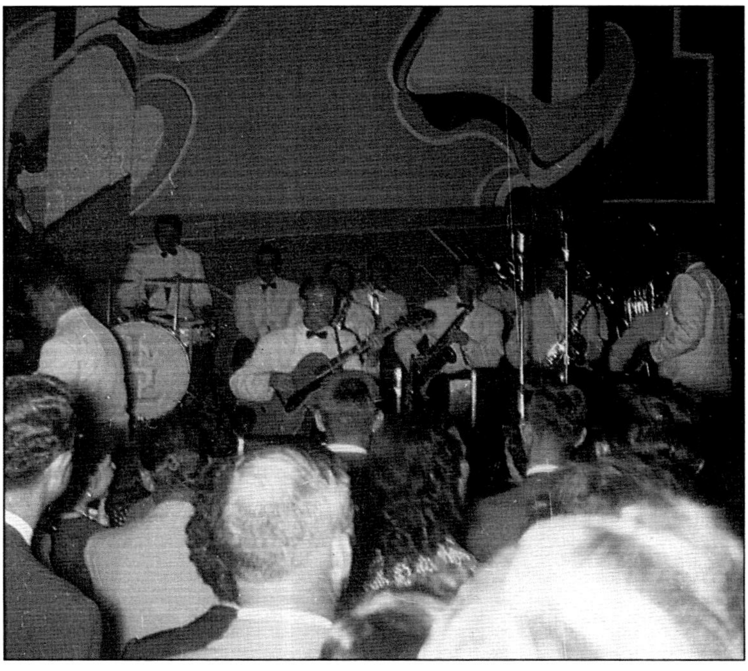

Here's another angle of the same performance of the Guy Lombardo Orchestra with Guy directing. Notice that the audience appears more intent on hearing and seeing than dancing. (Photo from Al Williams.)

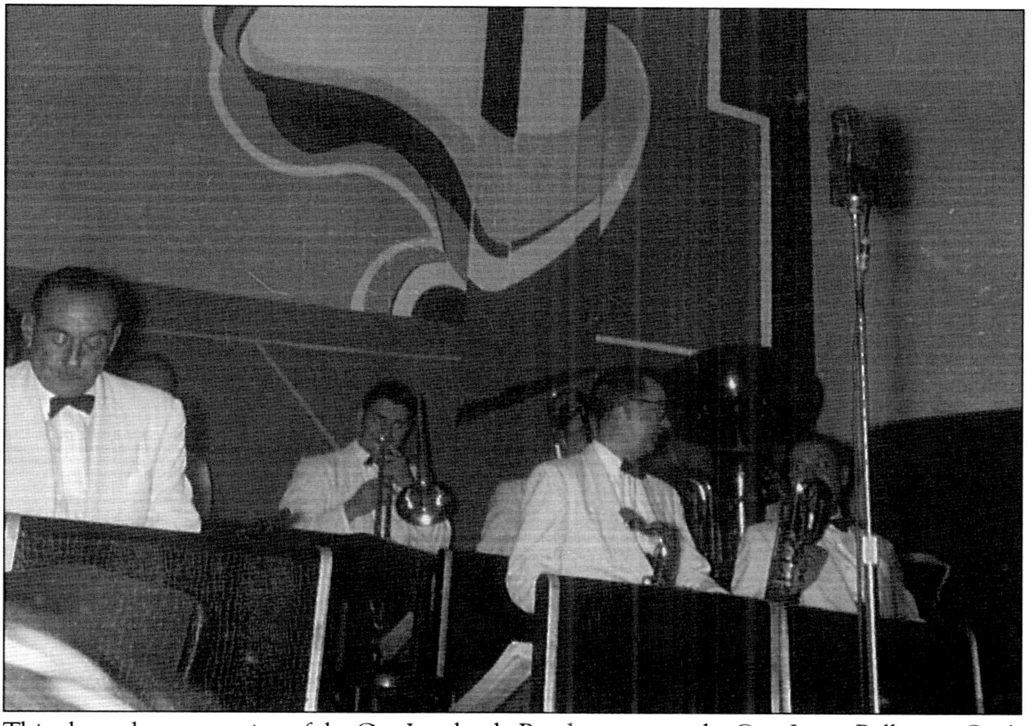

This photo shows a portion of the Guy Lombardo Band on stage at the Casa Loma Ballroom. Guy's brother, Carmen Lombardo, who played sax and sang, is on the left. (Photo from Al Williams.)

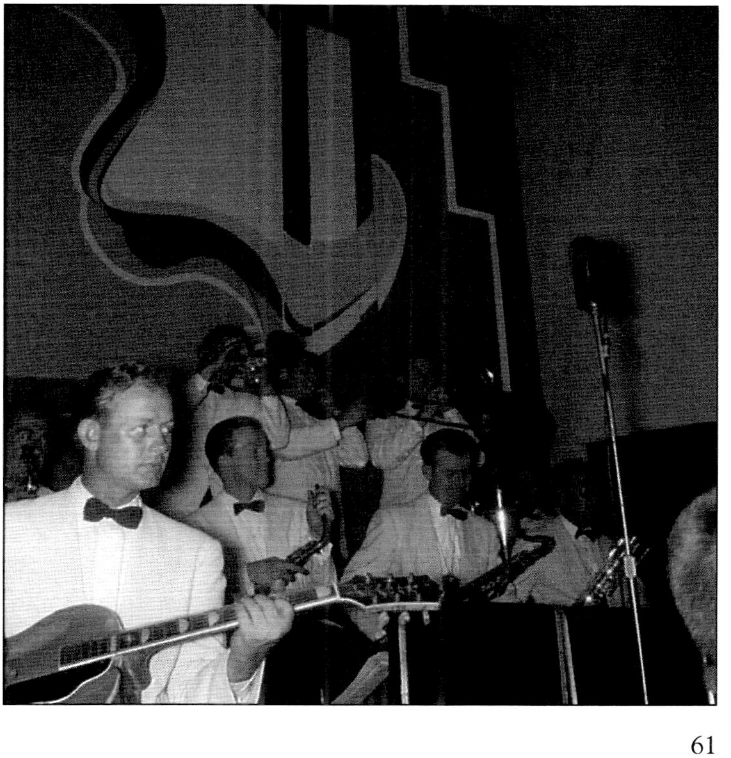

Another photo of the Guy Lombardo Band on stage at the Casa Loma Ballroom. (Photo from Al Williams.)

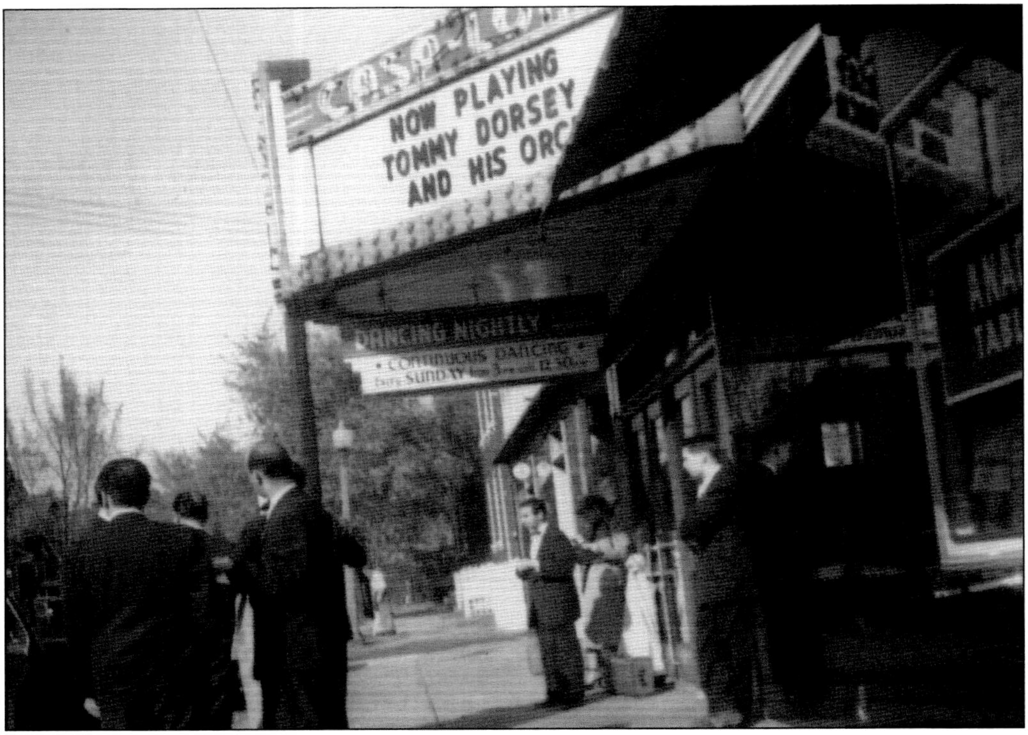

The Tommy Dorsey Band is waiting to get into the Casa Loma Ballroom on a Sunday afternoon. This photo, taken in 1952, shows the Iowa Street entrance to the Ballroom. (Photo from Al Williams.)

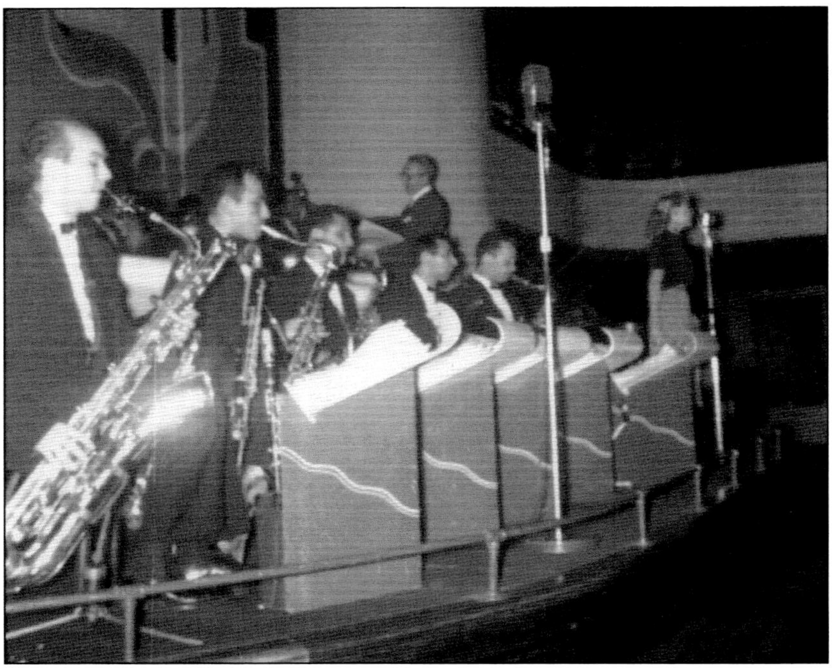

The Tommy Dorsey Band performs live on stage at the Casa Loma. (Photo from Al Williams.)

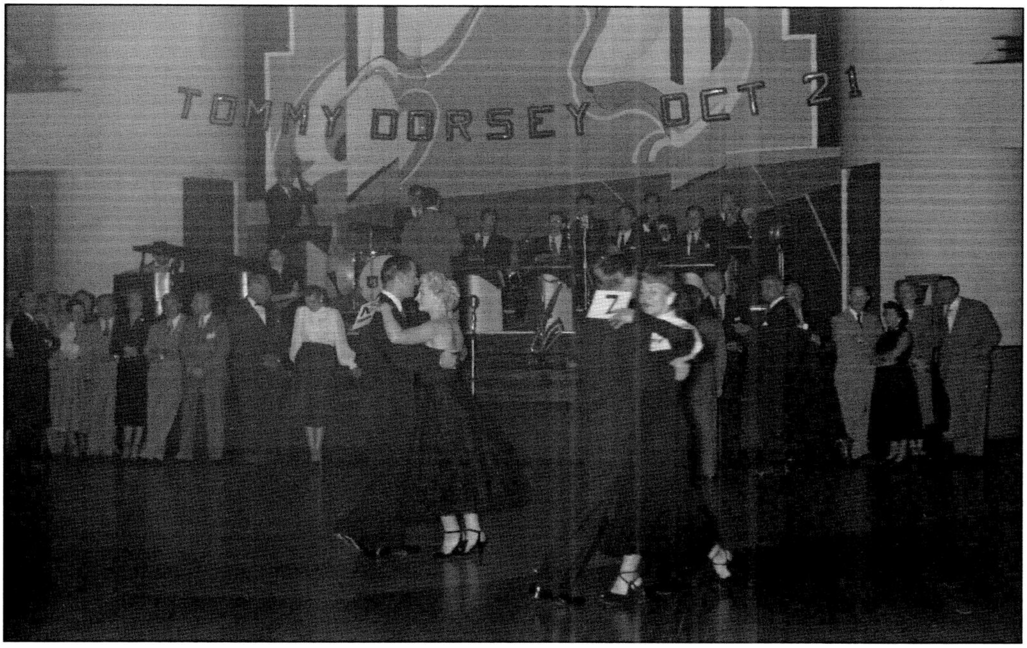

Just before the Dorsey Brothers were reunited in 1953, the Tommy Dorsey Orchestra played at a dance contest held in the Casa Loma Ballroom. After the reunion, the Dorsey Brothers, led mainly by Tommy, but with Jimmy prominently featured, earned national publicity in 1955–56 through the Dorseys' own TV program on CBS. (Photo from Carol Kawell Ellis.)

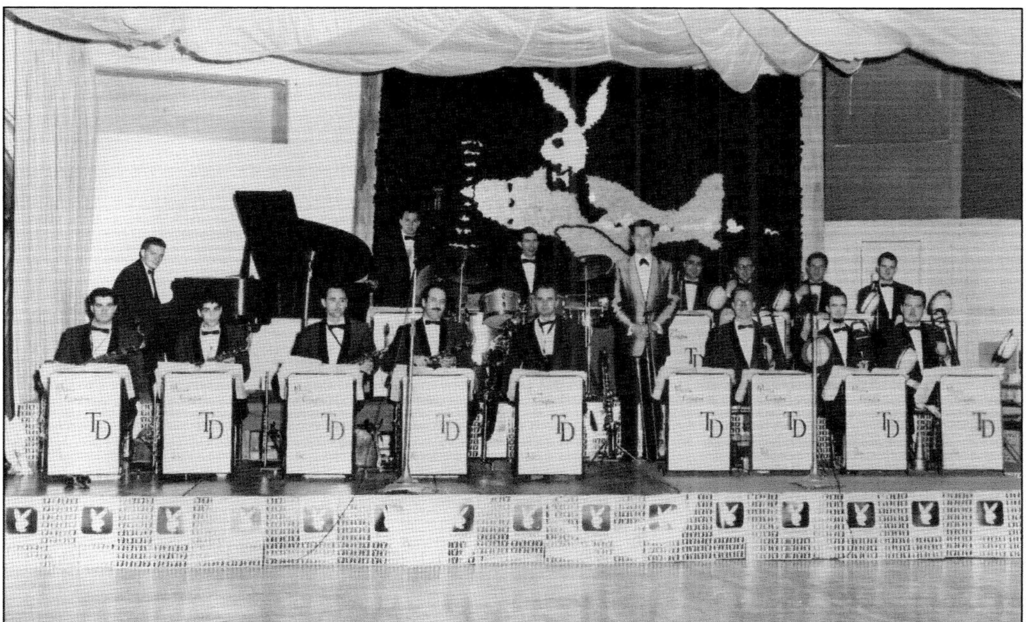

In the fall of 1957, after the sudden death of Tommy Dorsey the year before, an orchestra designed as the Tommy Dorsey band, under the direction of trombonist Warren Covington, was organized and toured dance halls throughout the country. (Photo from Carol Kawell Ellis.)

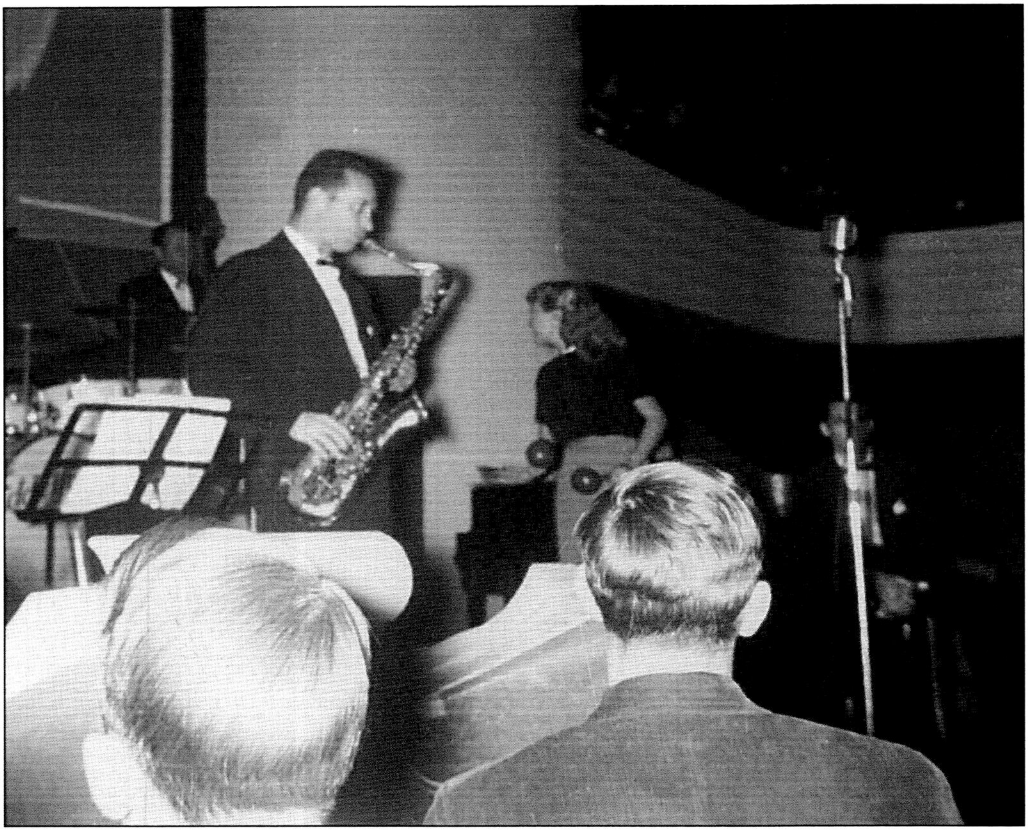

Sam Donahue on tenor sax takes center stage at the Casa Loma Ballroom. A member of the Tommy Dorsey Band, Sam took over the band when Tommy Dorsey died in 1956. (Photo from Al Williams.)

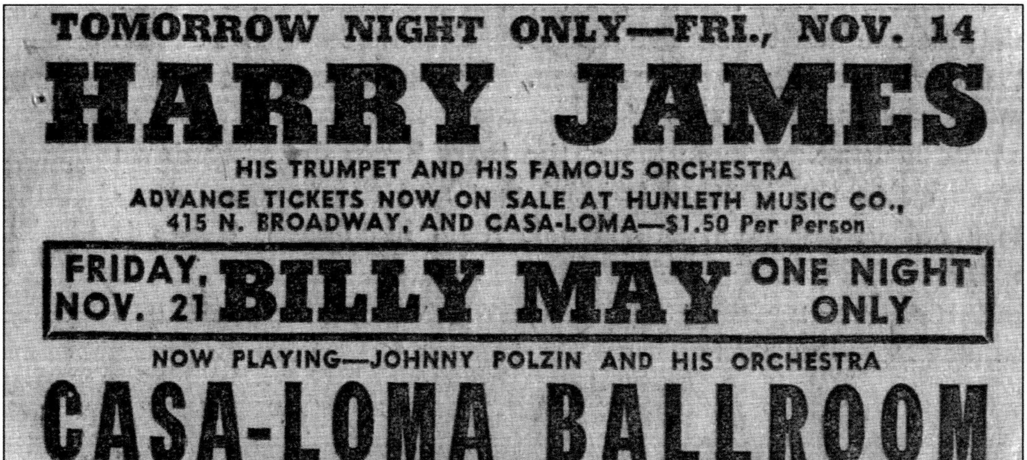

TOMORROW NIGHT ONLY—FRI., NOV. 14

HARRY JAMES

HIS TRUMPET AND HIS FAMOUS ORCHESTRA

ADVANCE TICKETS NOW ON SALE AT HUNLETH MUSIC CO., 415 N. BROADWAY, AND CASA-LOMA—$1.50 Per Person

FRIDAY, NOV. 21 BILLY MAY ONE NIGHT ONLY

NOW PLAYING—JOHNNY POLZIN AND HIS ORCHESTRA

CASA-LOMA BALLROOM

DANCING NIGHTLY EXCEPT MONDAYS—CONTINUOUS SUNDAYS 3 'til 12:30

Harry James and Billy May newspaper advertisement—Friday, November 14 and 21, 1952. (Newspaper clipping from Al Williams.)

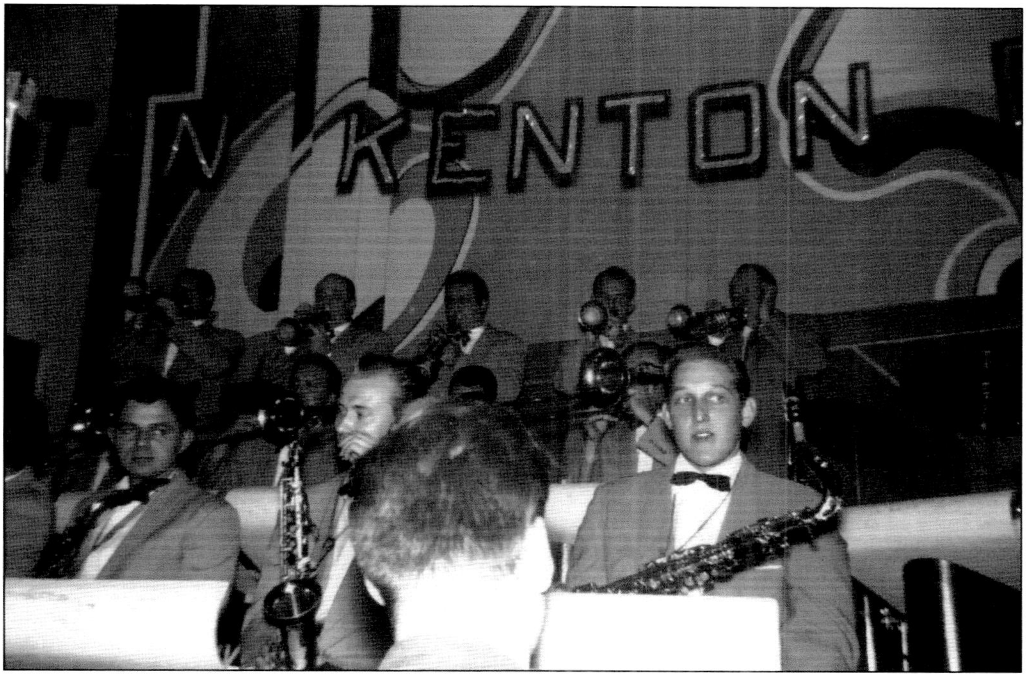

Billy May with the trumpet section—Casa Loma had put a sign for Stan Kenton over the Billy May Band advertising Kenton's upcoming appearance. This photo was taken during a performance in 1952. (Photo from Al Williams.)

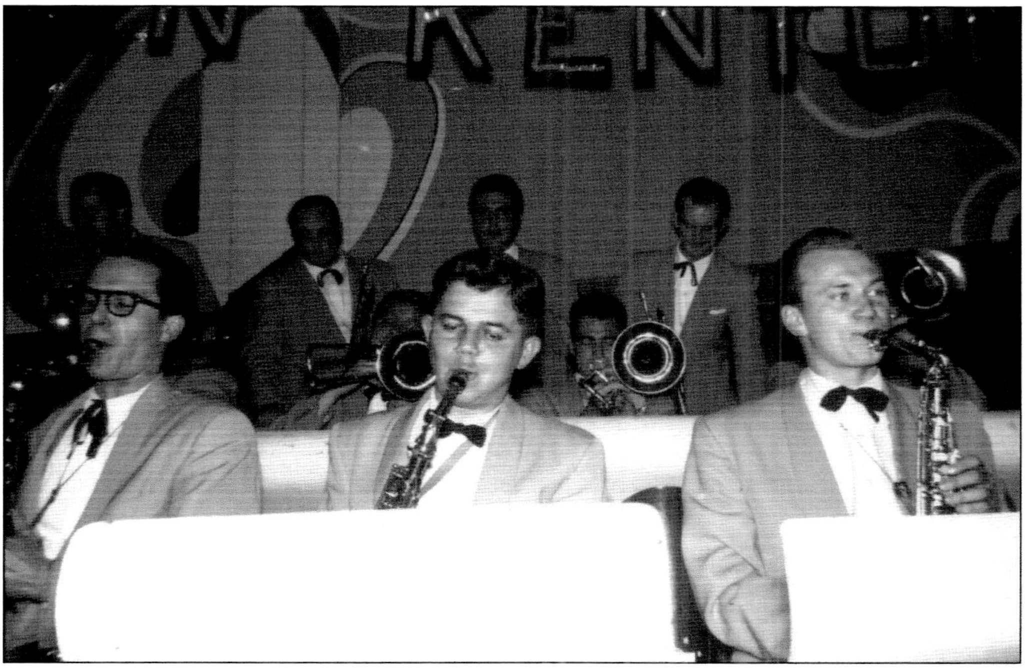

Part of the Billy May saxophone section seem all concentration. (Photo from Al Williams.)

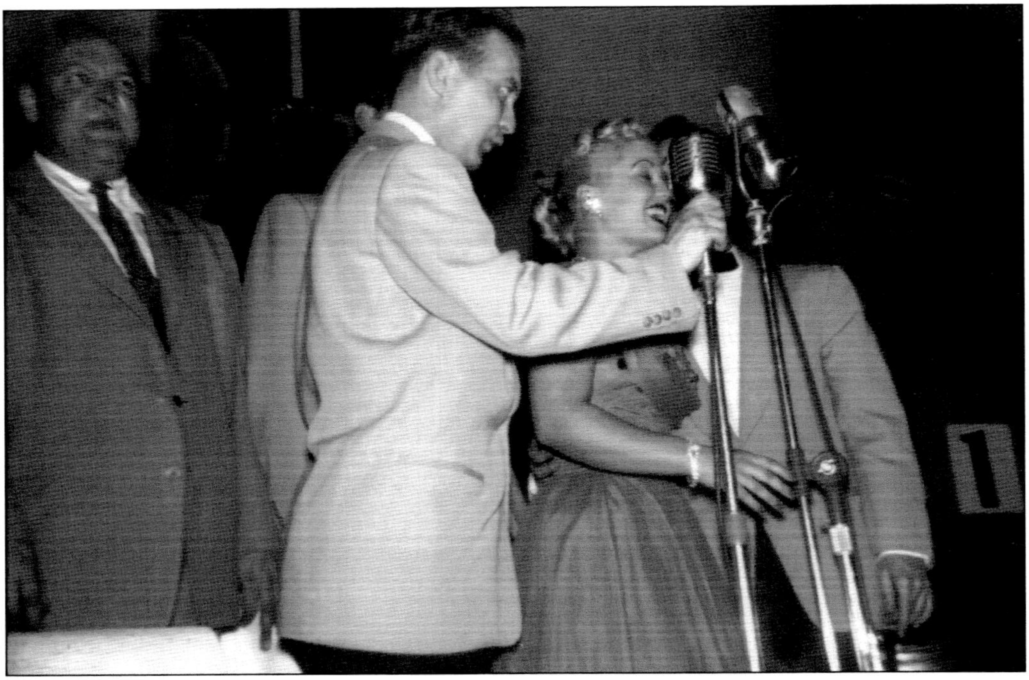

Billy May (left) makes faces on the bandstand. (Photo from Al Williams.)

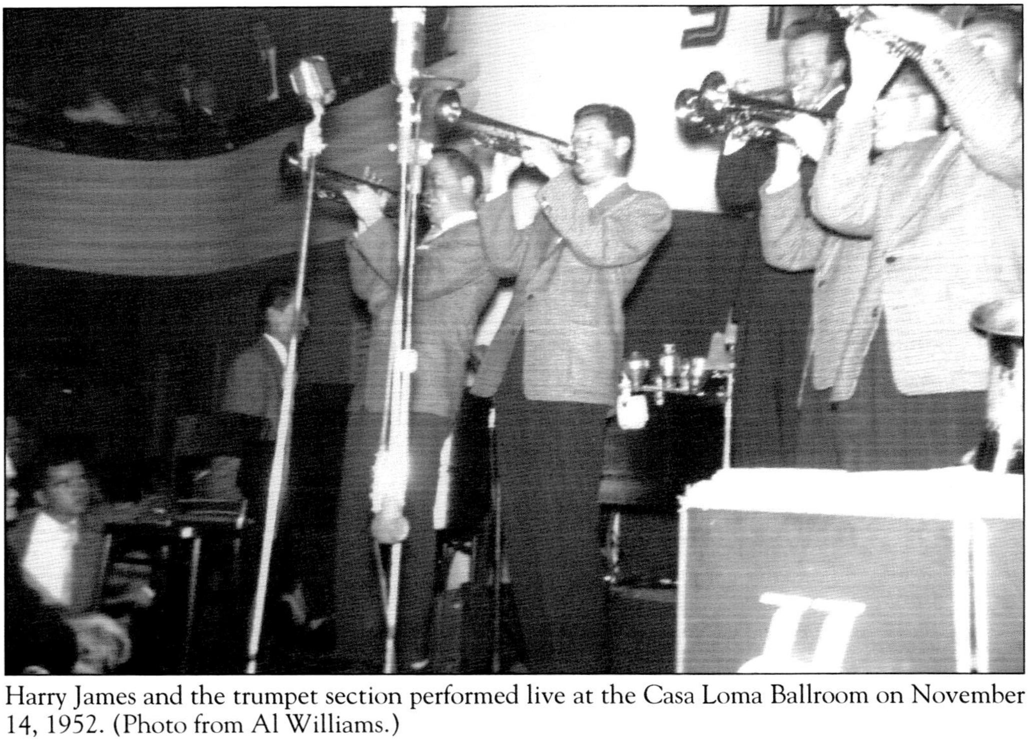

Harry James and the trumpet section performed live at the Casa Loma Ballroom on November 14, 1952. (Photo from Al Williams.)

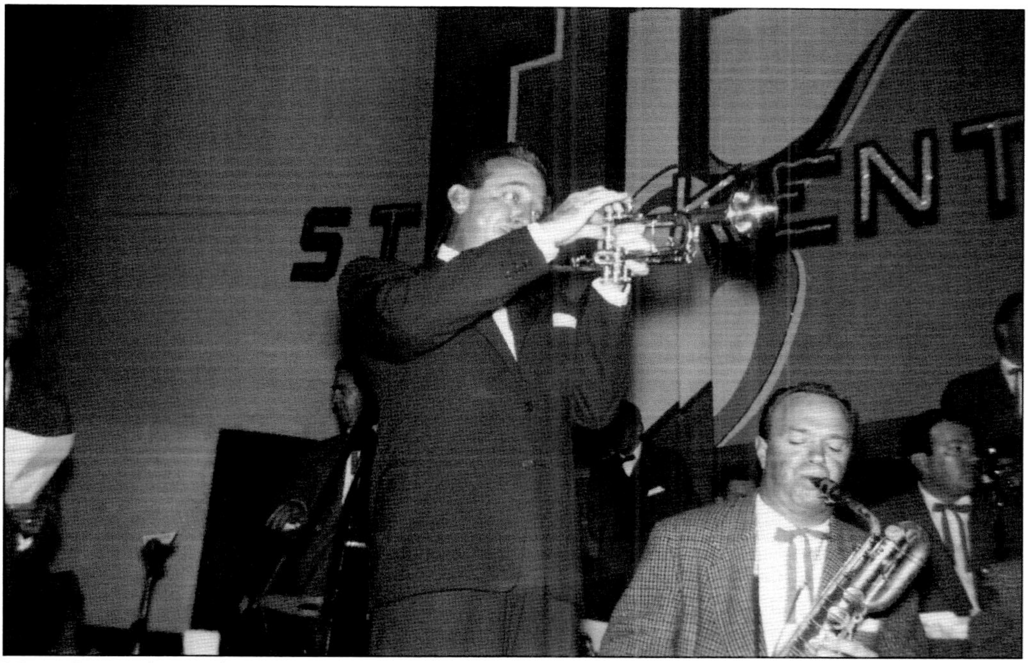
Harry James shares the Casa Loma Ballroom stage with his band. (Photo from Al Williams.)

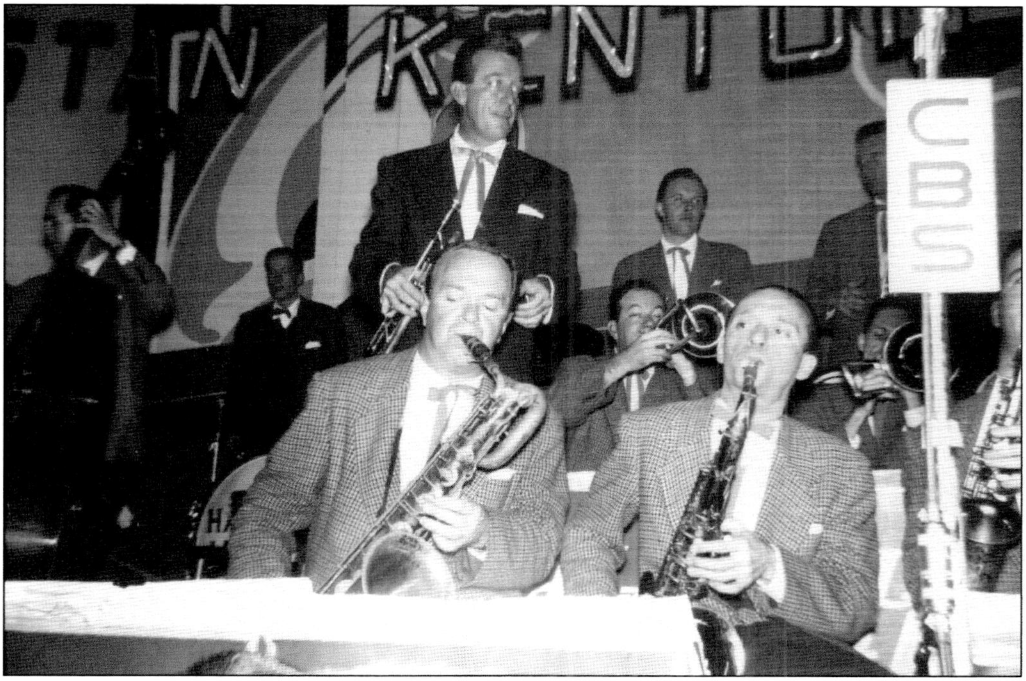

The Harry James Band features Harry and Bob Poland on baritone sax. (Photo from Al Williams.)

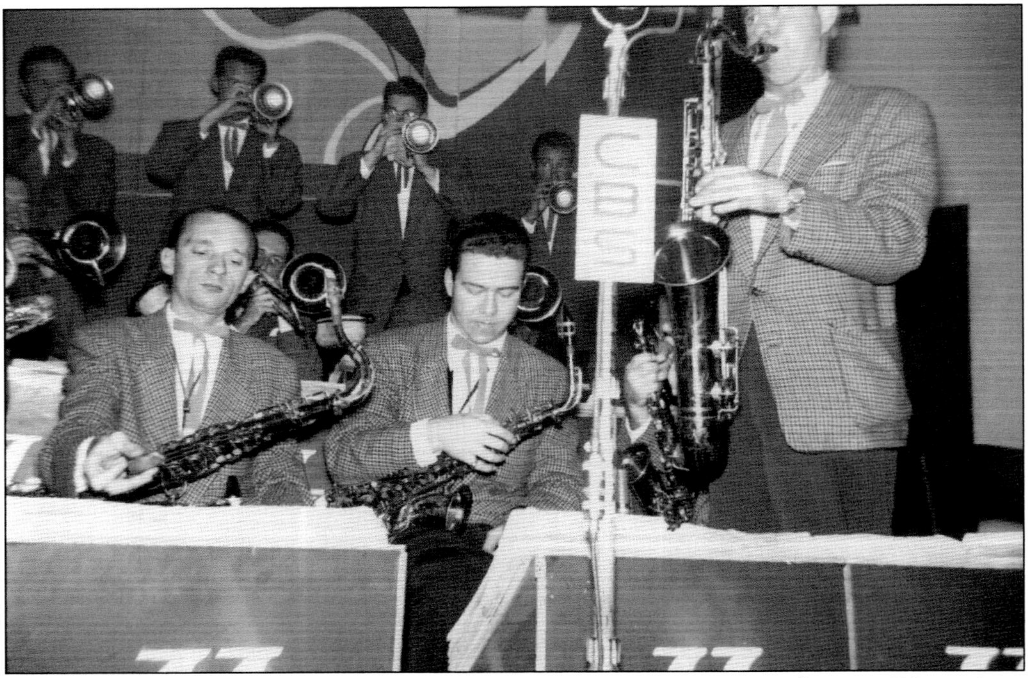

Harry James Band broadcasting live on CBS from the Casa Loma Ballroom. (Photo from Al Williams.)

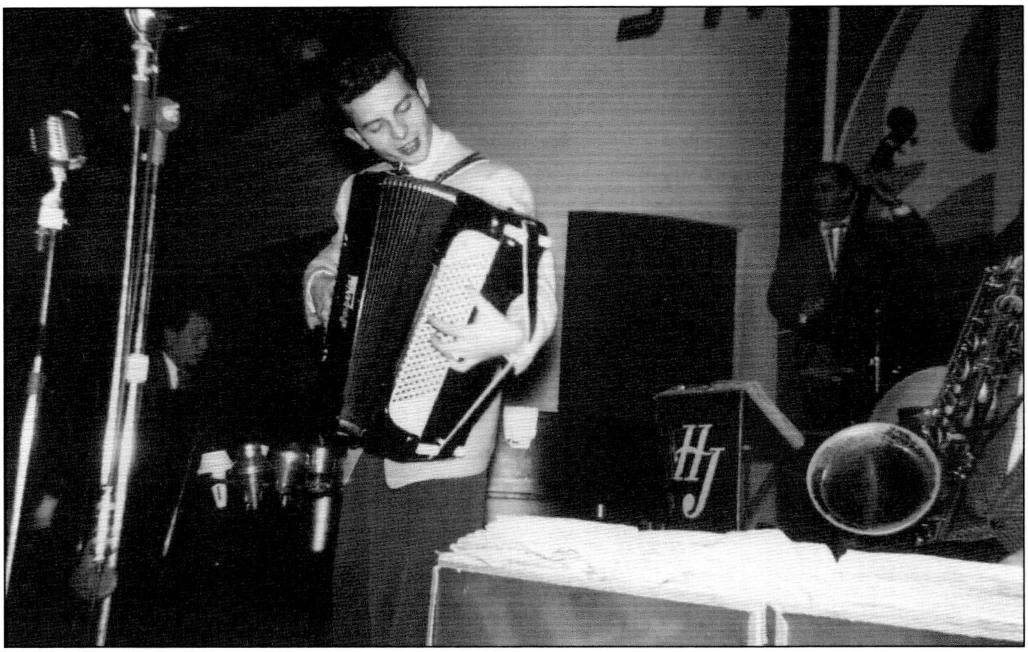

A young accordion player goes solo with the Harry James Band. (Photo from Al Williams.)

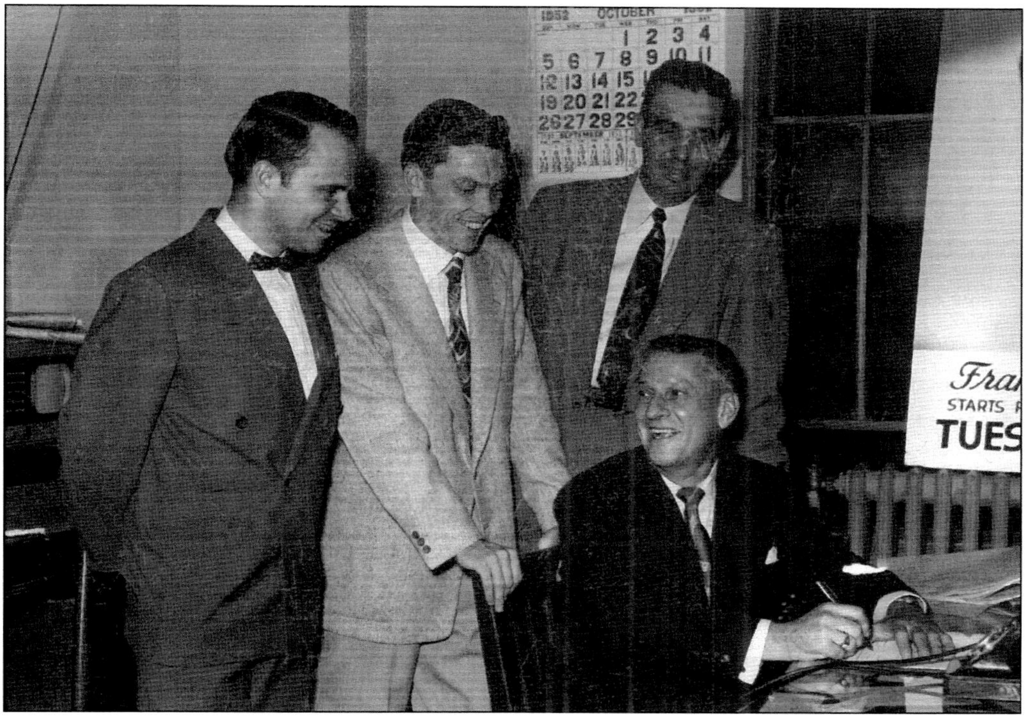

H. J. (Nap) Burien, co-owner of the Casa Loma Ballroom, is shown seated at his desk in the above photo taken in October 1952. That's Ed Bonner standing in the middle. Ed began his "DJ" career on KXOK radio the year before, when he was only 28. His first program, *St. Louis Ballroom* soon gave way to the station's afternoon drive slot, and his large audience encompassed teens and adults. He left KXOK in 1958, taking his listeners with him to WIL. (Photo from Carol Kawell Ellis.)

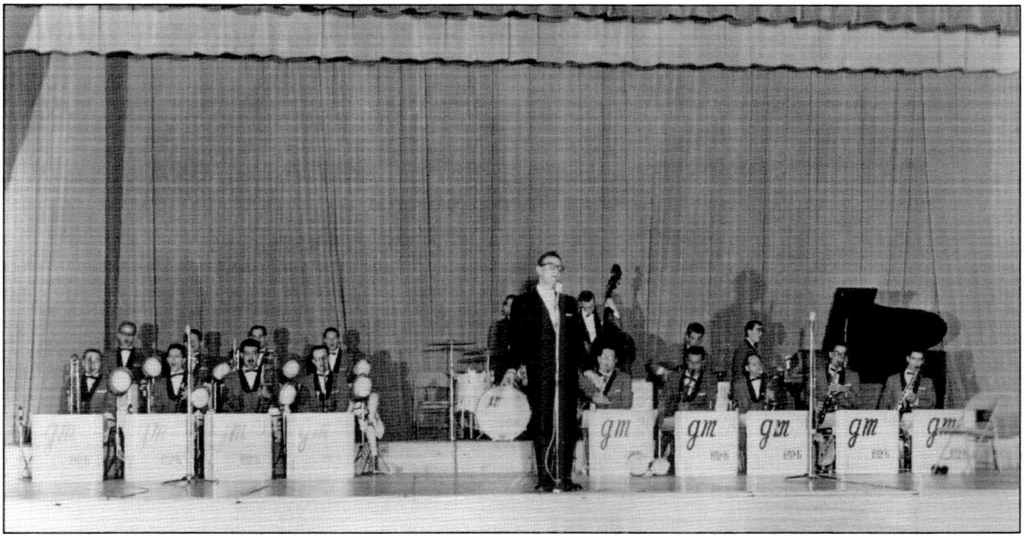

The new Glenn Miller Orchestra under the direction of Ray McKinley played the Casa Loma Ballroom sometime after they organized in 1957. (Photo from Carol Kawell Ellis.)

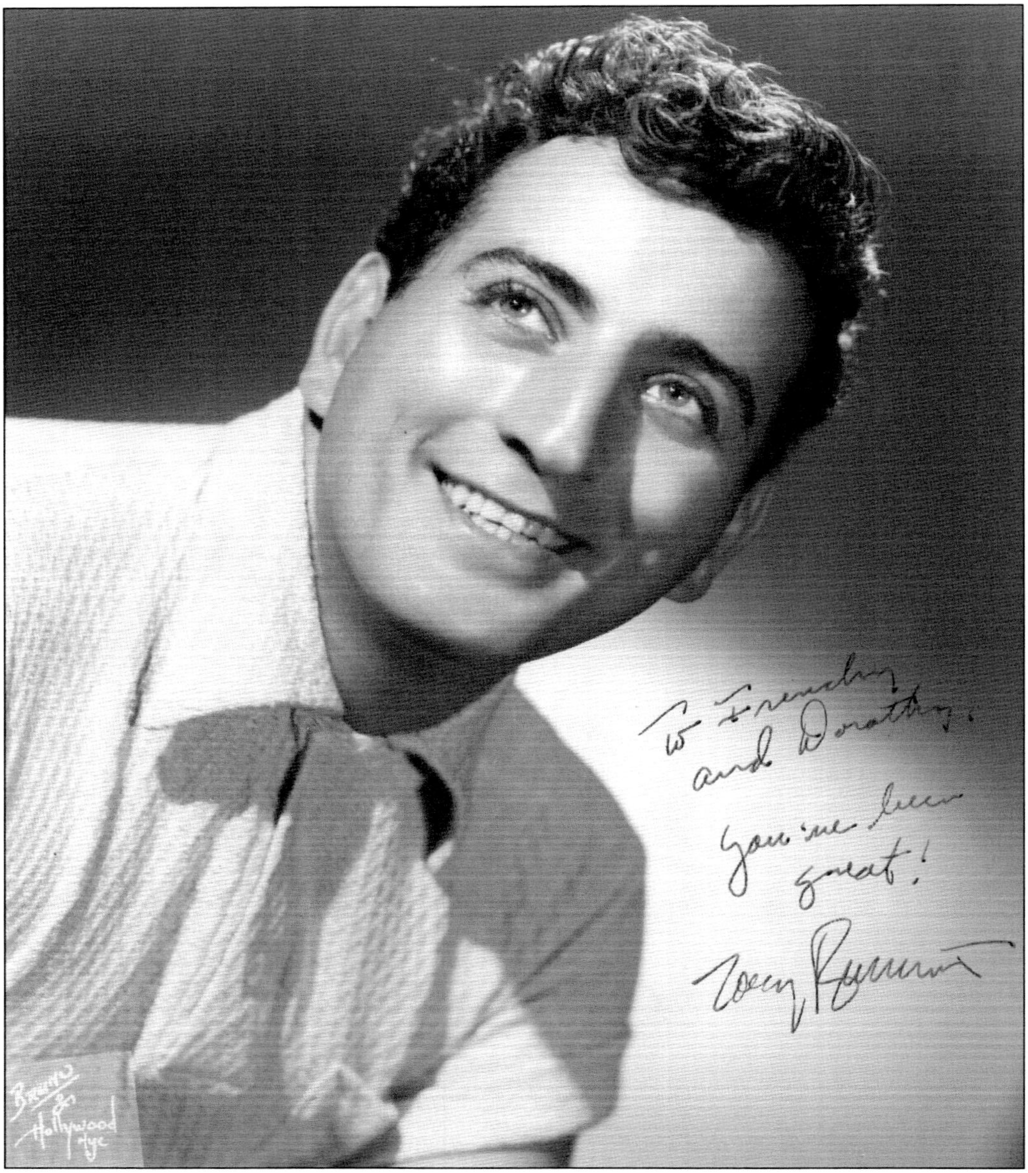

Tony Bennett's big break came in 1949 when comedian Bob Hope spotted him working with Pearl Bailey in Greenwich Village. With over 50 million records sold world-wide and platinum and gold albums to his credit, Bennett has won ten Grammy Awards including the Grammy Lifetime Achievement Award. His initial successes came via a string of singles in the early 1950s, including such hits as "Because of You," "Rags To Riches," and "Cold, Cold Heart." He had 24 songs in the Top 40, including "I Wanna Be Around," "The Good Life," "Who Can I Turn To (When Nobody Needs Me)," and his signature song, "I Left My Heart In San Francisco," which garnered him two Grammy Awards. One can assume that a number of these songs reverberated through the Casa Loma Ballroom during his appearance in the 1950s. (Photo from Dorothy Vincent. Inscription reads "To Frenchy and Dorothy, You've been great! Tony Bennett.")

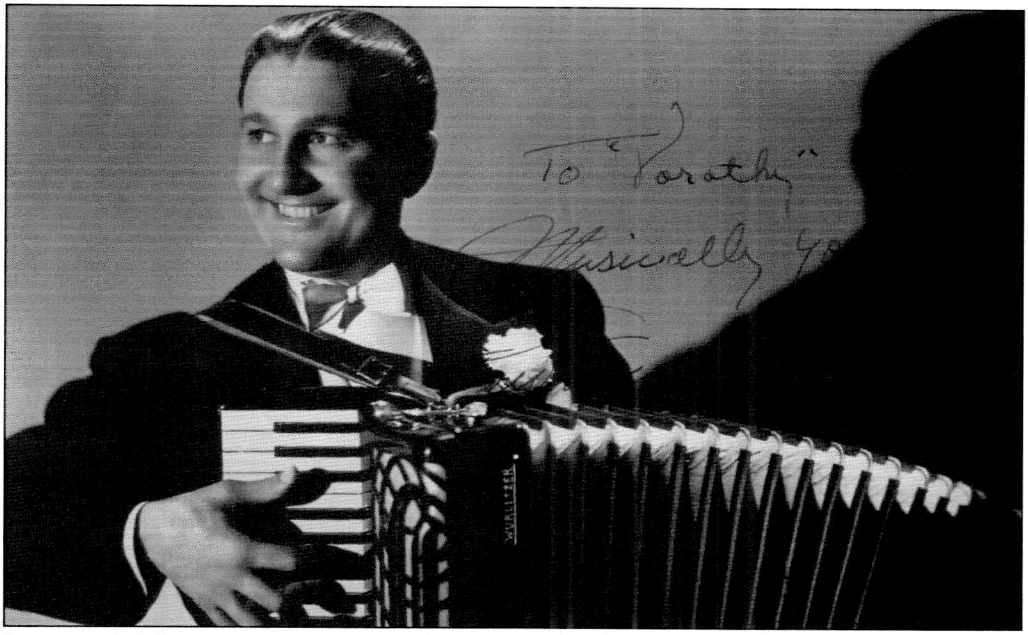

Lawrence Welk was a musician, accordion player, band leader, and television star. His music was conservative, concentrating mostly on pop song standards, polkas, and novelty songs, all delivered in a smooth, calming, good-humored, easy-listening style. His show was warm and family-oriented. His "Champagne Music" has been considered the epitome of "square." During the 1930s and 1940s, Welk led a traveling big band, specializing in dance tunes and 'sweet' music. In 1955, he began producing *The Lawrence Welk Show*. (Photo from Dorothy Vincent. Inscription reads "To Dorothy" Musically Yours, Lawrence Welk.")

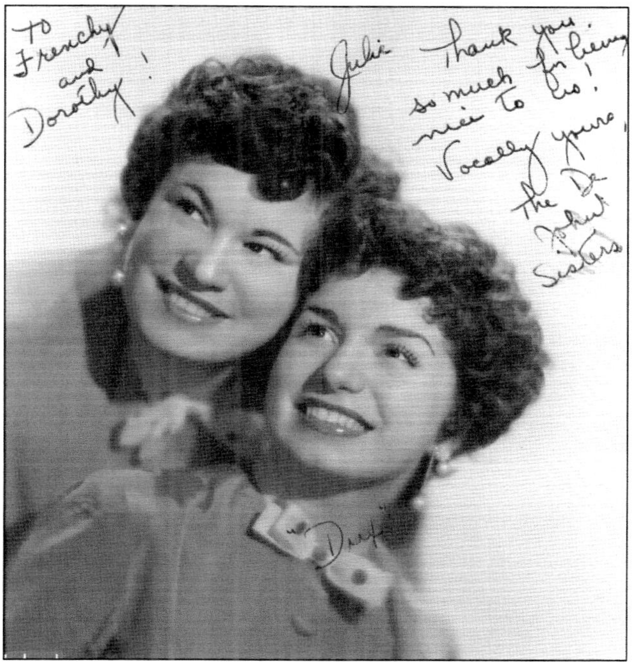

Julie and Dux (the De John Sisters) played at the Casa Loma Ballroom in the late fifties, having gained popularity on Dick Clark's *American Bandstand*. (Photo from Dorothy Vincent. Inscription reads "To Frenchy and Dorothy" Thank you so much for being nice to us, Vocally Yours, the De John Sisters.")

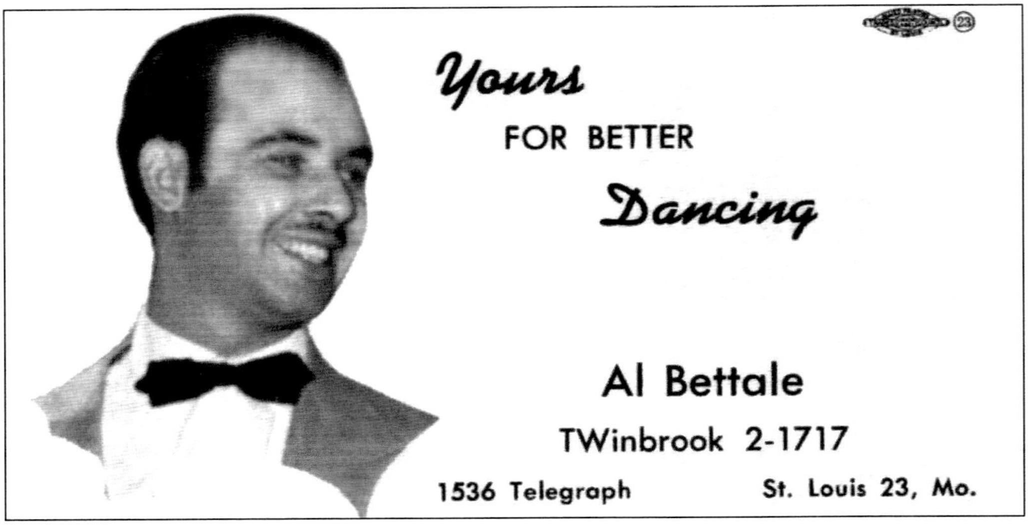

Al Bettale is approaching his 50th anniversary of first dancing the night away at the Casa Loma Ballroom. A ballroom dancer for more than 60 years, and a dance instructor at the Casa Loma, as well as at the Avalon Ballroom in Chicago, and many other noted clubs all across the nation, Al, and his wife, Rose, have seen the dance steps change through the years. From fox trot to jitterbug to waltz, Al has taught it all. As Al said in an interview with Max Kaiser in 1995, "The Casa Loma was, and is, one of the unique dance clubs in the city. (Information gathered from *St. Louis Times* edition of January 1995, article by Max Kaiser.)

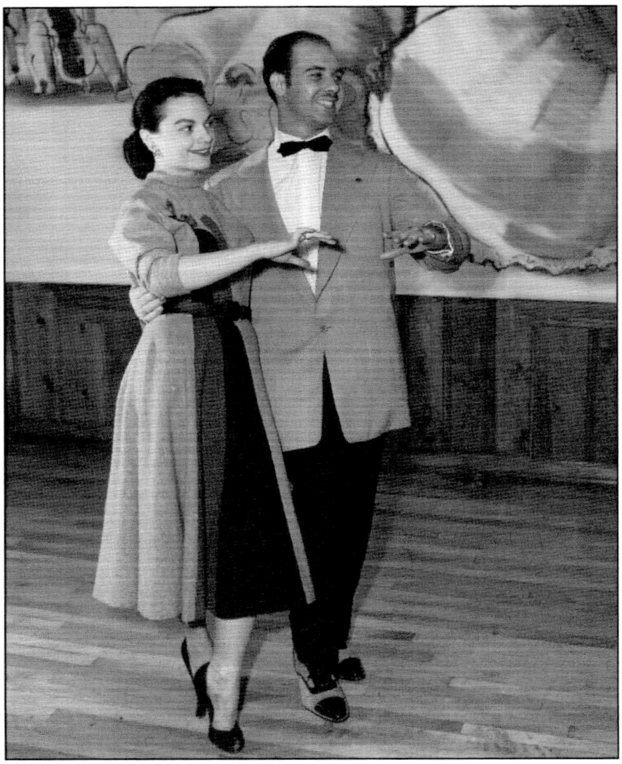

Al Bettale and his dance partner perform in one of the many dance contests in which he participated in the St. Louis area. (Photo from Carol Kawell Ellis.)

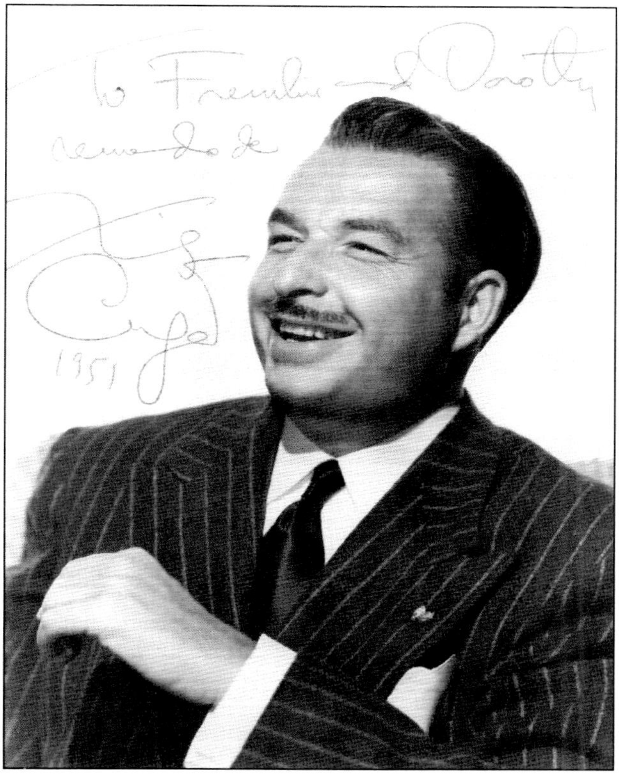

Xavier Cugat trained as a classical violinist. In the late 1920s, as sound began to be used in movies, he assembled a tango band that had some success in very early musical shorts. By the early 1930s, he began appearing in feature films. Cugat took his band to New York to open the new Waldorf Astoria Hotel and they became the hotel's resident group. Married four times, Cugat's wife at the time they played at the Casa Loma Ballroom in 1951 was Abbe Lane. (Photo from Dorothy Vincent.)

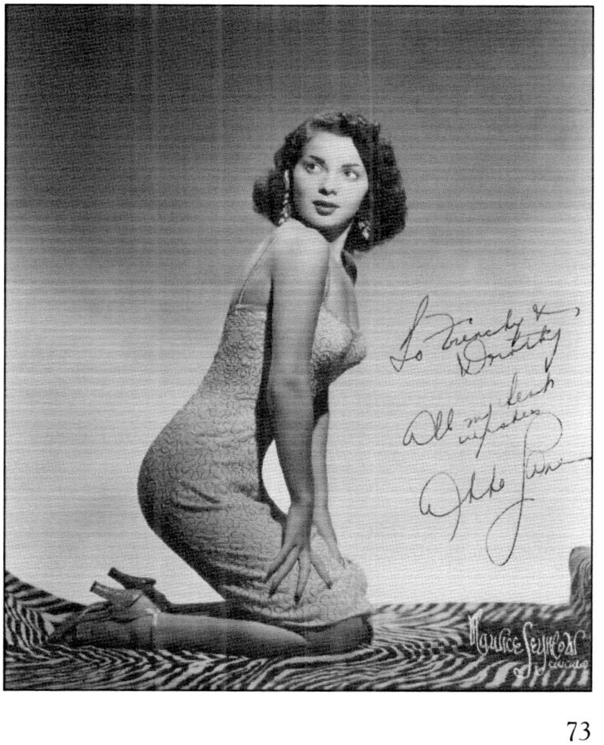

Abbe Lane was only 19 years old when she appeared with her husband Xavier Cugat and his orchestra at the Casa Loma Ballroom. (Photo from Dorothy Vincent. Inscription reads "To Frenchy & Dorothy, All my best wishes, Abbe Lane.")

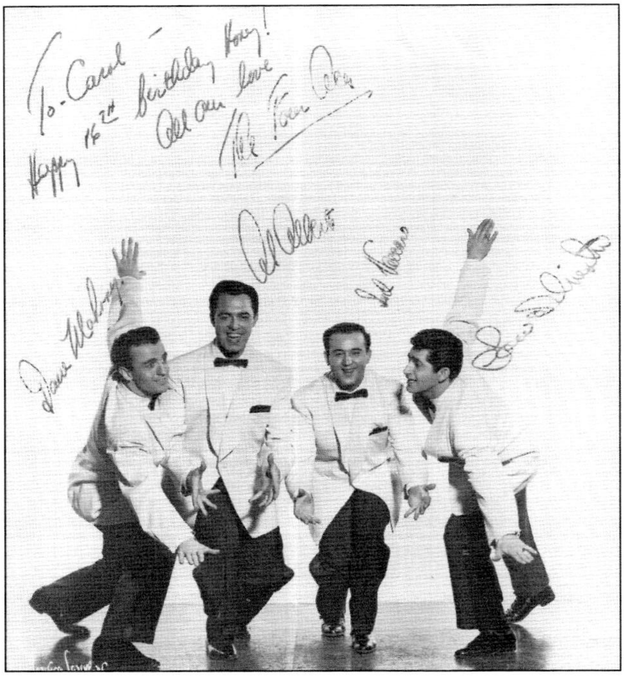

One of the most successful pre-rock vocal groups, the Four Aces did well during the early 50s. Founded by Navy shipmates Al Alberts and Dave Mahoney, the act added Lou Silvestri and Sol Vaccaro before making a name for themselves around their native Philadelphia. A few Top Ten hits followed, during the early 50s, before the theme to *Three Coins in the Fountain* hit number one in 1954. Another movie theme, "Love Is a Many-Splendored Thing," spent over a month at the top during 1955. This inscription reads "To Carol—Happy 16th birthday honey! All our love, The Four Aces" (Photo from Carol Kawell Ellis.)

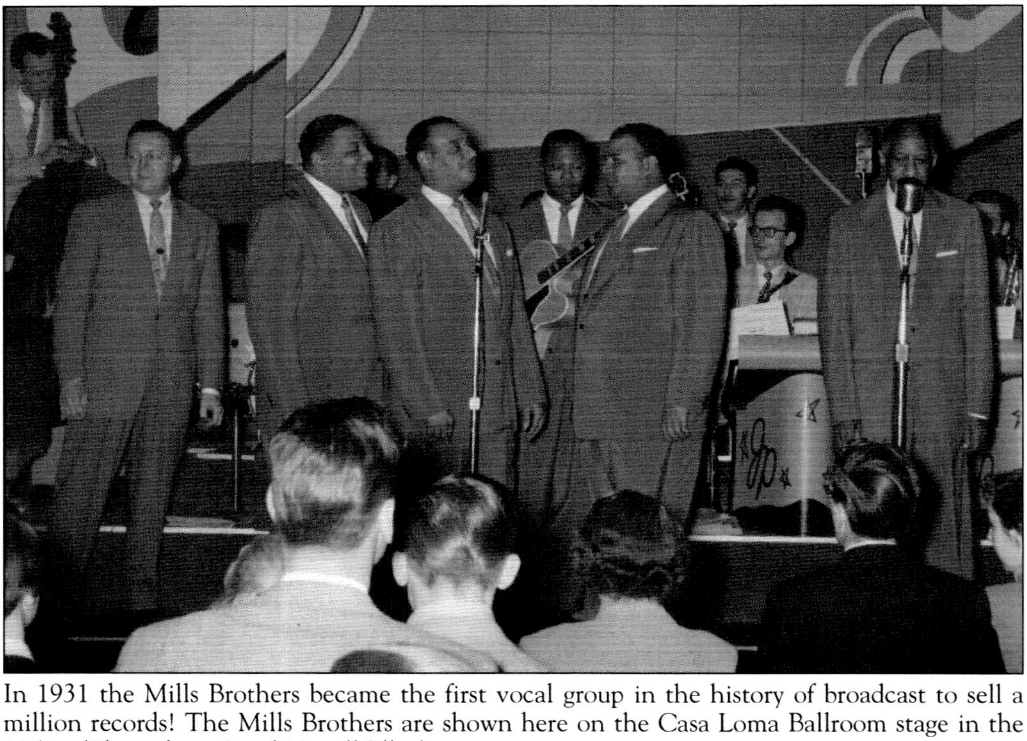

In 1931 the Mills Brothers became the first vocal group in the history of broadcast to sell a million records! The Mills Brothers are shown here on the Casa Loma Ballroom stage in the 1950s. (Photo from Carol Kawell Ellis.)

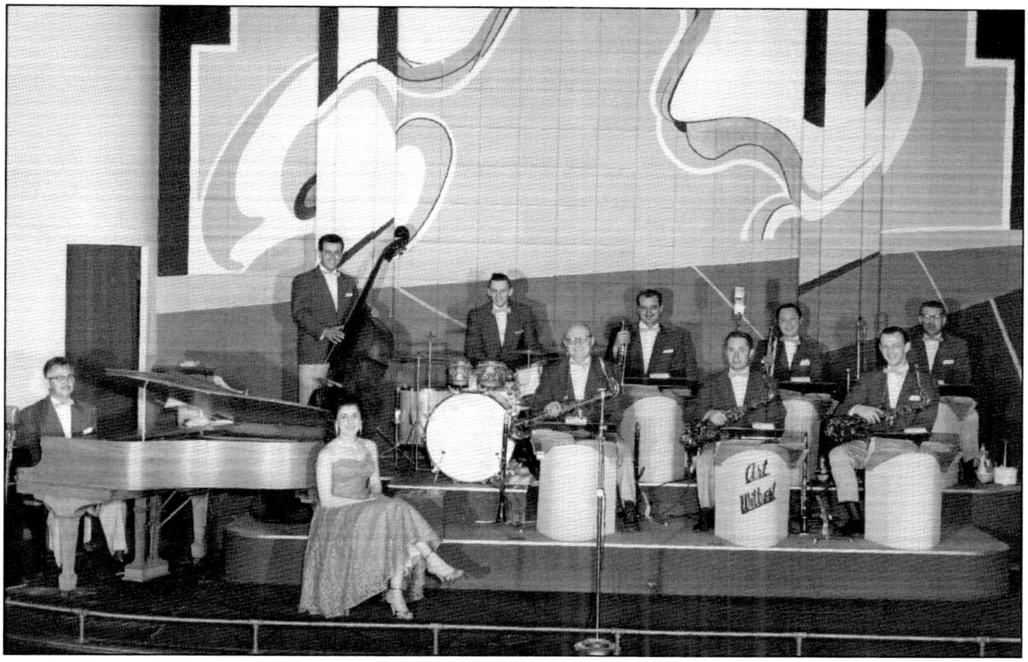

Art Wilbert and his Orchestra as they appeared on the stage of the Casa Loma Ballroom. (Photo from Carol Kawell Ellis.)

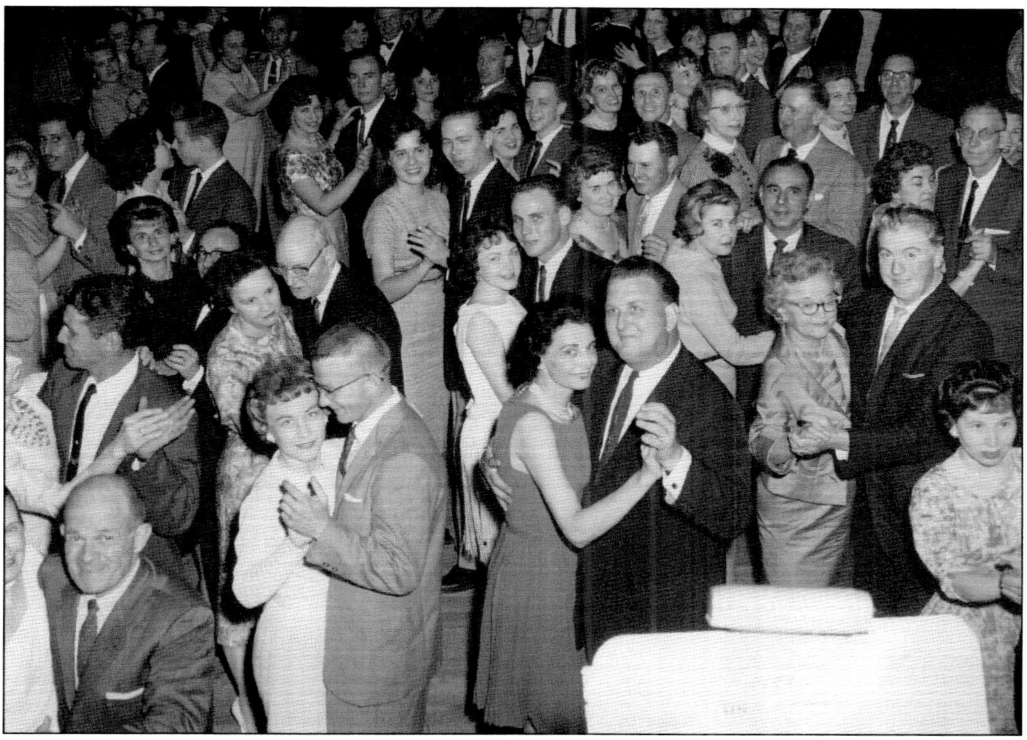

. . . And this is a view from the bandleader's perspective. (Photo from Carol Kawell Ellis.)

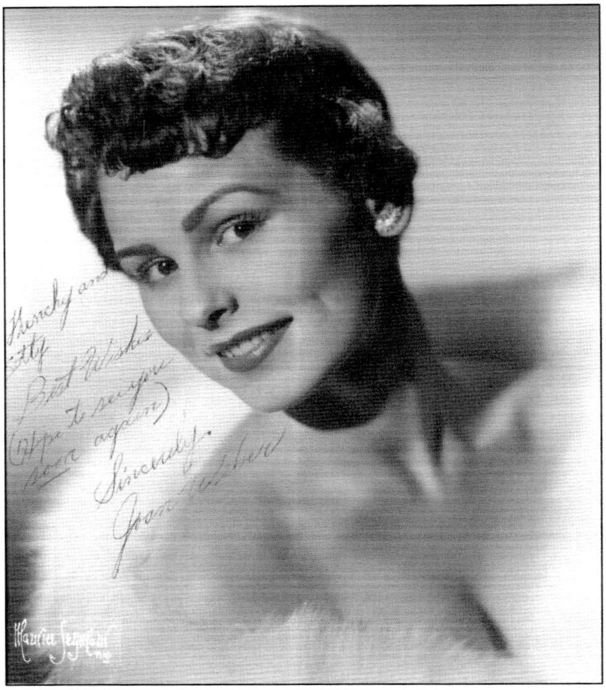

Joan Weber's smash hit "Let Me Go, Lover," of 1954, was one of the songs sung during her visit to the Casa Loma Ballroom. (Photo from Dorothy Vincent. Inscription reads: "To Frenchy and Dotty, Best Wishes, (Hope to see you soon again), Sincerely, Joan Weber.")

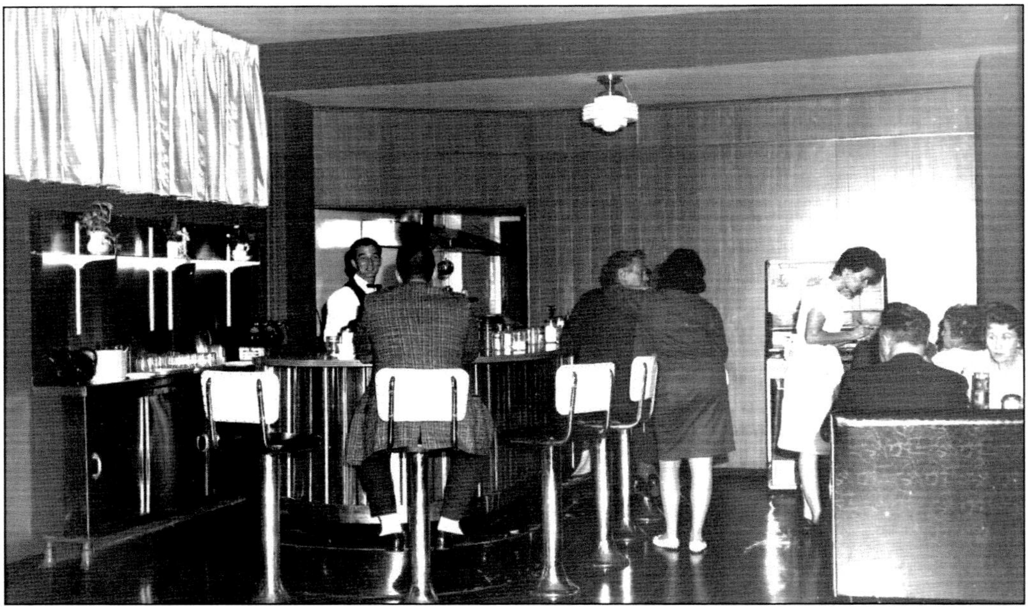

In the 1950s this snack bar/restaurant at the Casa Loma Ballroom served refreshments to patrons as they took a break from the dancing. Edna Kawell did the cooking and baking. (Photo from Carol Kawell Ellis.)

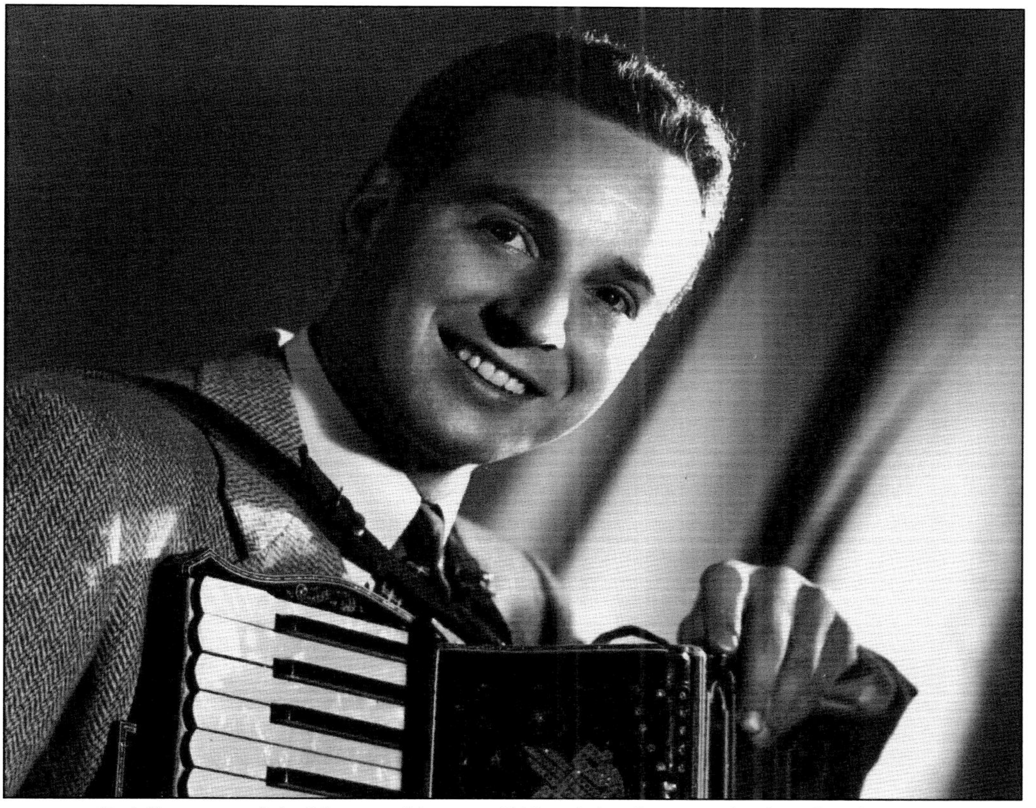

Dick Renna joined the Musicians Union in 1939 and then began to play for a lot of society parties. "Lawn parties they called them then." said Renna. Then came three and a half years in the Navy. He took his accordion with him to the service. "Always had my duffle bag and my accordion," said Renna. "So, we had music aboard ship, too." Dick served aboard L.ST.s in the Pacific. When Renna's time in the military was over he played at the Palladium in East St. Louis. He also played with Bobby Swain in the House Band at the Chase Hotel. Later he and Eileen Brown formed a duo and played at the Jefferson and the Gatesworth Hotels and at Mound City Country Club in East St. Louis. Then Tommy Reardon, the booking agent, wanted a House Band at the Casa Loma Ballroom. "I told him that I didn't have a band," said Renna. "And he just said, 'Oh, call a few of the guys and get a group together.' I did and he gave us a one year contract. We were there for ten years. In fact, we set a record run as House Band there." A few special highlights of Renna's career include playing for Bob Hope at the Ambassador Theatre, Johnny Carson's Show at Keil, a political rally for Lyndon Johnson, and a campaign rally for Hubert Humphrey. There were also Teresa Brewer, Johnny Mathis, and Andy Williams. "We played on the Admiral in the summer, and the Casa Loma Ballroom in the winter," he said with a chuckle. "This was before air conditioning. We also played at the Missouri Athletic Club." In 1979 he was elected Treasurer of the Musicians Union, and in 1982, he moved up to President of the Union and was no longer allowed to play professionally. He played his swan song at Norwood Hills Country Club New Years Eve 1982, his last Big Band job.

Sports fans still treasure memories of Dick Renna and his strolling musicians at old Sportsman Park, Busch Stadium, and his big Band at the Football Cardinal games. And, just for the record, Dick Renna's band played for the opening of the new Busch Stadium in 1966.

(Edited excerpt from *Big Bands Of St. Louis* by Taffy Wilber, reproduced with permission of *Senior Circuit*, July 1998, publisher, Carol Trauth. Photo from Dick and Bea Renna.)

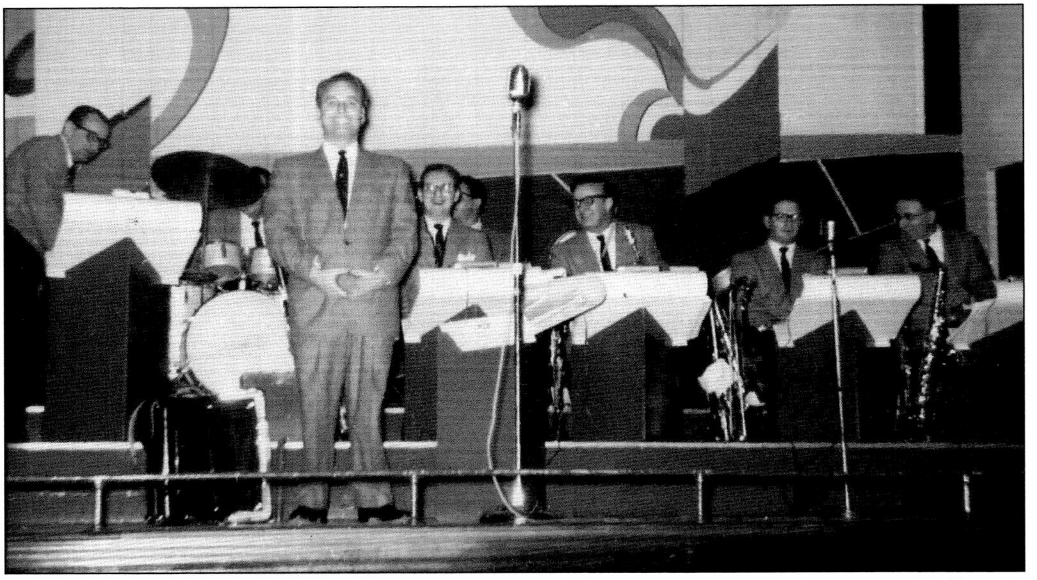

Dick Renna and his Orchestra smile for the camera while onstage at the Casa Loma Ballroom. Pictured here, from left to right, are Frank Gauding on bass, Dick Renna out front, Bobby Fryer on the drums—partially hidden, Wally Zwilbelman on trumpet, Chuck Polzin on sax, John Littich on sax/violin, Danny Goffstein on sax/violin, and Ben Pearlmutter on sax/violin. (Photo from Dick and Bea Renna.)

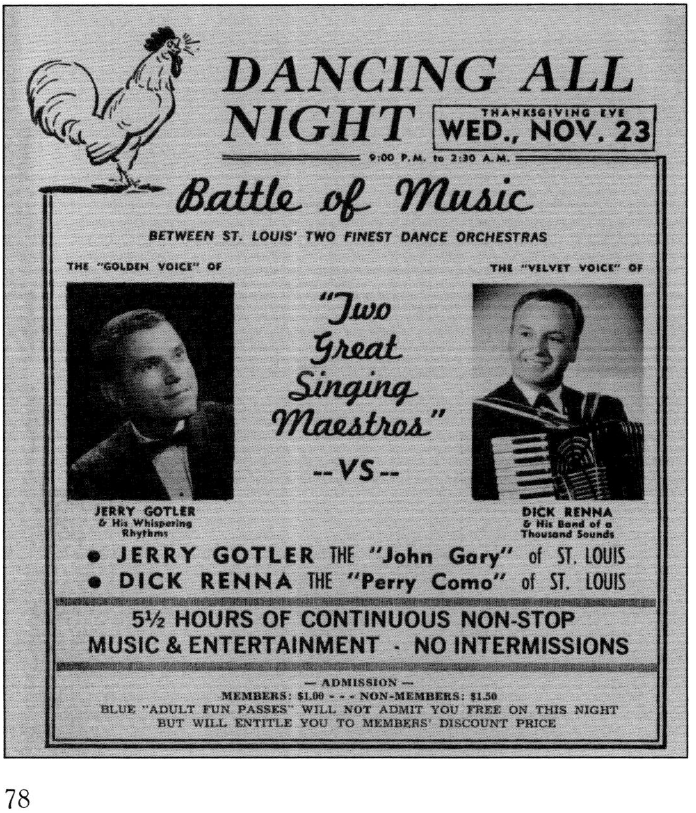

As this 1950s brochure states, Dick Renna had the distinction of being known as the "Perry Como" of St. Louis. (Copy of brochure from Dick and Bea Renna.)

Minnie Witte (Art Kawell's sister) and her niece Carol Kawell (Art's daughter) manage the snack counter at the Casa Loma Ballroom. This photo was taken in the mid 1950s.(Photo from Carol Kawell Ellis.)

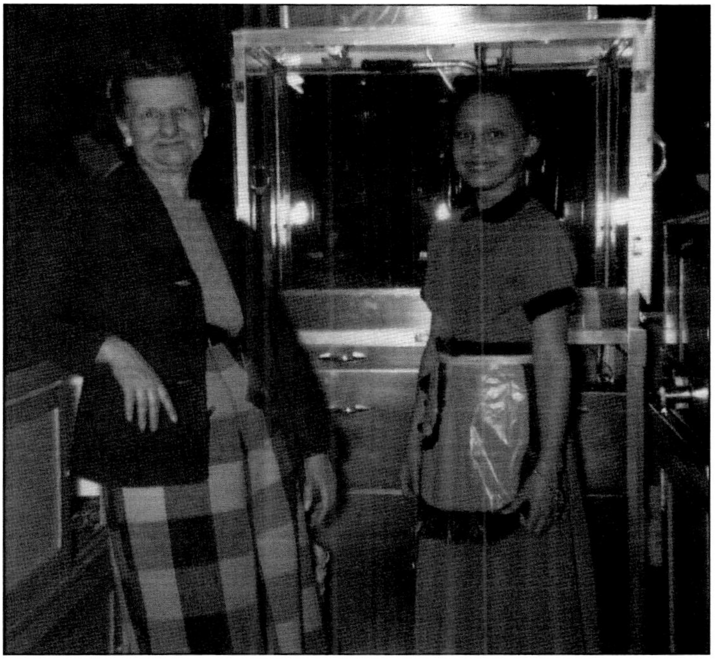

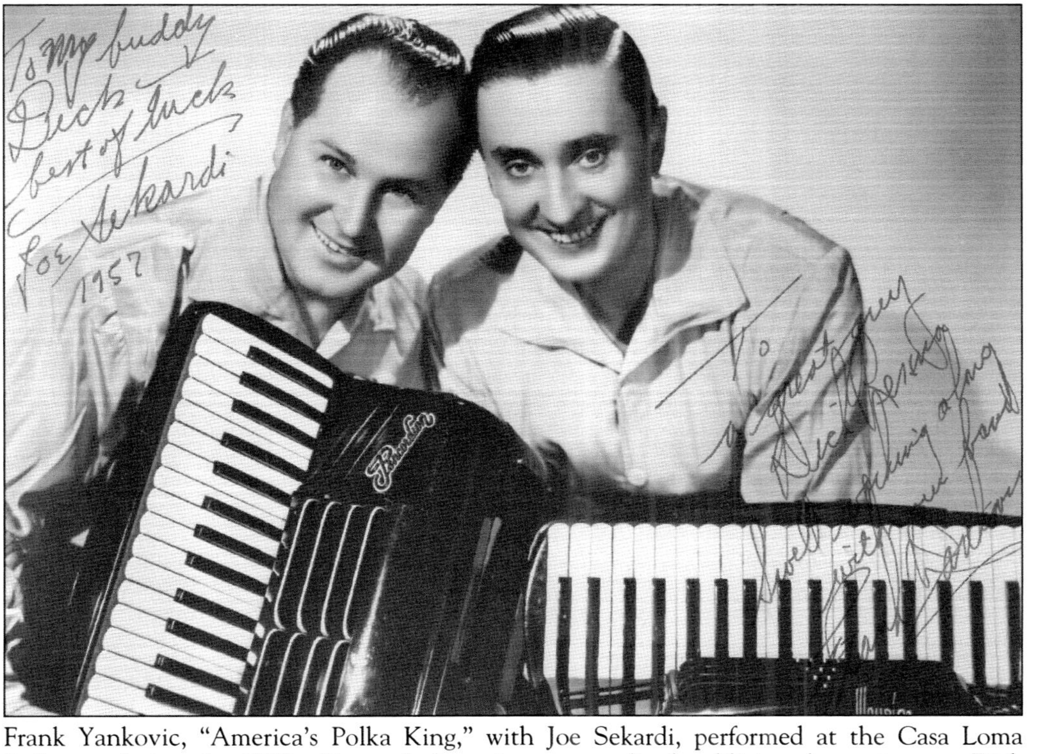

Frank Yankovic, "America's Polka King," with Joe Sekardi, performed at the Casa Loma Ballroom during the 1950s. Pictured above is a personalized publicity photo given to Dick Renna. (Photo from Dick and Bea Renna.)

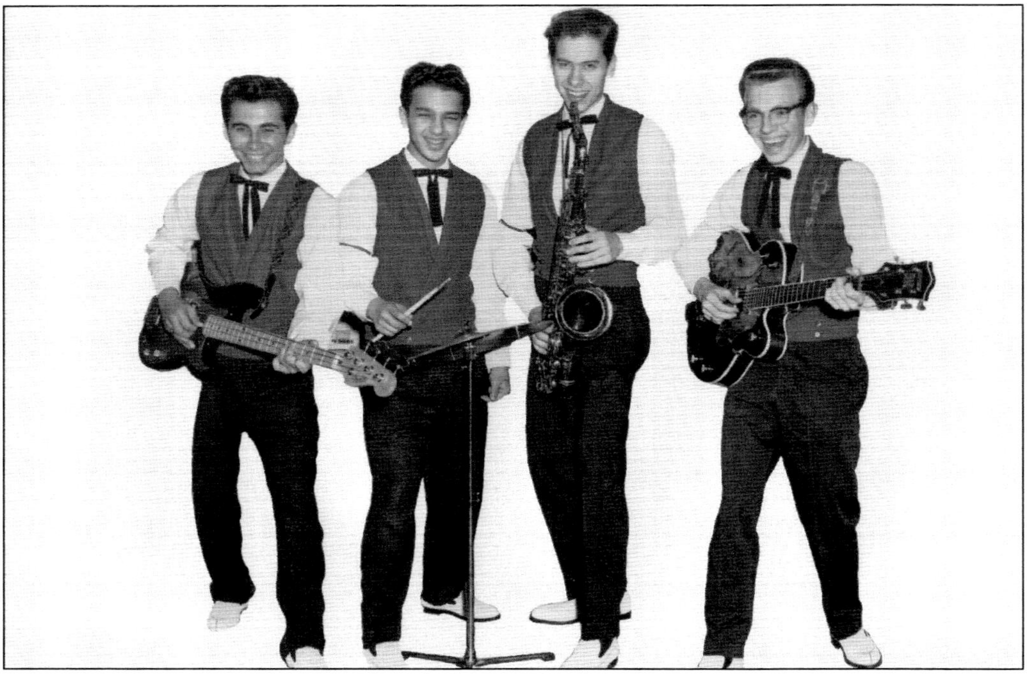

Around 1956, St. Louis native Jules Blattner and some of his schoolmates from Affton High School got together and formed the group Jules Blattner & The Teen Tones. They played at many local high school dances and St. Louis Teen-towns. Rock 'n' roll music was still a new sound back then. Before becoming a regular at Gaslight Square, Jules played many times at the Casa Loma Ballroom. (Photo from Carol Kawell Ellis.)

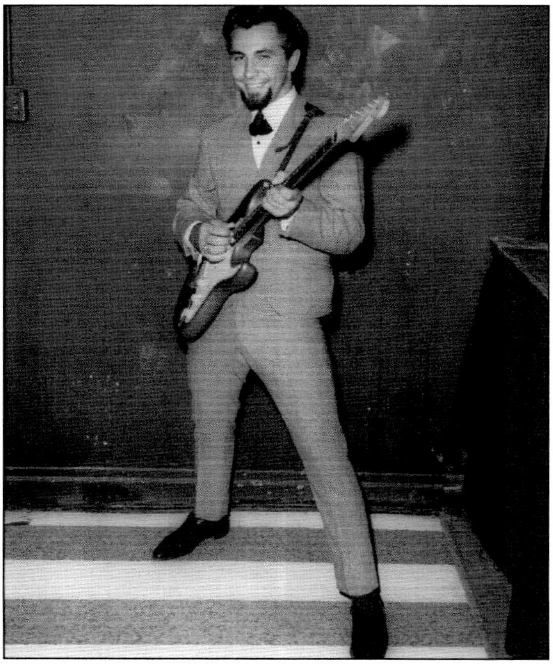

Casa Loma Ballroom patrons can still catch Jules Blattner on stage. He still comes around once in a while to put on a show for his loyal fans. (Photo from Carol Kawell Ellis.)

With Cary Grant-like looks, Ray Anthony began leading his own big band before being signed by Glenn Miller at the height of the Miller Band's popularity. After returning from the war, Anthony formed his own big band. His biggest hit came in 1954, when he recorded the theme to Jack Webb's cop show, *Dragnet*. He also earned a Top 10 hit with a dance tune that sparked a craze that will never go away—The Bunny Hop. On the personal side, Ray Anthony was known as the husband of Mamie Van Doren. (Photo from Dorothy Vincent. Inscription reads "To Frenchy & Dorothy, the very best of everything, Sincerely, Ray Anthony.")

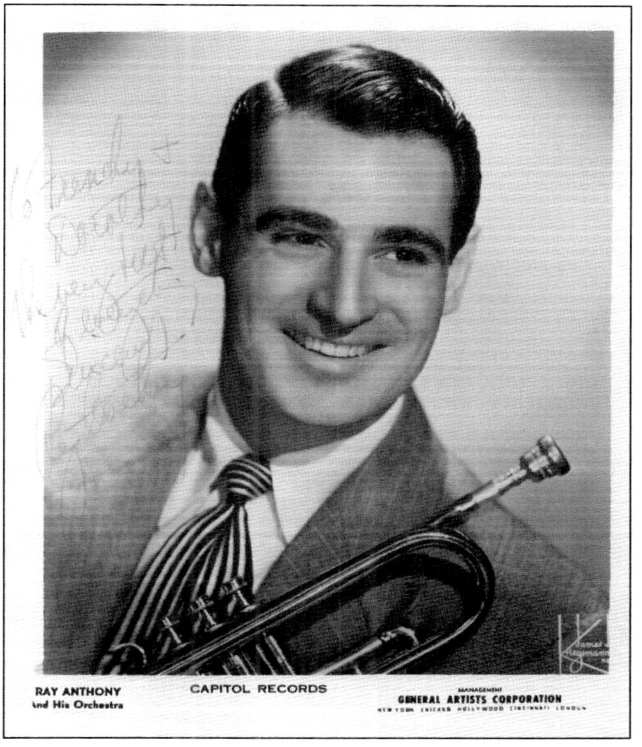

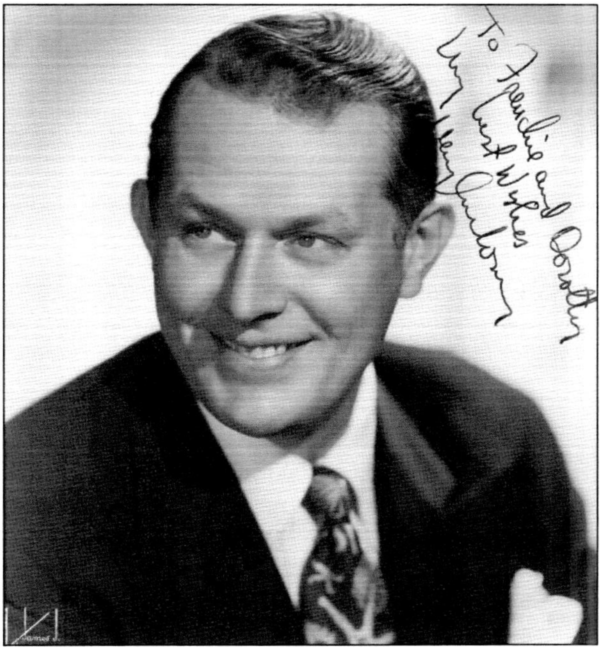

Vaughn Monroe was one of the popular male vocalists to come out of the big band phenomenon. He had a rich baritone voice that he used masterfully. He played trumpet and trombone with the same virtuosity. His six-foot frame and likable personality put him out in front of the orchestra and behind the baton. (Photo from Dorothy Vincent.)

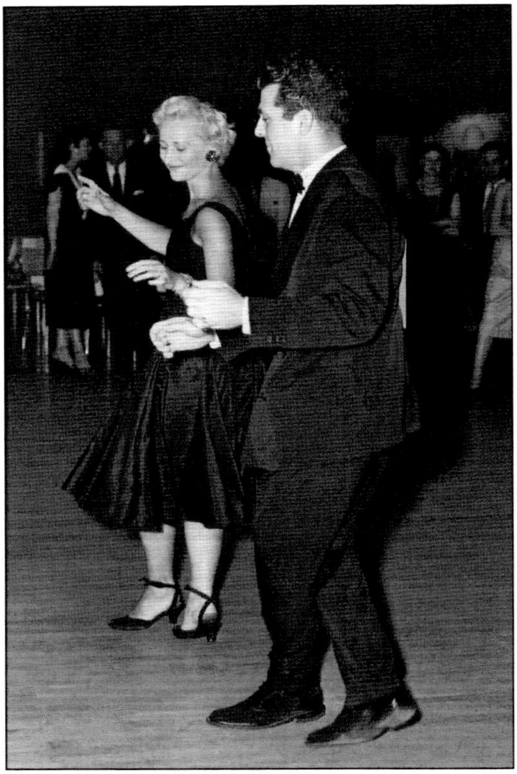

Alfredo Ciolek and Virginia Ramshaw display their dancing skills in 1953. (Photo from Alfredo Ciolek.)

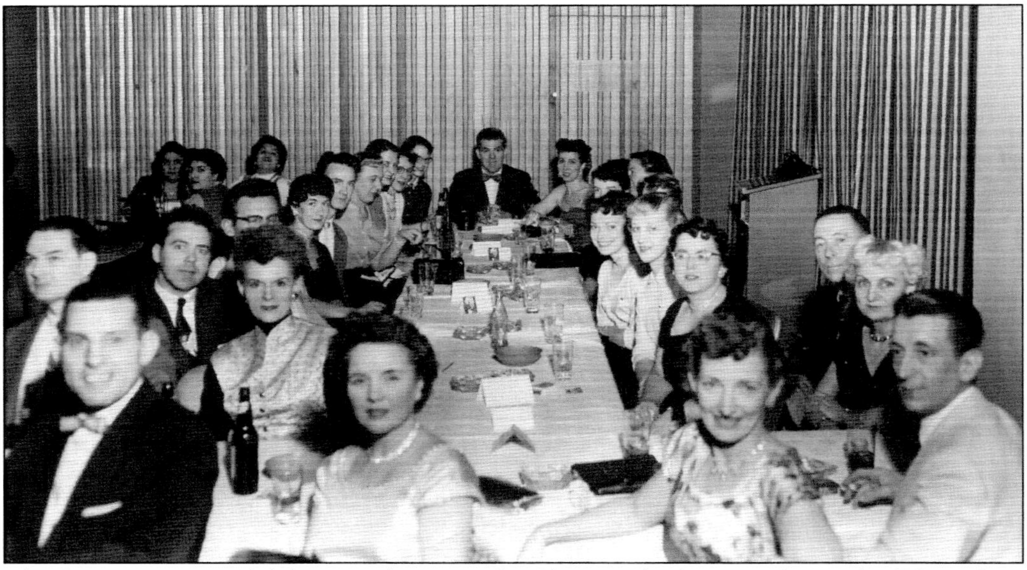

The Casa Loma 400 Club has a night out at the Chase-Park Plaza Hotel in 1952. (Photo from Alfredo Ciolek.)

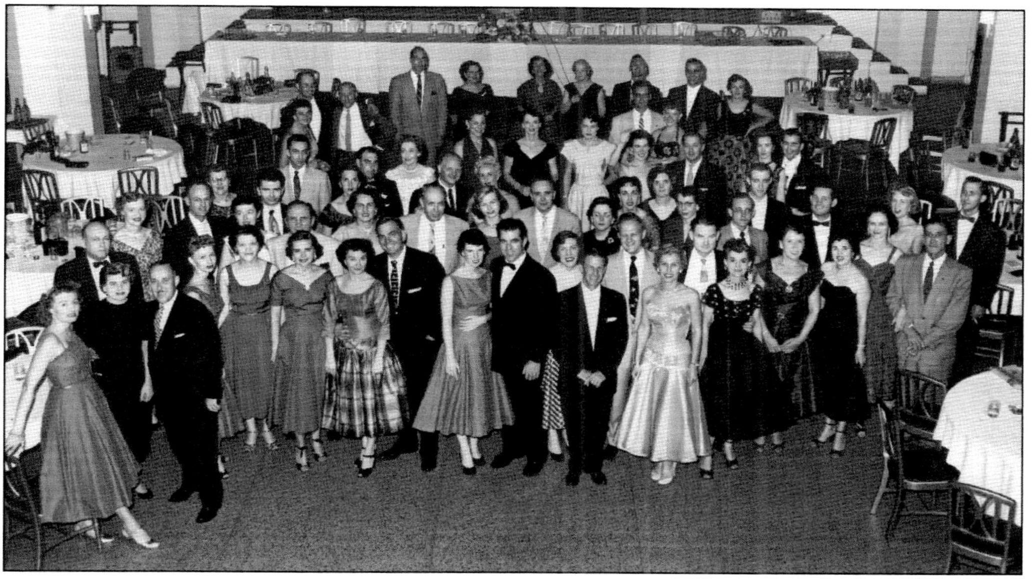

This group photo of the Casa Loma 400 Club was taken in the early 1950s. (Photo from Alfredo Ciolek.)

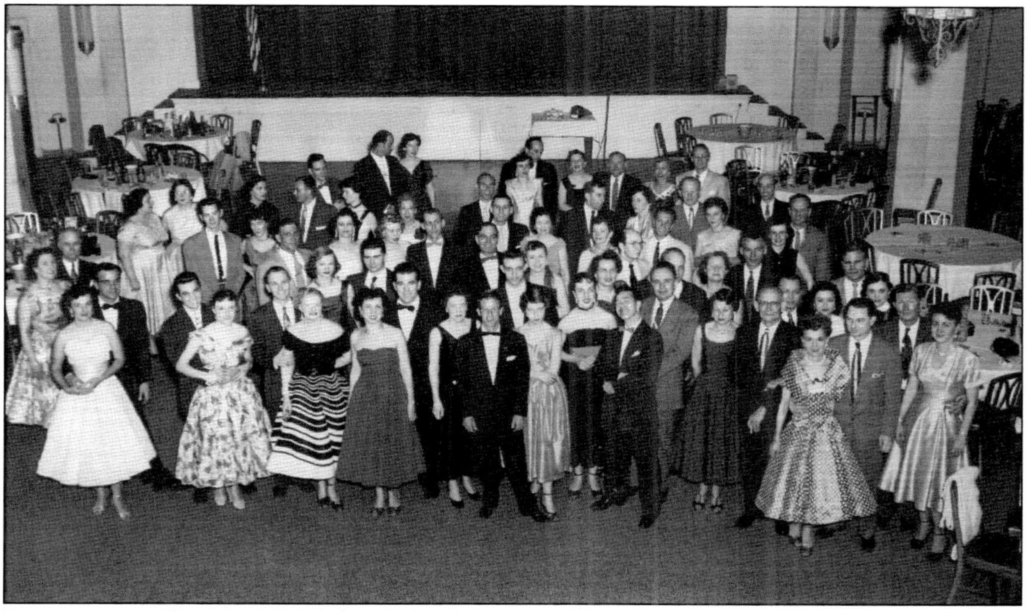

In an even earlier picture of the group, some names of those in the crowd include Jeannie Burg, Tom and Tess Ashton, Leta and Jim Chapman, Bud and Sally Gregory, Vic Koenig, Paul and Jane Terweston, Juke Box George Schoen, Delors Schlomer, Dorothy Aebli, Al Paygen, Alfredo Ciolek, and Shirley Weggie. (Photo from Alfredo Ciolek.)

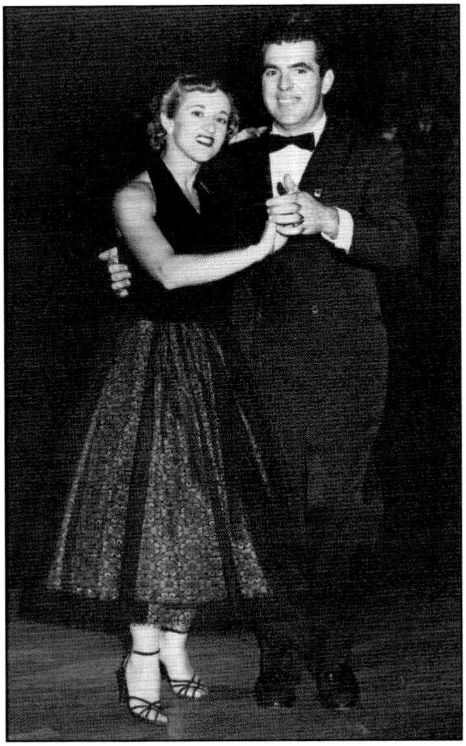

Lynn Lamb and Alfredo Ciolek show proper form on the Casa Loma Ballroom dance floor. (Photo from Alfredo Ciolek.)

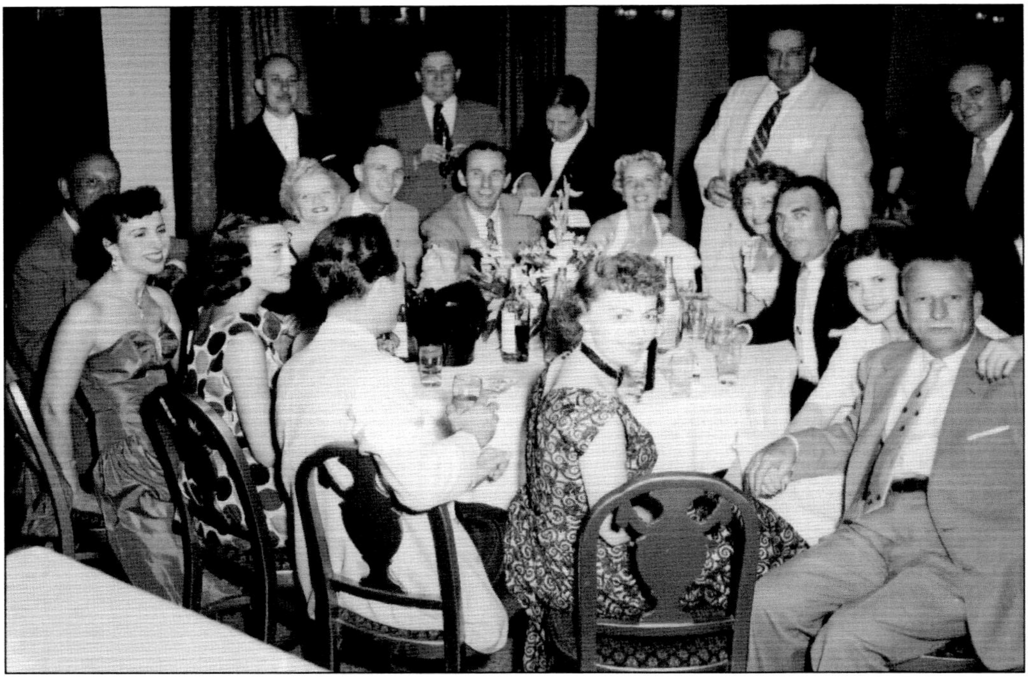

It's another dinner dance for the Casa Loma 400 Club. (Photo from Alfredo Ciolek, taken by Virgil Vossmeyer.)

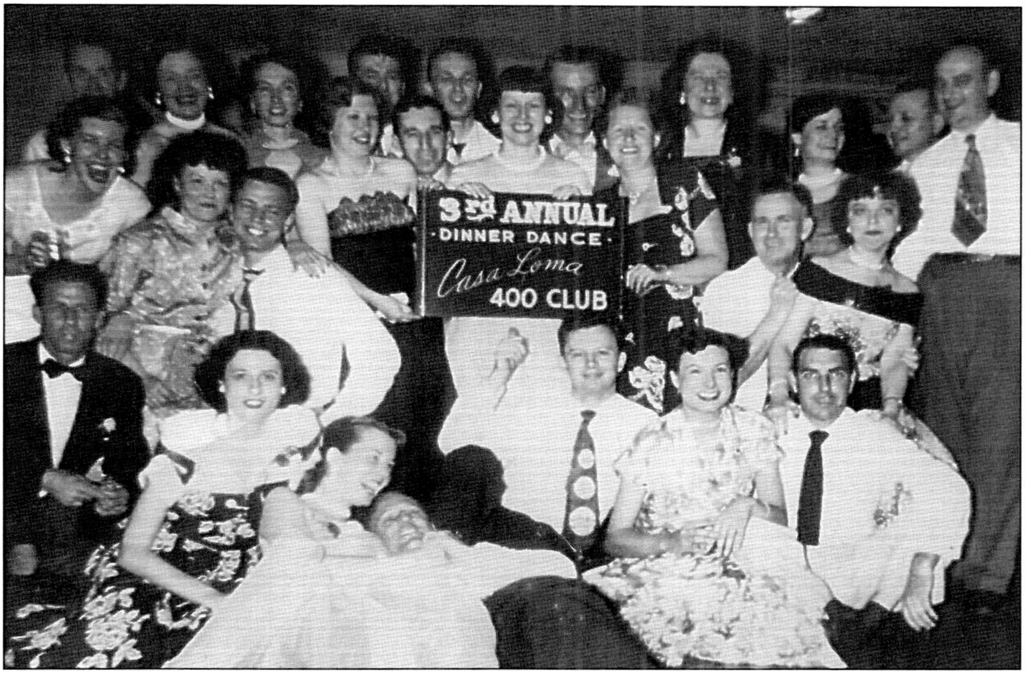

The Casa Loma 400 Club gathers for the Third Annual Dinner Dance held at Edgewater Club in the late 1940s. (Photo from Alfredo Ciolek.)

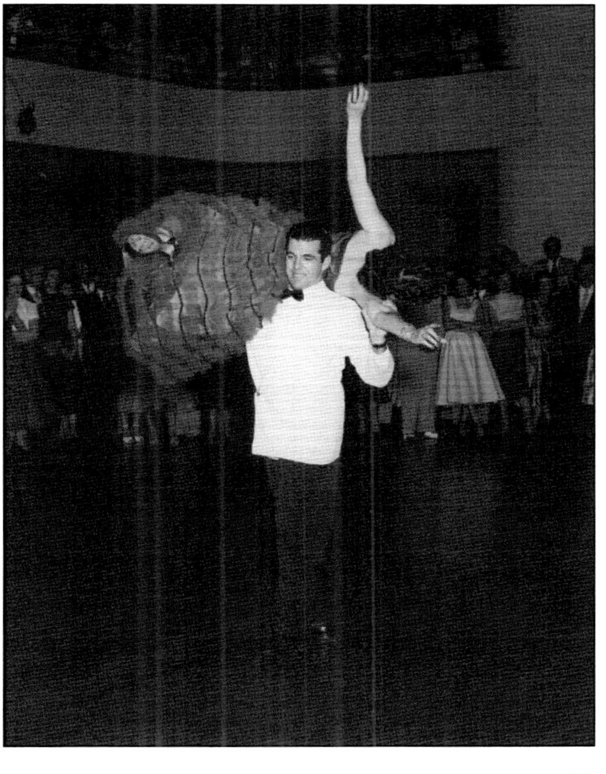

Alfredo Ciolek and Jeannie Burg display their impressive dancing skills at the Casa Loma Ballroom in 1952. (Photo from Alfredo Ciolek.)

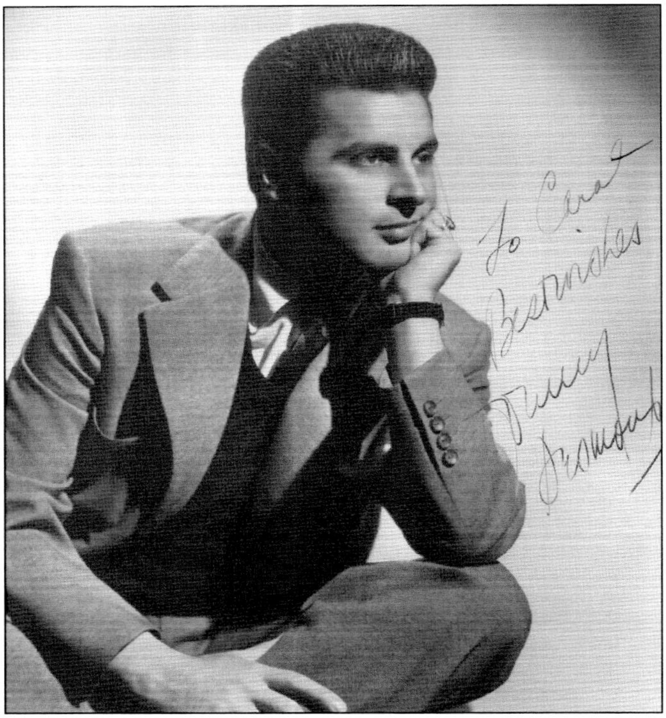

Johnny Desmond was a heartthrob when he sang with Bob Crosby and the Glenn Miller Band during World War II, and later as an actor in films and TV. This is a copy of the promo photo showing him when he appeared at the Casa Loma Ballroom. Inscription reads: "To Carol, Best wishes, Johnny Desmond." (Photo from Carol Kawell Ellis.)

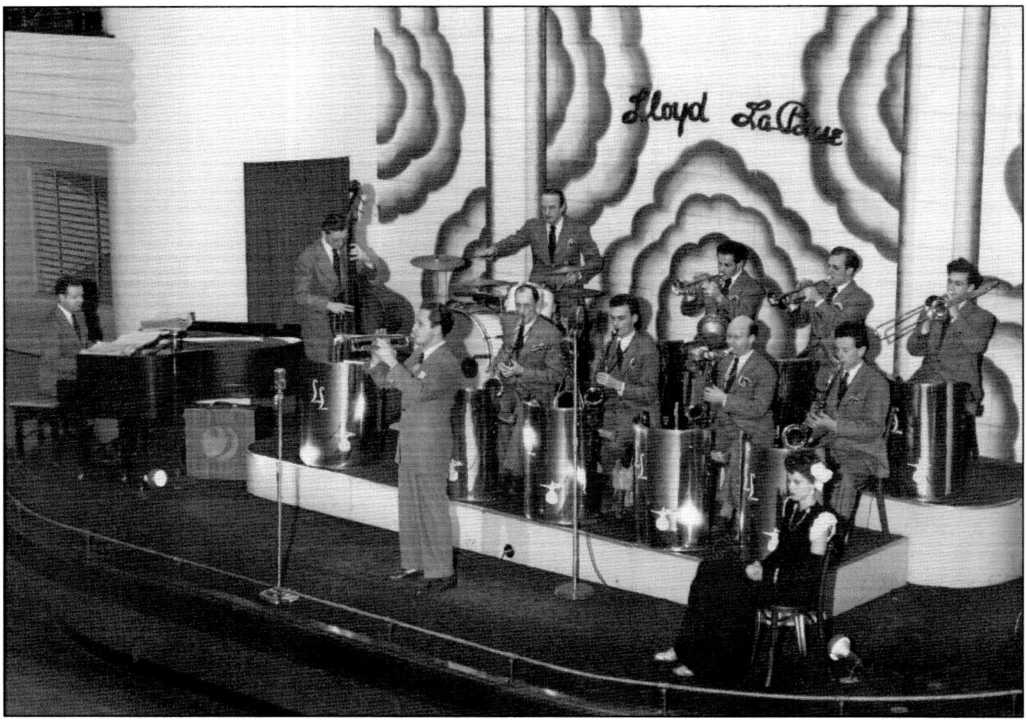

The Lloyd LaParie Orchestra takes the stage at the Casa Loma. (Photo from Carol Kawell Ellis.)

Five

"St. Louis Hop" Years

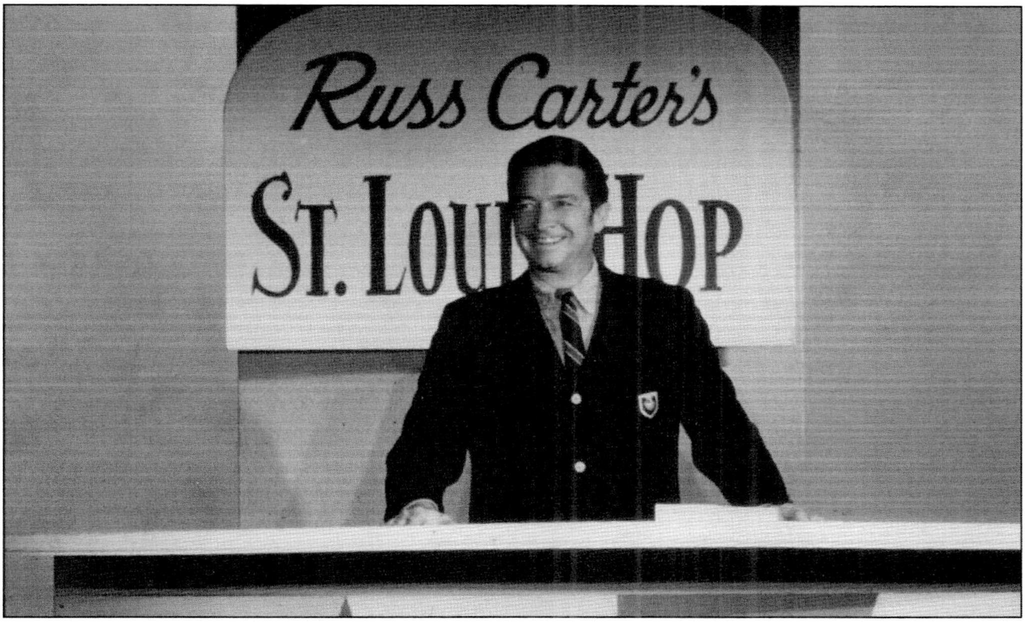

A mainstay of Saturday TV in St. Louis during the 50s and 60s was a program called the *St. Louis Hop*. The hometown version of the hugely popular Dick Clark's *American Bandstand* was hosted by Russ Carter. He was the emcee of this dance show in St. Louis from 1958 to 1973. The show had several homes, including the Arena Roller Rink, the Casa Loma Ballroom, and the Sheraton Jefferson Hotel before finally ending its run in 1973 at KSD studios. (Photo from Mrs. Russ (Gracia) Carter.)

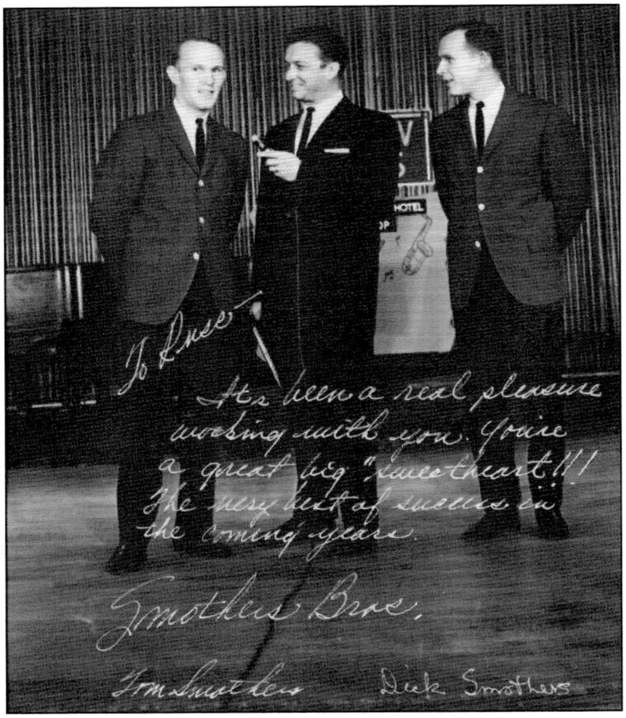

Many nationally know acts appeared on the *St. Louis Hop* TV show in St. Louis. Pictured here is Russ Carter chatting with the "new" comedy/singing duo: Tom and Dick Smothers. The inscription reads: "To Russ—Its been a real pleasure working with you. You're a great big "sweetheart"!!! The very best of success in the coming years. Smother Bros." (Photo from Mrs. Russ (Gracia) Carter.)

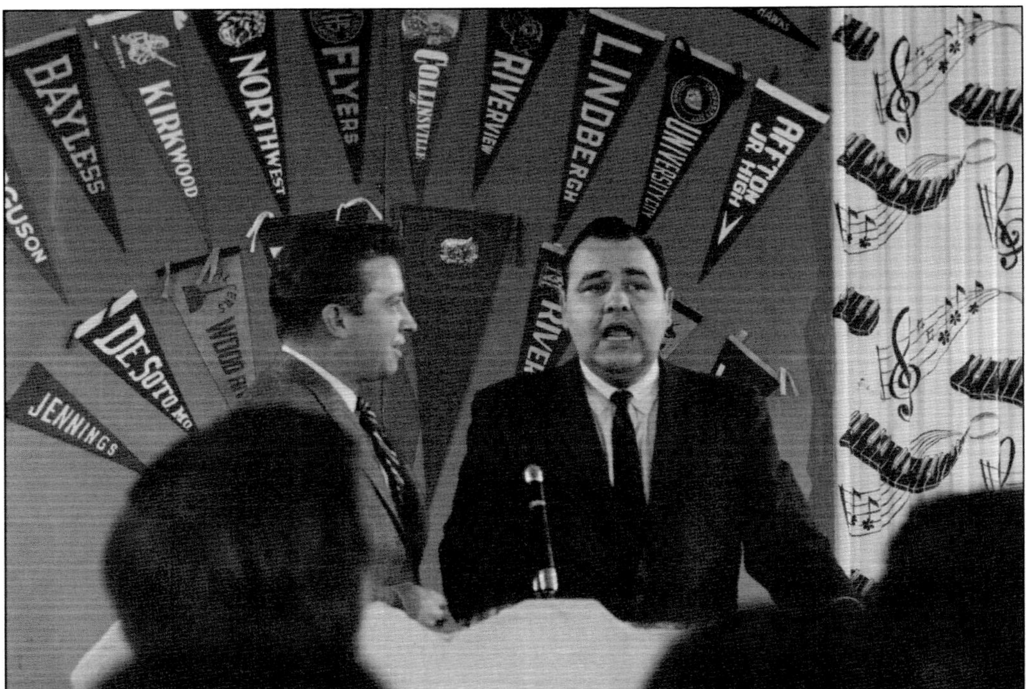

Another well known guest on the TV show was Jonathan Winters, shown here at the bandstand with Russ Carter. (Photo from Mrs. Russ (Gracia) Carter.)

Heartthrob Robert Goulet had the teenage girls of St. Louis breathless with his sultry singing style. (Photo from Mrs. Russ (Gracia) Carter.)

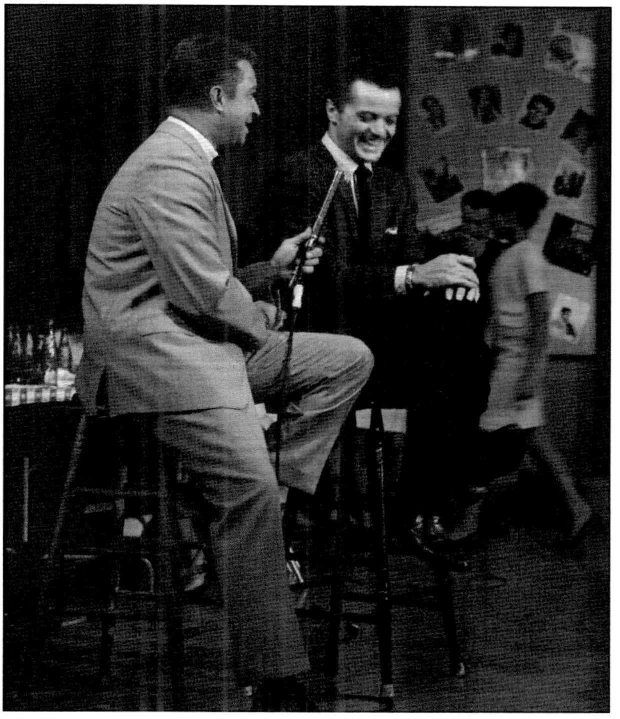

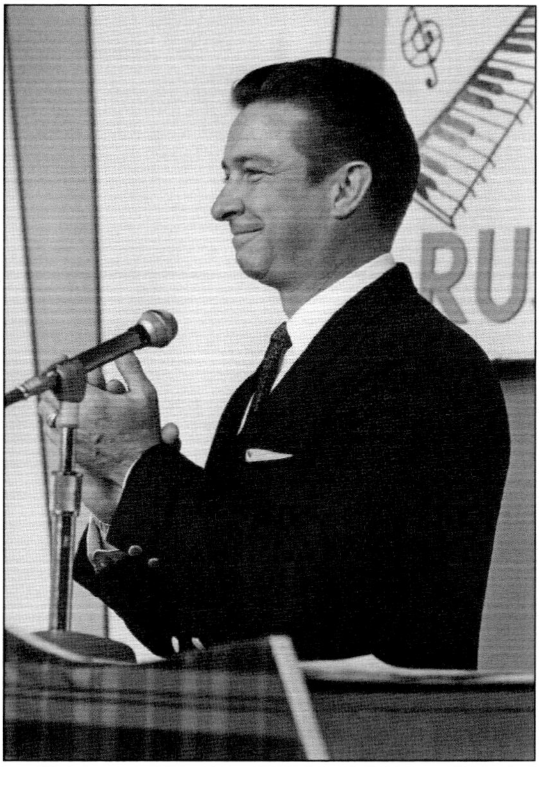

Russ Carter was hired as associate producer on the new KSDTV show *St. Louis Hop*, which debuted in 1958. Three months later, Mr. Carter became host of the show, a role he held for 15 years. (Photo from Mrs. Russ (Gracia) Carter.)

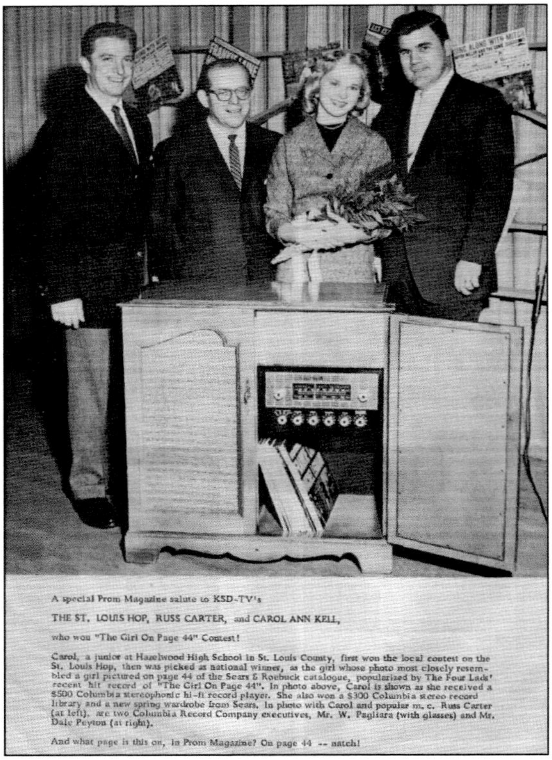

A special Prom Magazine salute to KSD-TV's

THE ST. LOUIS HOP, RUSS CARTER, and CAROL ANN KELL,

who won "The Girl On Page 44" Contest!

Carol, a junior at Hazelwood High School in St. Louis County, first won the local contest on the St. Louis Hop, then was picked as national winner, as the girl whose photo most closely resembled a girl pictured on page 44 of the Sears & Roebuck catalogue, popularized by The Four Lads' recent hit record of "The Girl On Page 44". In photo above, Carol is shown as she received a $500 Columbia stereophonic hi-fi record player. She also won a $300 Columbia stereo record library and a new spring wardrobe from Sears. In photo with Carol and popular m. c. Russ Carter (at left), are two Columbia Record Company executives, Mr. W. Pagliara (with glasses) and Mr. Dale Peyton (at right).

And what page is this on, in Prom Magazine? On page 44 -- natch!

Another very popular staple of teen life in the 1950s and 60s in St. Louis was a publication called *Prom Magazine*. This page appeared in that publication. Pictured here are "St. Louis Hoop" winners Russ Carter and Carol Ann Kell. Carol, a junior at Hazelwood High School in St. Louis County, first won the local contest on the *St. Louis Hop*, then was picked as national winner, as the girl most closely resembling a girl pictured on page 44 of the Sears & Roebuck catalogue, popularized by The Four Lads' recent hit, "The Girl on Page 44." In this photo Carol is shown as she receives a $500 Columbia stereophonic hi-fi record player. She also won a $300 Columbia stereo record library and a new spring wardrobe from Sears. In the photo with Carol and popular emcee Russ Carter (at left) are two Columbia Record Company executives." (Photo from Mrs. Russ (Gracia) Carter.)

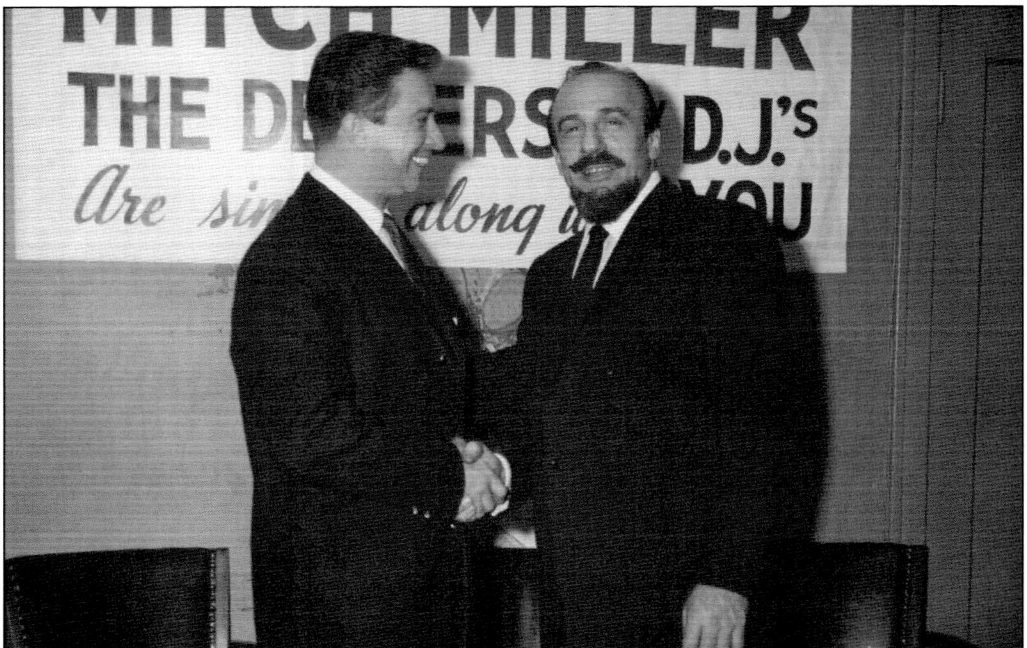

Another guest on the *St. Louis Hop* was none other than Mitch Miller. (Photo from Mrs. Russ (Gracia) Carter.)

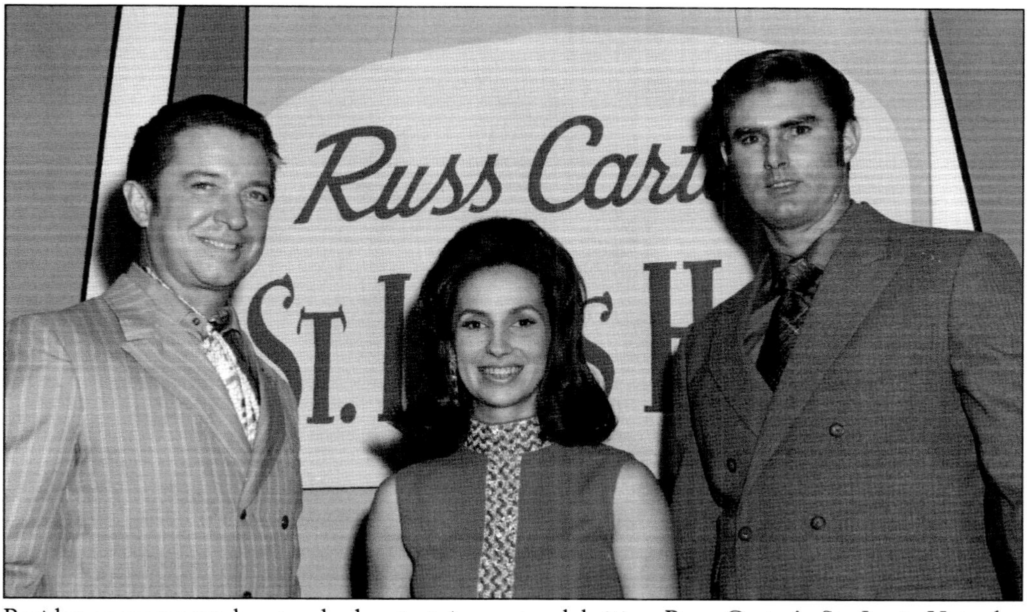

Besides appearances by standard entertainment celebrities, Russ Carter's *St. Louis Hop* also welcomed some prominent St. Louis personalities, such as St. Louis Cardinal's pitcher Steve Carlton and his wife, pictured here. Steve, a four time Cy Young Award winner played for the Cardinals from 1965 through 1971. (Photo from Mrs. Russ (Gracia) Carter.)

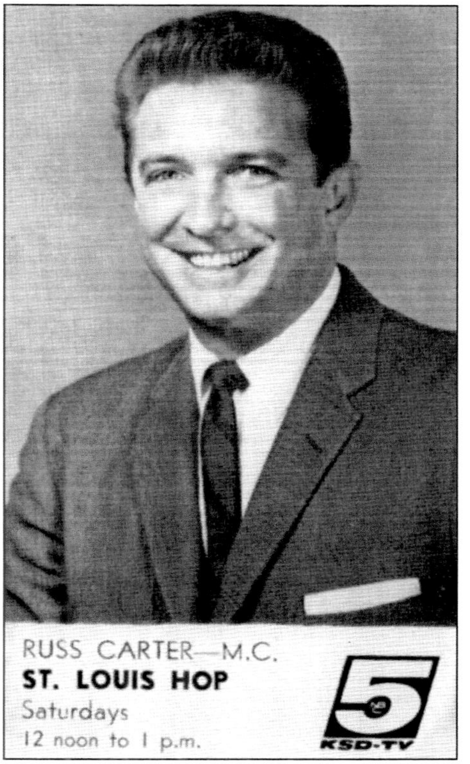

Russ Carter got his big break in entertainment as a replacement for Perry Como, singing for three years in The Ted Weems Orchestra. His second break happened when St. Louis bandleader Russ David wanted to produce a local version of Dick Clark's popular *American Bandstand. St. Louis Hop* was broadcast on Saturdays, featuring prize giveaways, area high school students dancing to rock 'n' roll records and appearances by national artists such as Tony Bennett, Bobby Vinton, Chubby Checker, and Johnny Mathis. Mr. Carter was inducted into the National Academy of Television Arts and Sciences Silver Circle in 1999. (Photo from Mrs. Russ (Gracia) Carter.)

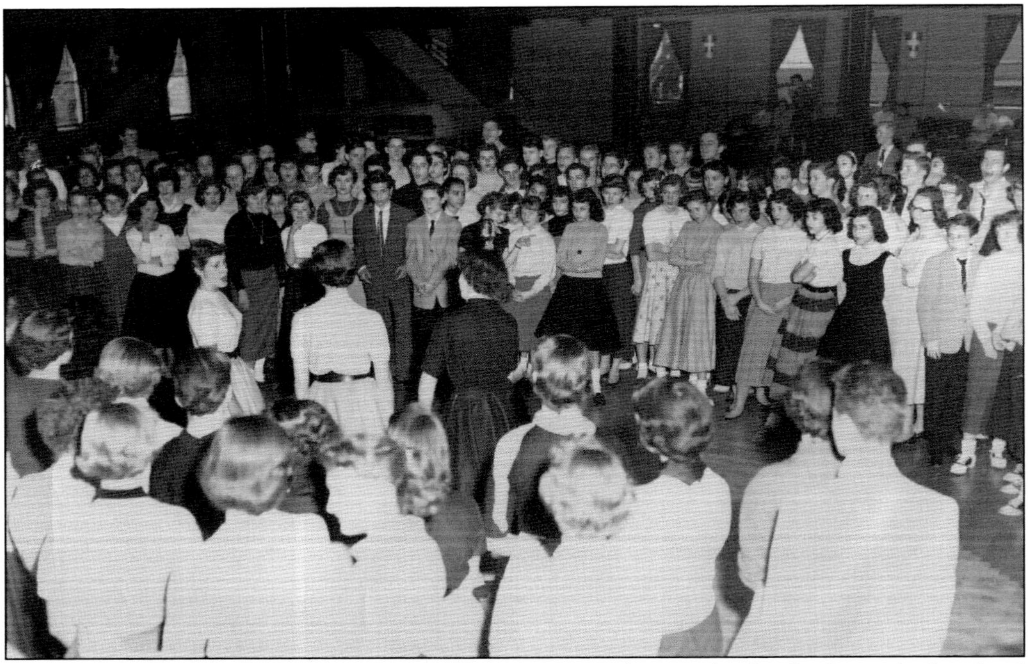

During the 1950s the Casa Loma Ballroom was THE place to be for St. Louis high school students on a Saturday afternoon. (Photo from Carol Kawell Ellis.)

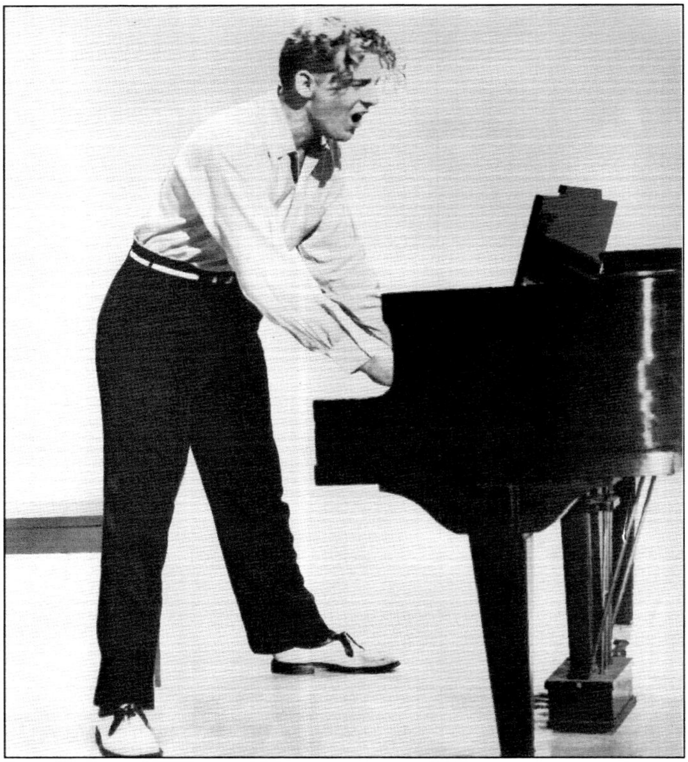

Great balls of fire! I'm sure that more than one set of parents had misgivings about allowing their teenagers to see Jerry Lee Lewis perform on the stage at the Casa Loma Ballroom. In spite of that, Jerry Lee Lewis was a mainstay of the rock 'n' roll scene during its most popular times. (Photo from Carol Kawell Ellis.)

The Poni-Tails were one of many "one hit wonders." Their record about an older boy, "Born Too Late," is a rock and roll classic and worldwide favorite. The trio, Toni Cistone, LaVerne Novak, and Karen Topinka, were students in school near Cleveland, Ohio, when they started singing together in 1956. "Born Too Late" made the Poni-Tails part of rock and roll history. It reached number seven on Billboard's Top 100 and number five in England. The group might have remained anonymous if ABC had had its way, as they were promoting the album's other side, "Come On Joey, Dance With Me." It was only after several Cleveland deejays pushed "Born Too Late" that the record took off. They appeared at the Casa Loma Ballroom during their brief fame. (Photo courtesy of Dorothy Vincent.)

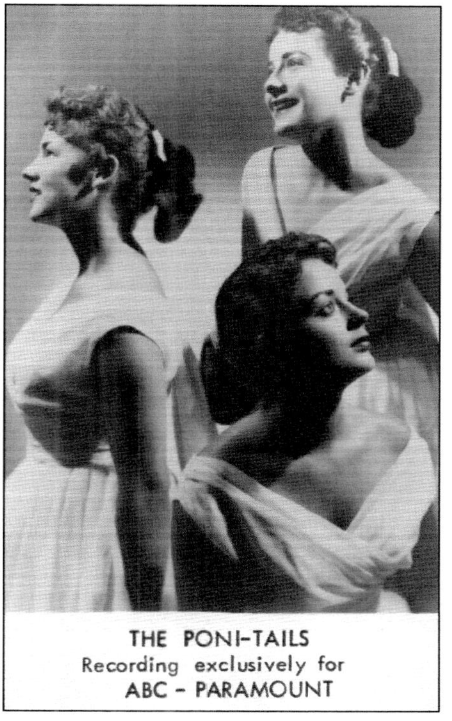

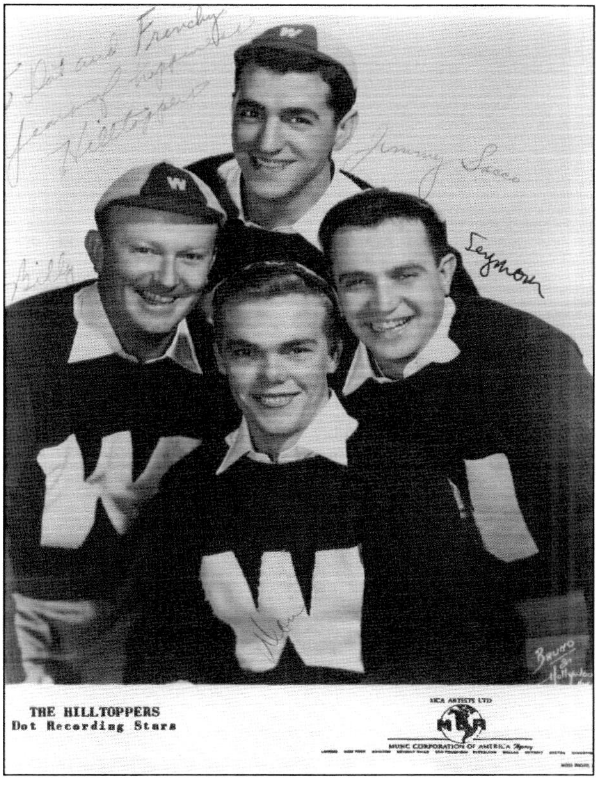

In April 1952, these four young men, calling themselves The Hilltoppers, recorded a song at Western Kentucky State College's Van Meter Auditorium. They were (clockwise from top): Jimmy Sacca, Seymour Spiegelman, Don McGuire, and Billy Vaughn. The song was "Trying," a composition of Vaughn's, and it would be the first of many chart-toppers by one of the most popular groups of the 1950s. (Photo courtesy of Dorothy Vincent. Inscription reads "To Dot and Frenchy, years of happiness, Hilltoppers.")

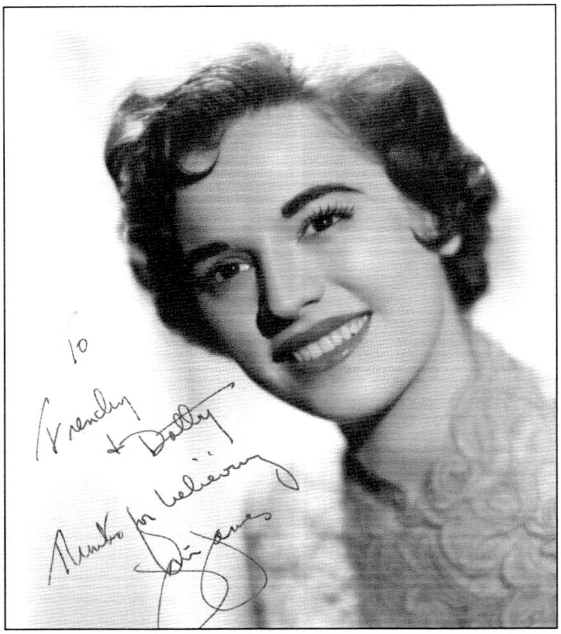

Joni James, a very popular singer during the 1950s and 1960s, played the Casa Loma Ballroom, singing hits that included "Why Don't You Believe Me?", "How Important Can It Be?", and "My Love, My Love". (Photo from Dorothy Vincent. Inscription reads "To Frenchy & Dotty, Thanks for believing, Joni James.")

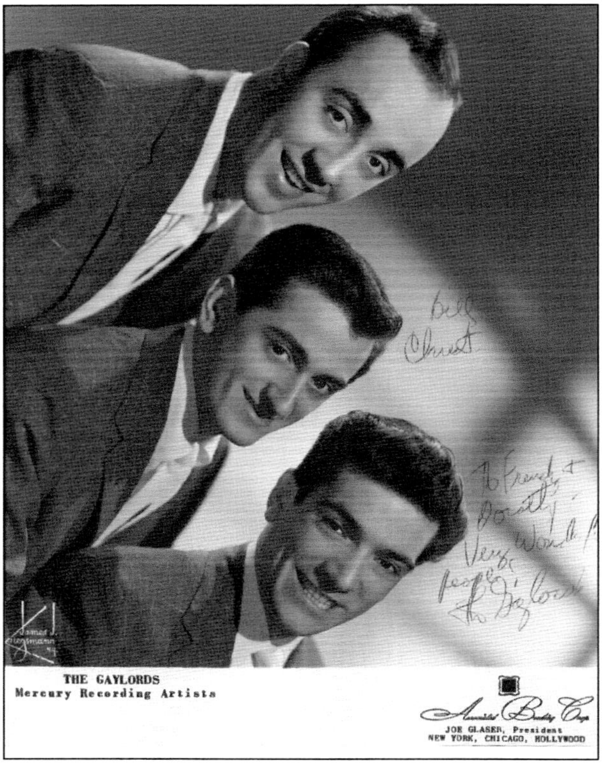

The Gaylords were a popular singing trio in the 1950s. The group had a number of Italian-flavored hits on the charts, often consisting of a song partly sung in Italian and partly in English. (Photo from Dorothy Vincent. Inscription reads "To Frenchy & Dorothy, Very Wonderful People, the Gaylords.")

Bill Haley and His Comets played at the Casa Loma Ballroom for the first time in November of 1954. This was at the height of the new "rock'n'roll" craze that was sweeping the country, inspired in great part by his hit release earlier that year called "Rock Around the Clock." They were to appear at the Casa Loma a few more times, and owners Harold Burian and Art Kawell admitted that Bill Haley's Comets were the Casa Loma's biggest recent draws in an interview published in May of 1956. However, in the same article, they missed the mark when they stated that "Rock'n'roll is just a fad and it's rapidly fading." (Photo from Carol Kawell Ellis.)

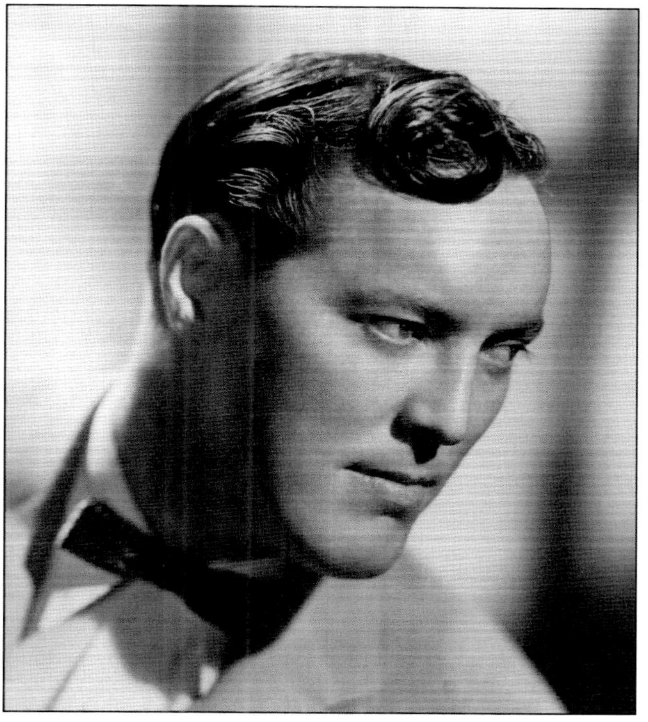

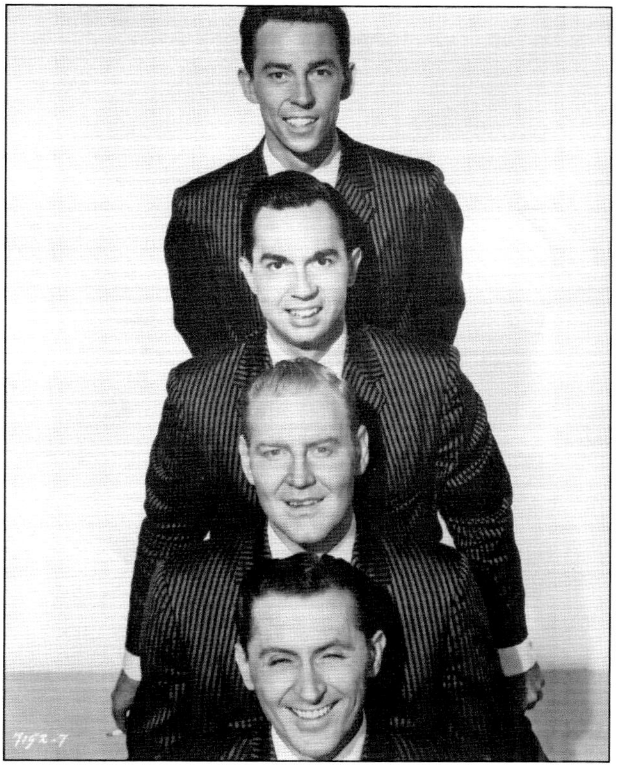

It was Stan Kenton that first recognized the talent of the Four Freshmen. Stan bugged Capitol Records until they gave the Freshmen a recording contract. It was their third single, "Blue World," that started them on the road to success. The group has made more than 50 albums between 1955 and 1994. Here they are pictured as they looked when they played the Casa Loma Ballroom in the early 1950s. (Photo from Carol Kawell Ellis.)

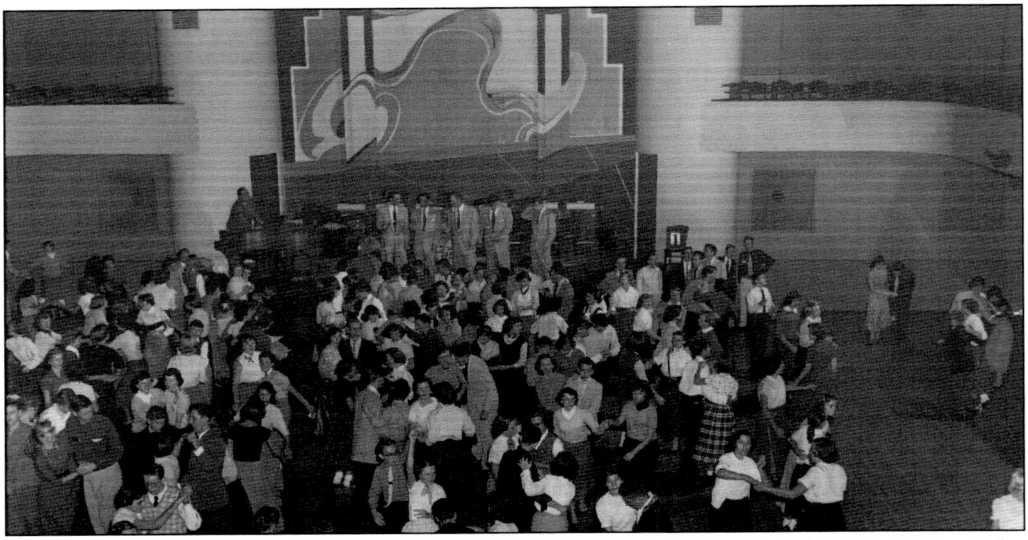

A young crowd packs the Casa Loma Ballroom dance floor on a Saturday afternoon in the 1950s. (Photo from Carol Kawell Ellis.)

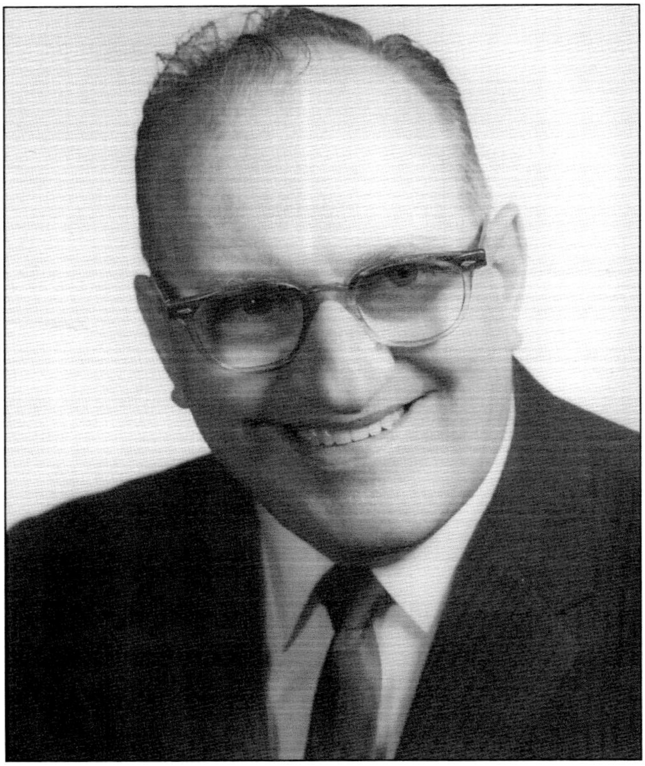

Jack Staulcup and his Orchestra still played the Casa Loma Ballroom in the 1960s, having to share the venue with the wave of rock that was sweeping the country. (Photo from Carol Kawell Ellis.)

Six

The Changing Times

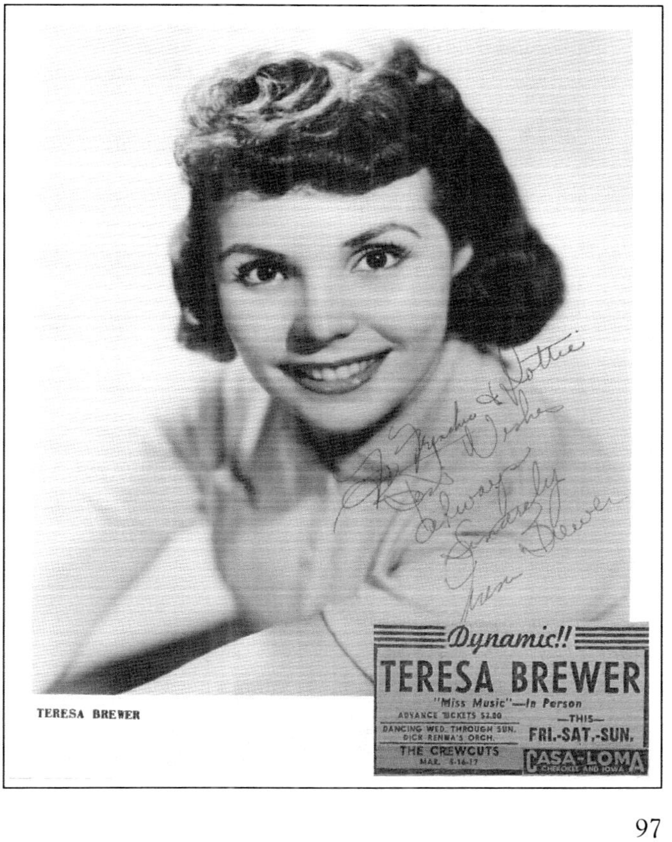

Teresa Brewer has been a star of motions pictures and television, but is remembered most for the unique sound of her music. She recorded numerous hits during the 1950s and 1960s, and she's still going strong. If I had my pick of all the fabulous performers who have graced the Casa Loma Ballroom stage, I would go back in time to witness Teresa Brewer. (Photo from Dorothy Vincent.)

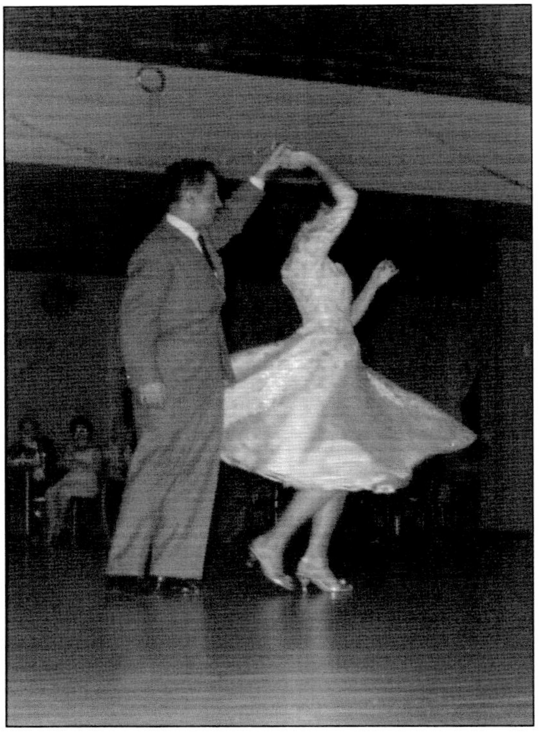

Dancing in the Tango solo at the Casa Loma Ballroom in December 1960 are Julius Gonstal and Marian Lubbers. (Photo from John and Marian Hargis.)

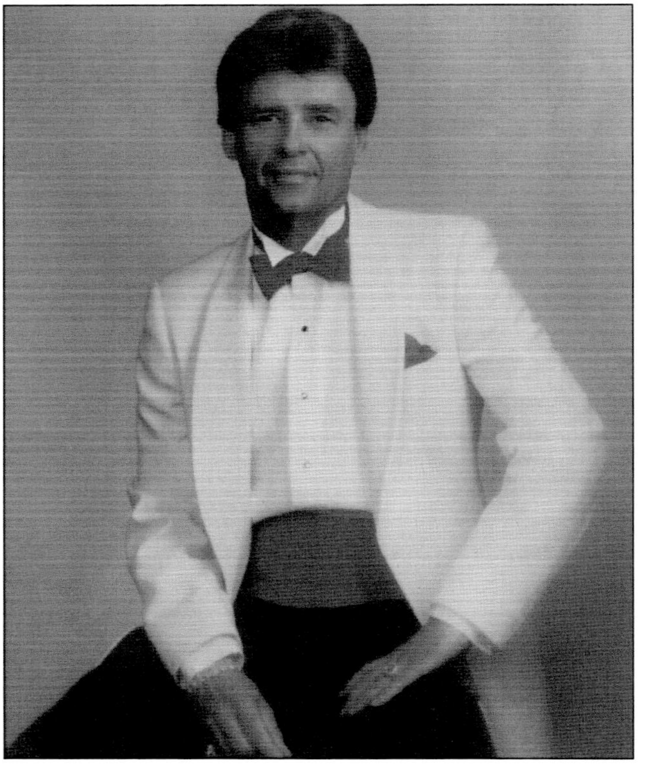

A well-known performer in St. Louis, Bob Kuban's popularity started back in 1966 with his top of the charts hit "The Cheater." (Photo from Pat Brannon.)

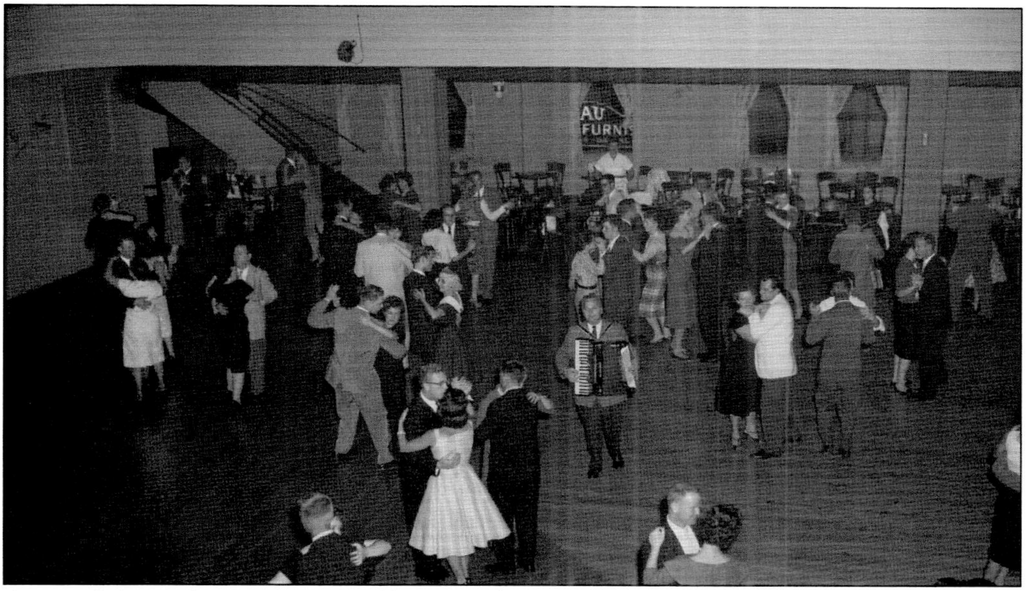

A typical day at the Casa Loma Ballroom in the early 1960s. Dick Renna takes a stroll around the dance floor, serenading the crowd with his accordion. (Photo from Carol Kawell Ellis.)

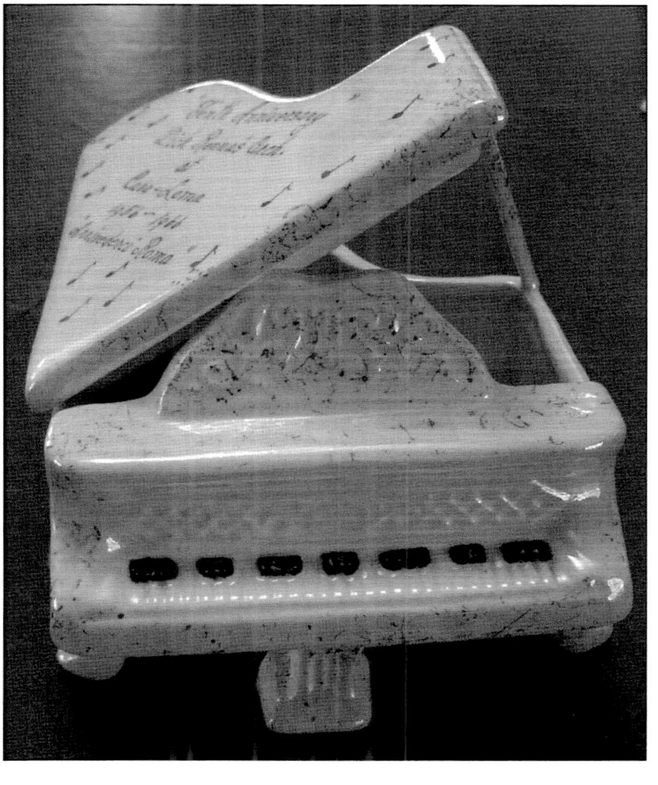

This beautiful ceramic piano still graces the home of Dick and Bea Renna. It was given to Dick and his orchestra in 1966 in recognition of their tenth anniversary as the Casa Loma Ballroom's "house band." The inscription reads "Tenth Anniversary Dick Renna Orchestra at Casa Loma 1956–1966, Arrivederci Roma." "Arrivederci Roma" was Dick Renna's signature song. (Photo taken by Dave Lossos.)

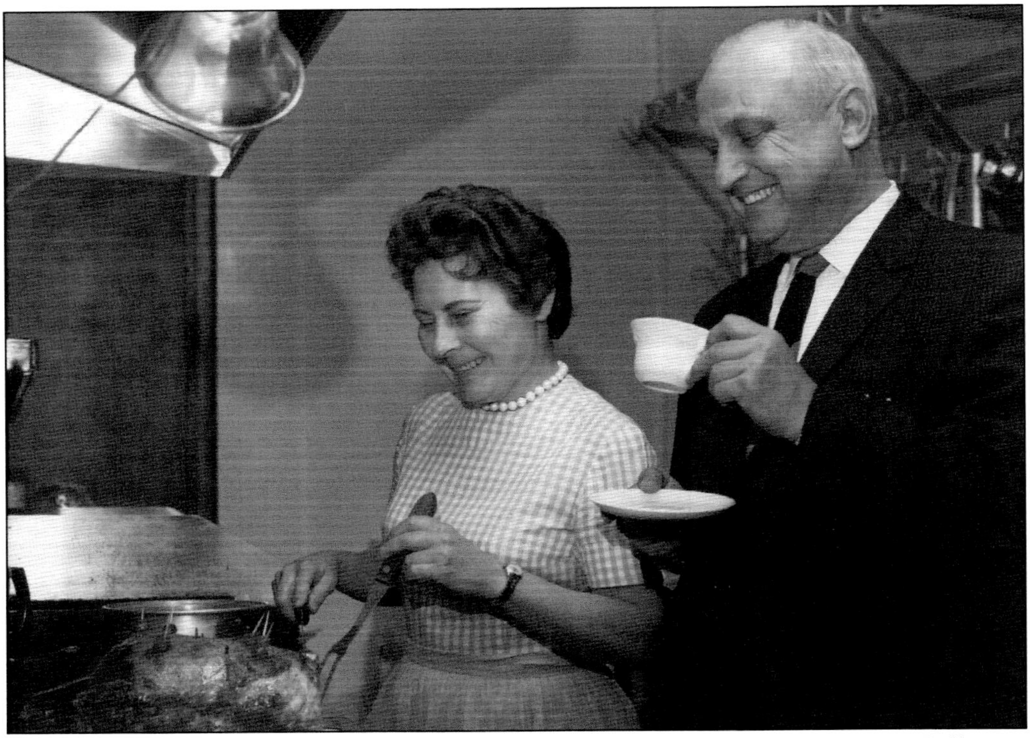

Edna and Art Kawell share some happy moments in the kitchen at the Casa Loma Ballroom. This photo was taken February 29, 1964. (Photo from Carol Kawell Ellis.)

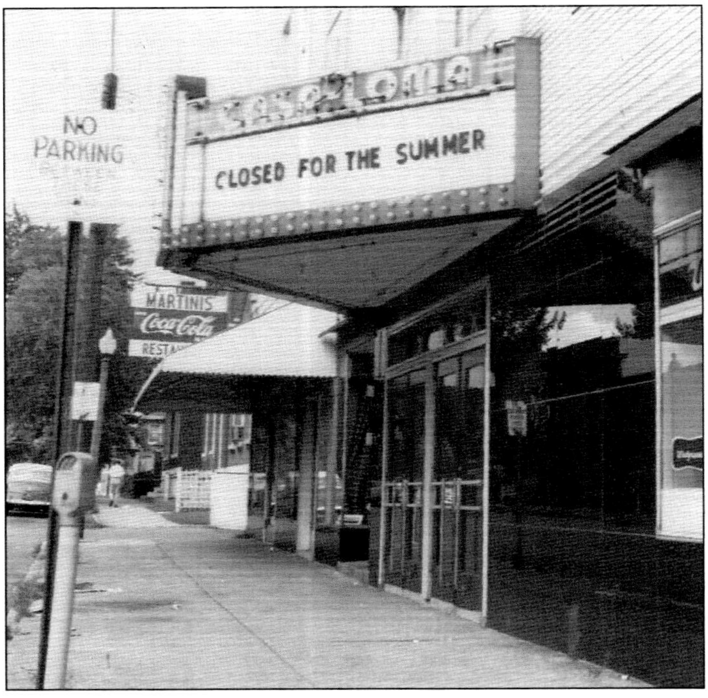

This was a common sight for patrons of the Casa Loma Ballroom, until the mid-1980s when the building finally had air conditioning installed, allowing entertainment to be scheduled year-round. Prior to that, the loyal patrons of the Casa Loma had to maintain their dancing skills at the Forest Park Highland and aboard the Admiral during the hot summer months. (Photo from Carol Kawell Ellis.)

"Exhibition Picture" of Julius Gonstal and Marian Lubbers taken in May of 1961. (Photo from John and Marian Hargis.)

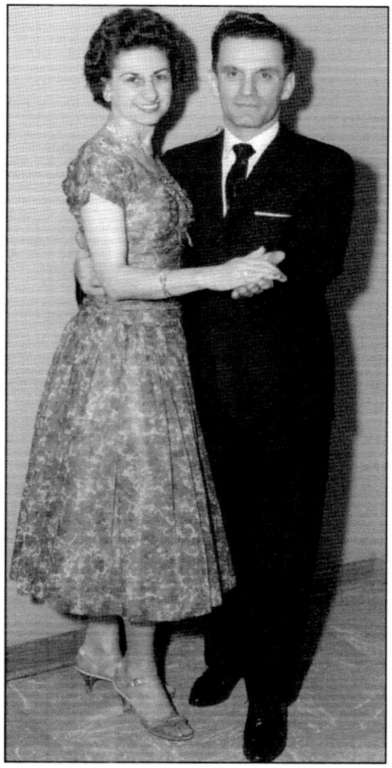

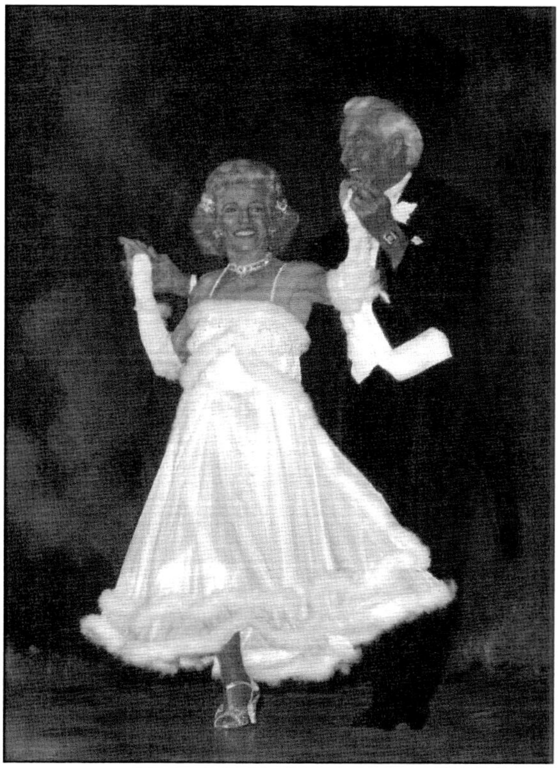

Lenore (Becky) Brunner and Charles (Tad) Pring are shown here dancing at the Casa Loma Ballroom where they met each other for the first time on April 4, 1980. The owners of the Casa Loma at that time, Ellen and Norman Reickard, entered them in the amateur category of the Ginger Rogers-Fred Astaire Dance-Alike Contest. It was held at the Fox Theater on July 9, 1984. Taking first place, the couple received a trophy, roses, and a party at the Fox. They also were sent on a three-day trip to New York. (Photo from Becky Bruner.)

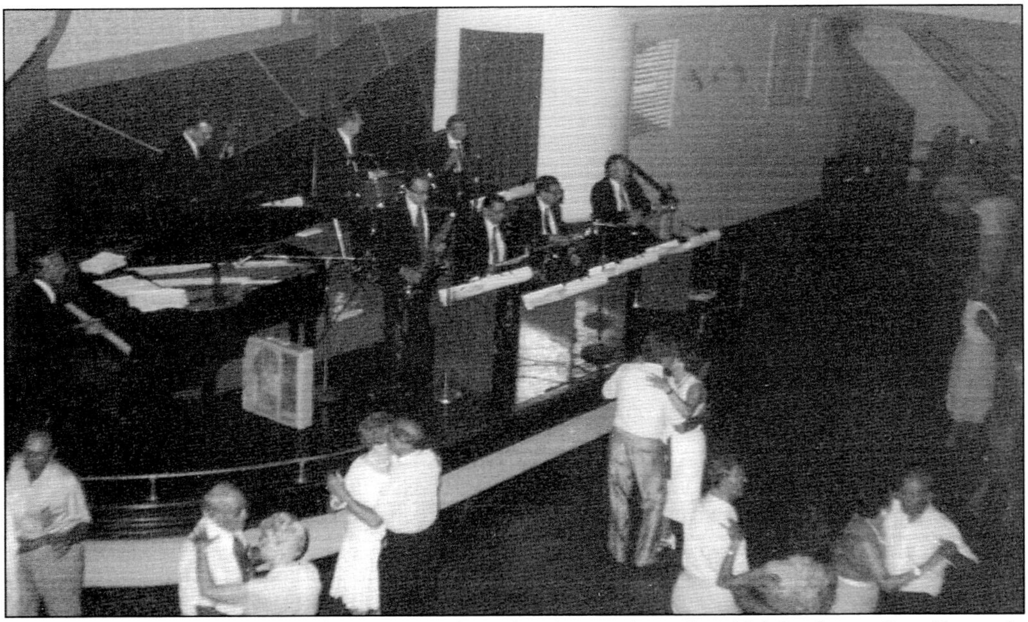

This is a copy of the photo that appeared in the September 15, 1985 *St. Louis Post-Dispatch*. A large article detailing much of the Casa Loma's past accompanied the photo. (Copy of newspaper article from Dick and Bea Renna.)

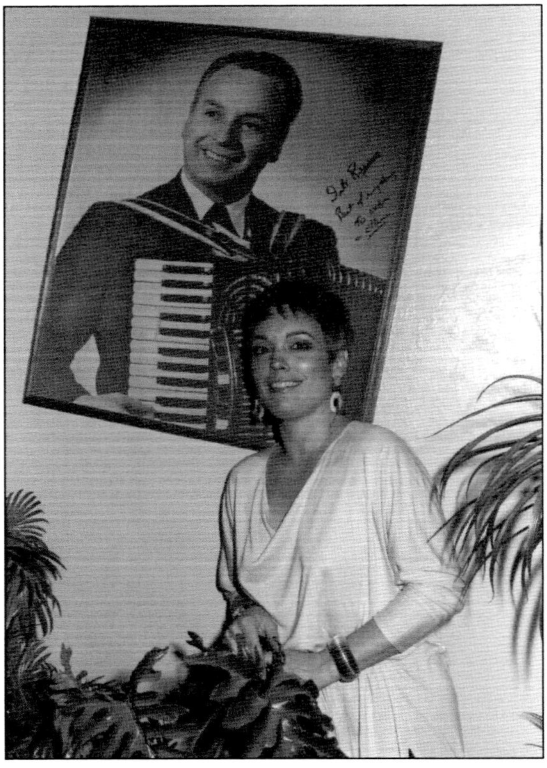

Most long-time patrons of the Casa Loma remember the many photos that adorned the walls of the ballroom, pictures of those who had performed there. Pictured here is Dick Renna's daughter, Ricki, posing below the photo of her father from when he played the Casa Loma in 1961. (Photo from Dick and Bea Renna.)

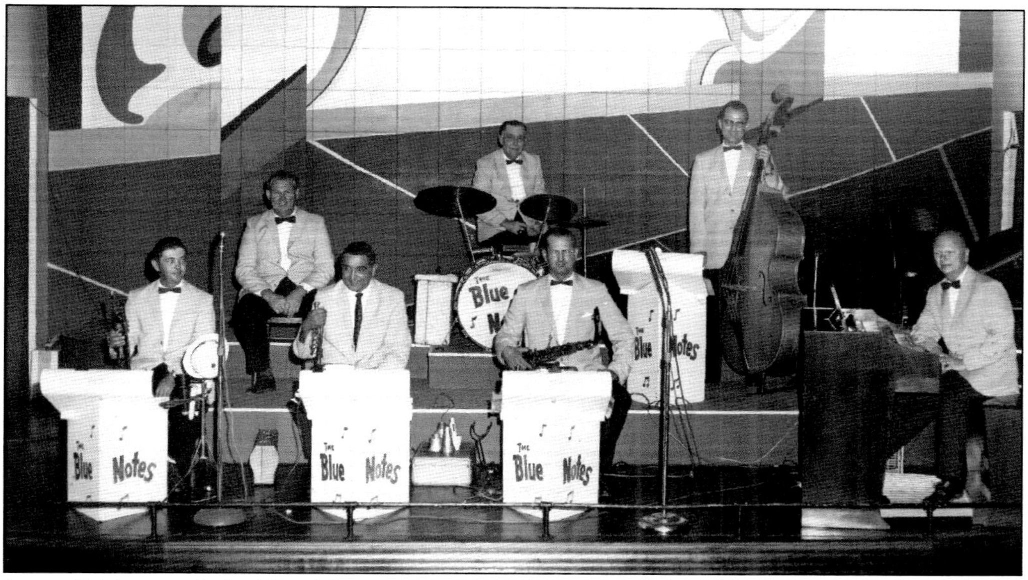

Louie Baldoni and the Blue Notes perform on the stage of the Casa Loma Ballroom. (Photo from Carol Kawell Ellis.)

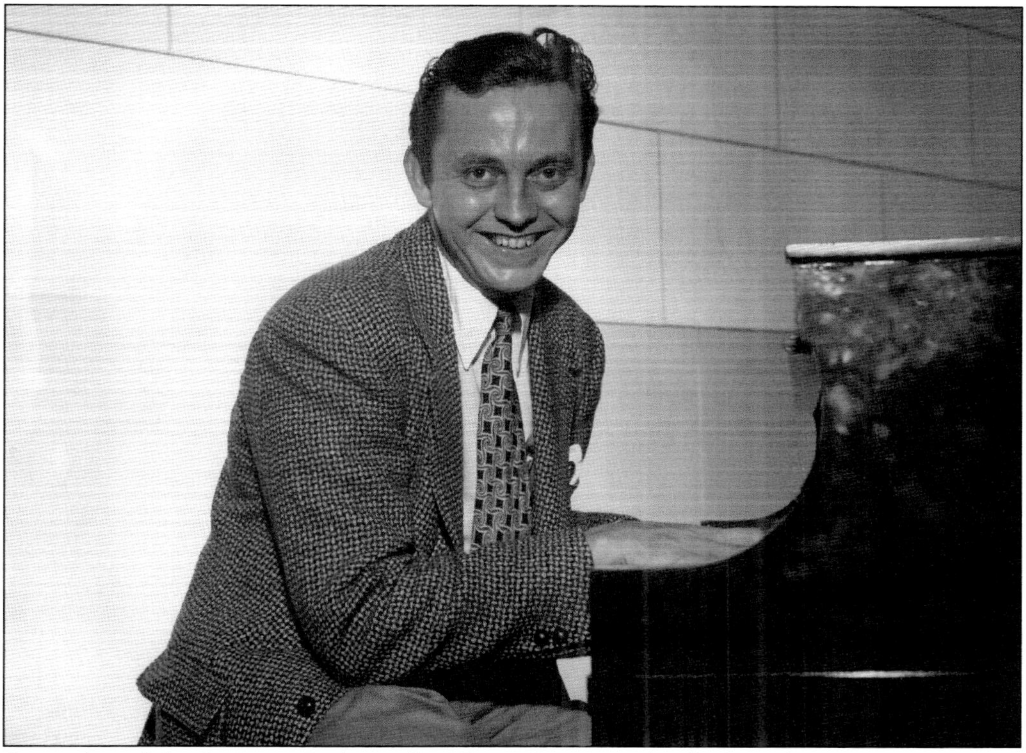

A member of the St. Louis Radio Hall of Fame, Russ David will always be remembered in St. Louis for his long-running music show which was heard on KSD. He was also no stranger to the Casa Loma Ballroom stage. (Photo from Carol Kawell Ellis.)

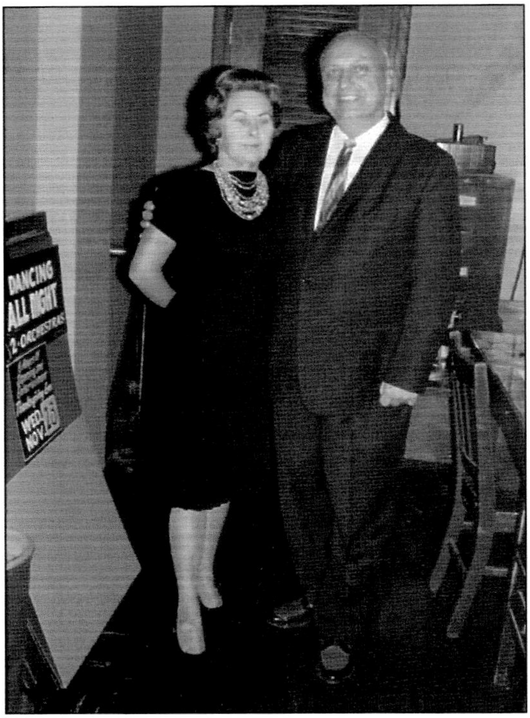

Shortly before they retired in 1967, Edna and Art Kawell posed for a photograph in the office at the Casa Loma Ballroom. (Photo from Carol Kawell Ellis.)

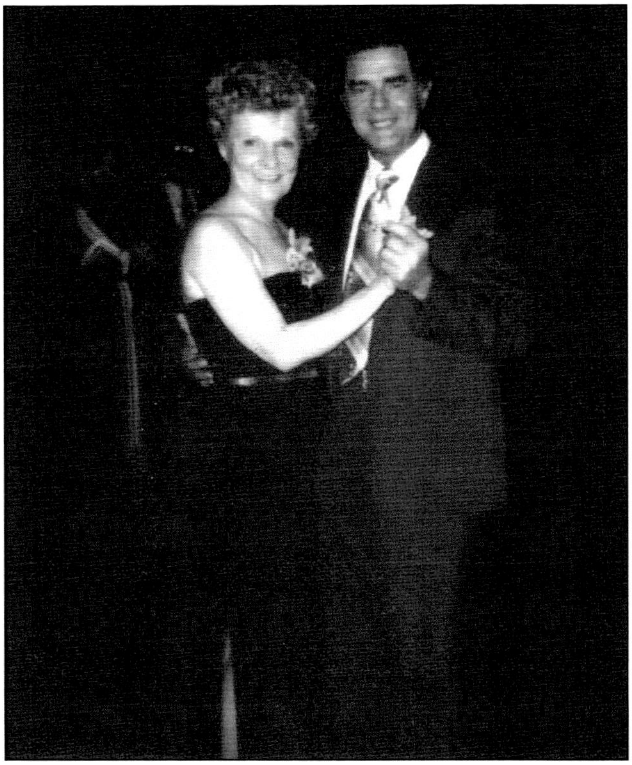

This photo, taken in the early 1980s, shows Ellen and Norman Reichert, owners of the Casa Loma Ballroom. They (along with Joe Roelle) purchased it in 1967. During the 1970s, the Reicherts sold their interest to the Roelles. However, in 1980, the Reicherts once again took over the operations at the Casa Loma. (Photo from Dennis and Laura Reichert.)

Seven

And the Beat Goes On

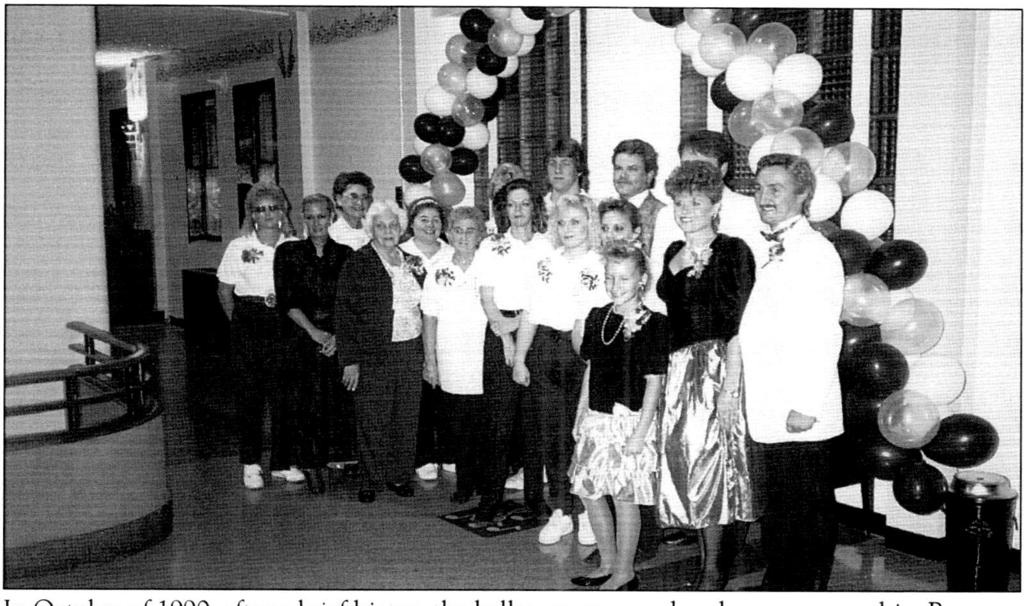

In October of 1990, after a brief hiatus, the ballroom reopened under new ownership. Roseann and Pat Brannon (on right) and their staff posed for this photo on opening night. Under the management of the Brannons, the Casa Loma Ballroom continued to evolve in order to stay current with today's ever-changing music styles. Two constants are the big-band sound and rock 'n' roll, both still very popular; however, just like in the past, innovation is the key to success, as you will see in the next few pages. (Photo from Pat Brannon.)

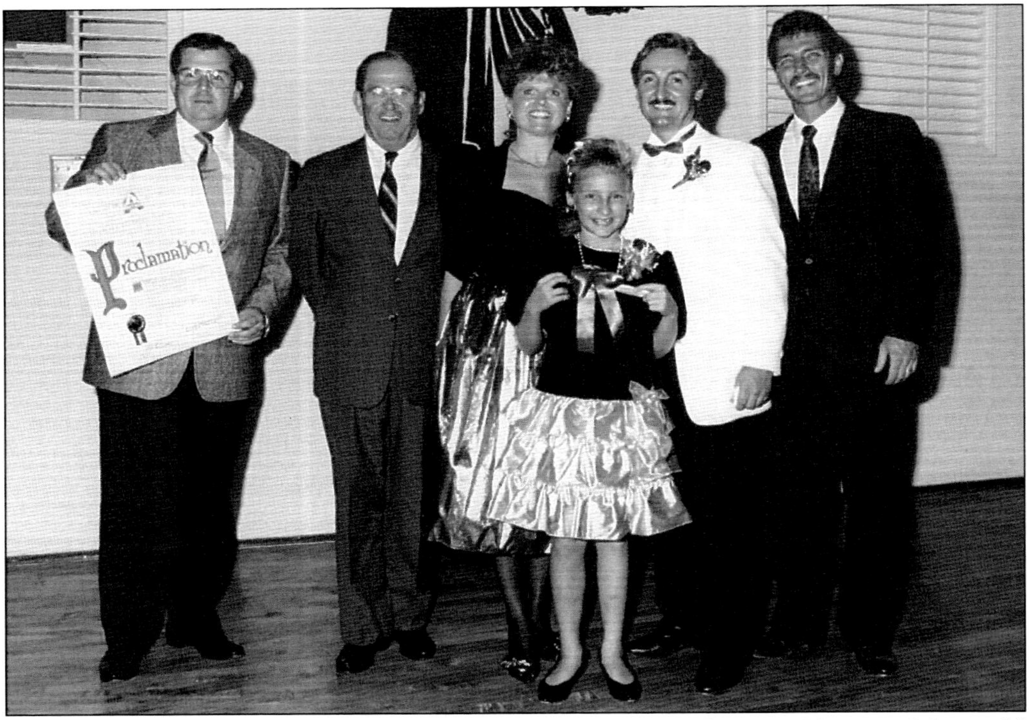

Another photo from opening night shows a representative of Mayor Vincent Schoemehl holding an official Proclamation honoring the Casa Loma Ballroom's reopening. H. C. Milford, a St. Louis County Executive, is next to Roseann and Pat Brannon and their daughter Kelly. On the far right is a State Representative from Jefferson County. (Photo from Pat Brannon.)

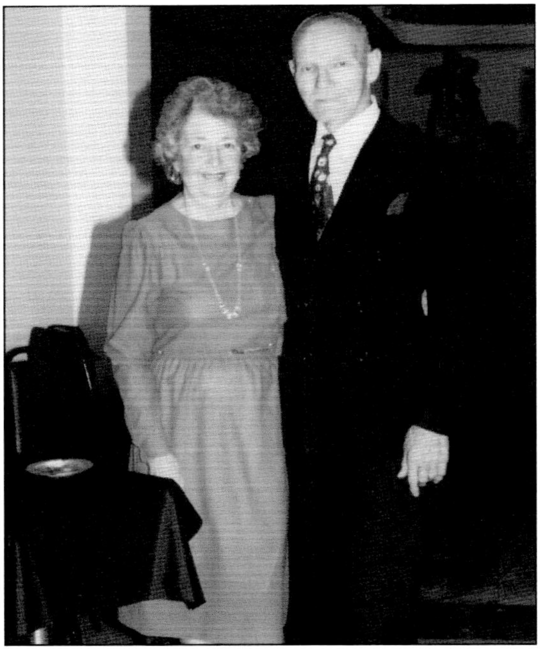

Almost all of the special wall photos of past performers were removed from the ballroom prior to the Brannons taking over. Another item noticeably missing was the rotating crystal ball that had hung over the dance floor for so many years. One of Pat Brannon's first tasks was to replace it. Mr. and Mrs. Adolph Meier approached Pat shortly after opening night and Adolf explained that he would like to purchase the replacement orb. Adolph explained that he and his wife had met at the Casa Loma Ballroom (one of seemingly hundreds of similar stories that I've heard) and that it was such a part of their lives that he wanted to give something back for all the wonderful memories. (Photo from Pat Brannon.)

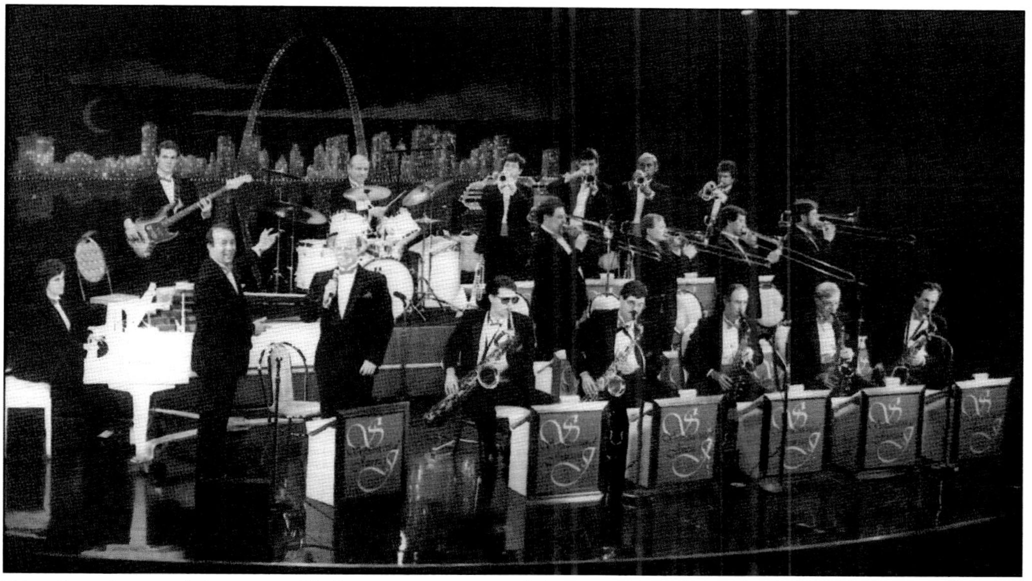

The Sentimental Journey Orchestra is pictured here on stage at the Casa Loma Ballroom. Notice that the backdrop proudly displays the St. Louis skyline and Gateway Arch. (Photo from Pat Brannon.)

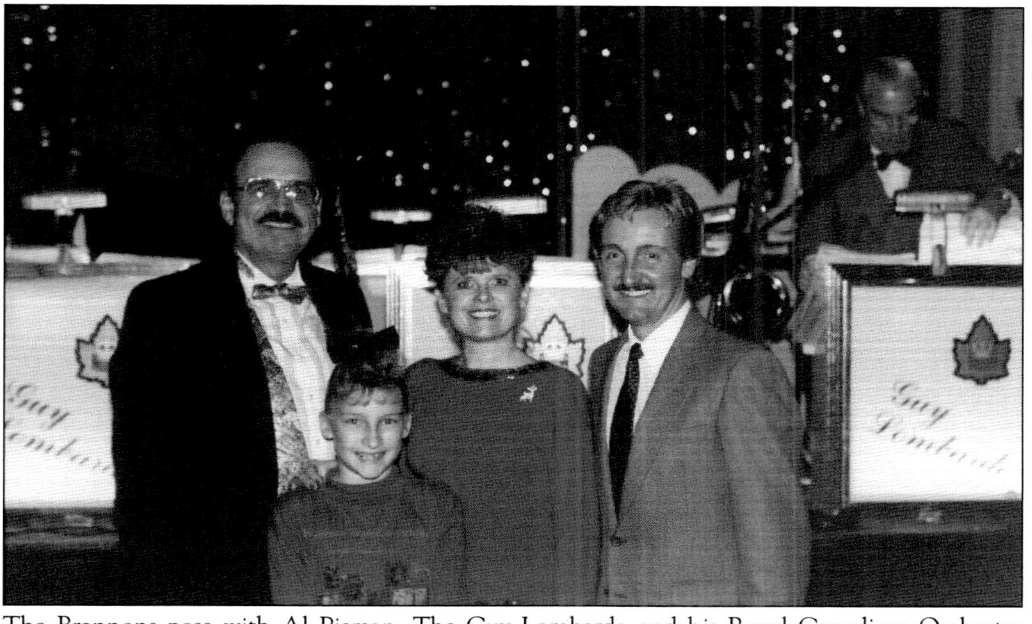

The Brannons pose with Al Pierson. The Guy Lombardo and his Royal Canadians Orchestra was founded in 1916. They played at New York's Waldorf Astoria on New Year's Eve for over 50 consecutive years. In 1989, Al Pierson took up the baton of the famed Guy Lombardo's Royal Canadians, with blessings from the Lombardo family. He continues the distinctive style that made the Lombardo Orchestra one of the greatest big bands of all time. (Photo from Pat Brannon.)

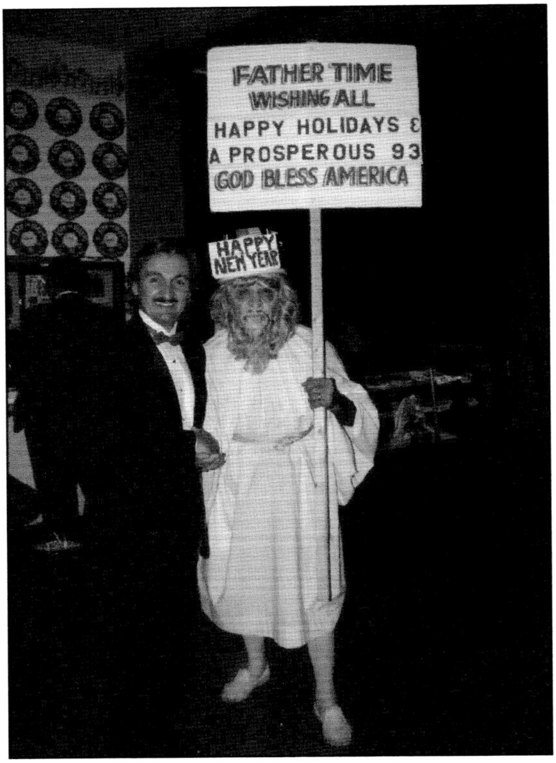

Pat Brannon greets Paul Pagano, a.k.a. "Father Time," during the New Year's celebration of 1993. Nearly everyone in St. Louis has seen Paul around. He shows up at almost all area festivals, sporting events, and parades decked out in costumes to match the occasion. He started this in 1985 after the death of Kate Smith. He decided to combine her trademark song, "God Bless America," with the Father Time figure. (Photo from Pat Brannon.)

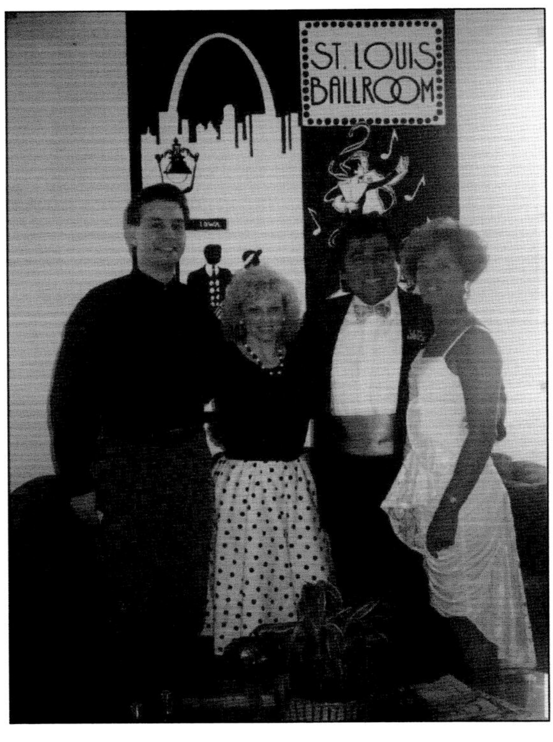

Pictured here are some of the dance instructors at the Casa Loma Ballroom in 1991. They are Stan Mayer and Linda Landwehr, and Nino Cruz and his dance partner. Free dance instruction continues today before most of the performances at the Casa Loma Ballroom. (Photo from Pat Brannon.)

Elaine Viets, noted columnist, author, and speaker on all things St. Louis (South St. Louis, that is), used the Casa Loma Ballroom as a backdrop for one of her mystery novels in the Francesca Vierling Series. In the book *Rubout*, she writes about the Leather and Lace Bikers Society Ball that takes place at the Casa Loma. She wasn't making it up—there really is an annual event by that name, during which a thousand Harley riders get together in St. Louis to party at the historic Casa Loma Ballroom in South St. Louis. Elaine was one of the first female judges for the Best in Leather and Best in Lace contests (on her website she confesses that she knows firsthand that biker men have nice buns). If you still don't believe it, see the photo below. (Copy of *Rubout* cover used with permission of Elaine Viets.)

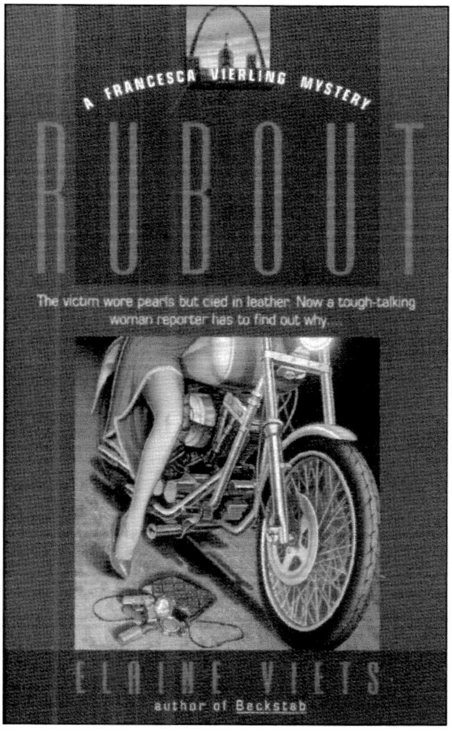

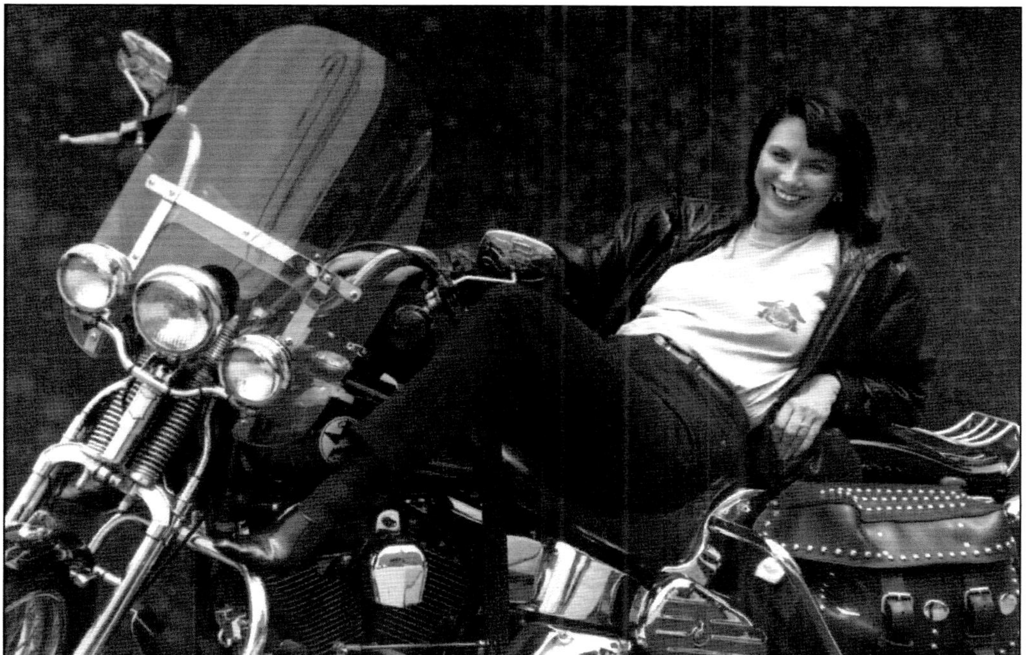

According to Pat Brannon, Elaine told him that this is one of her favorite photographs. (Photo from Pat Brannon. Elaine Viets informed me that it was taken by Jim Forbes of the St. Louis Post Dispatch.)

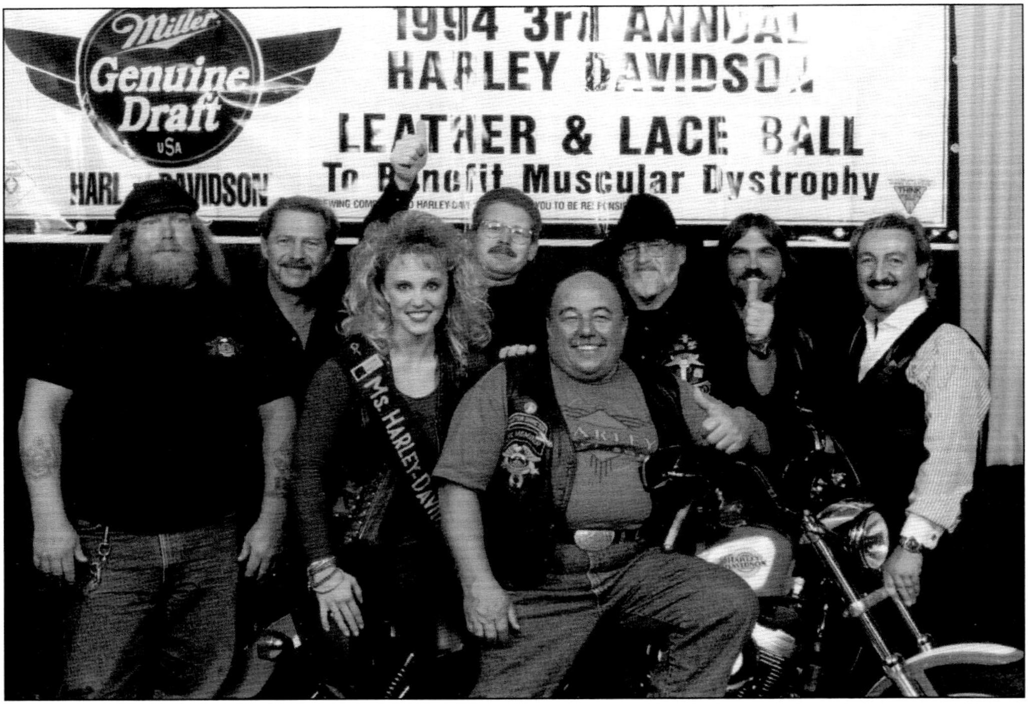

Some participants of the 1994 Annual Leather & Lace Ball are shown in this photo at the Casa Loma Ballroom. Ms. Harley Davidson is Krisann Whitley. Pat Brannon is on the right. (Photo from Terry Strahan.)

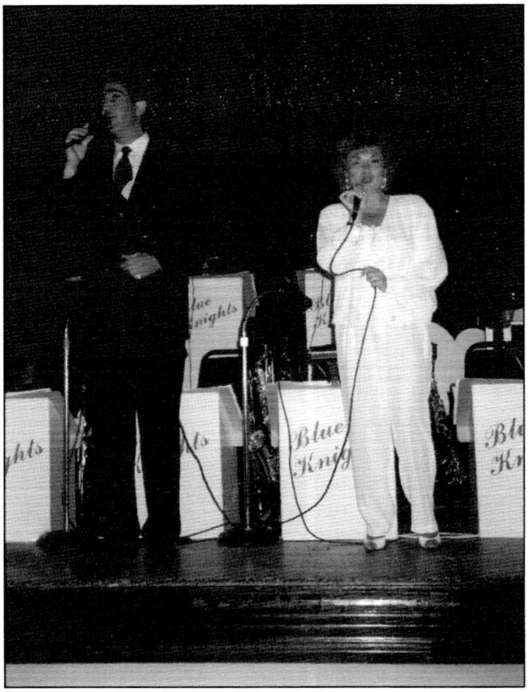

Owners of Falloni's Tavern on Manchester bring their trademark talents to the big stage at the Casa Loma Ballroom. (Photo from Pat Brannon.)

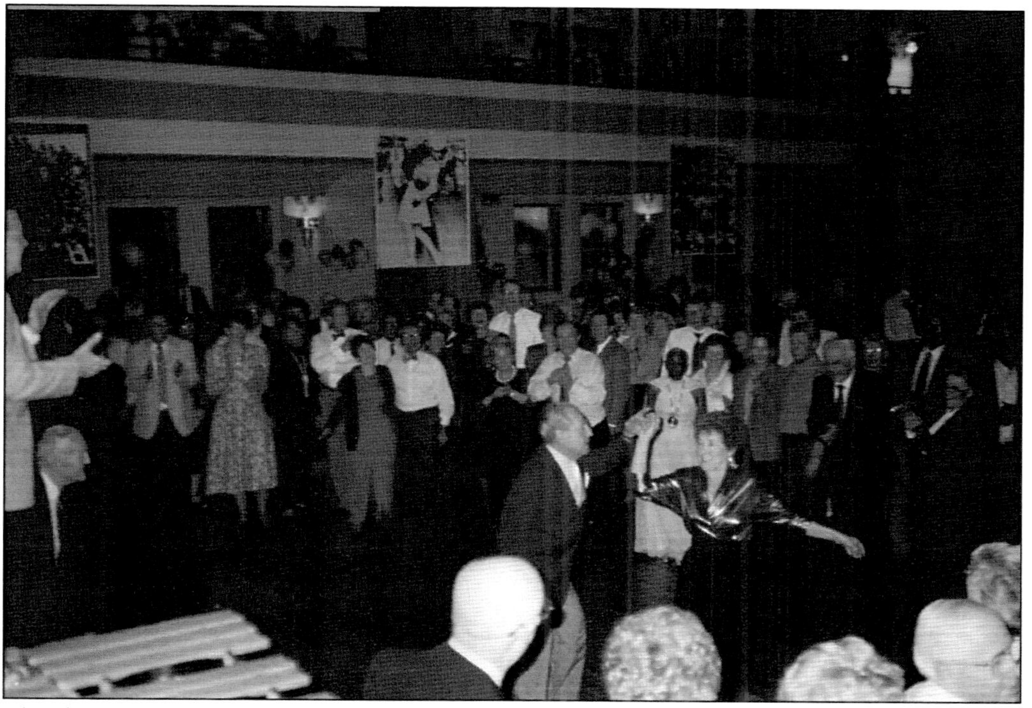

The dancing of Joe and Eva Renda caught the spotlight in this December 7, 1991 photo. Note popular St. Louis TV personality Jim Bolen on stage as the emcee. (Photo from Joe and Eva Renda.)

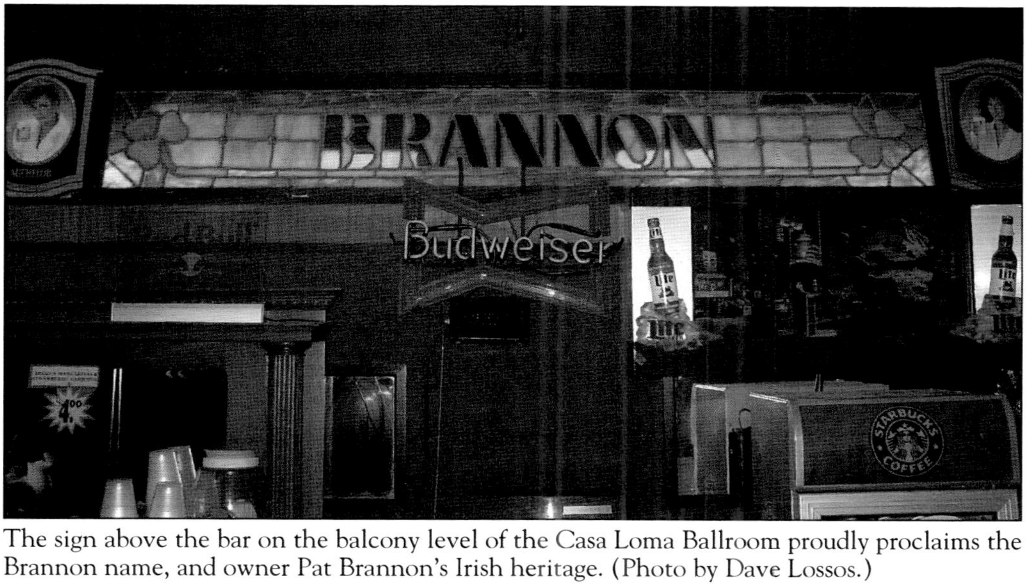

The sign above the bar on the balcony level of the Casa Loma Ballroom proudly proclaims the Brannon name, and owner Pat Brannon's Irish heritage. (Photo by Dave Lossos.)

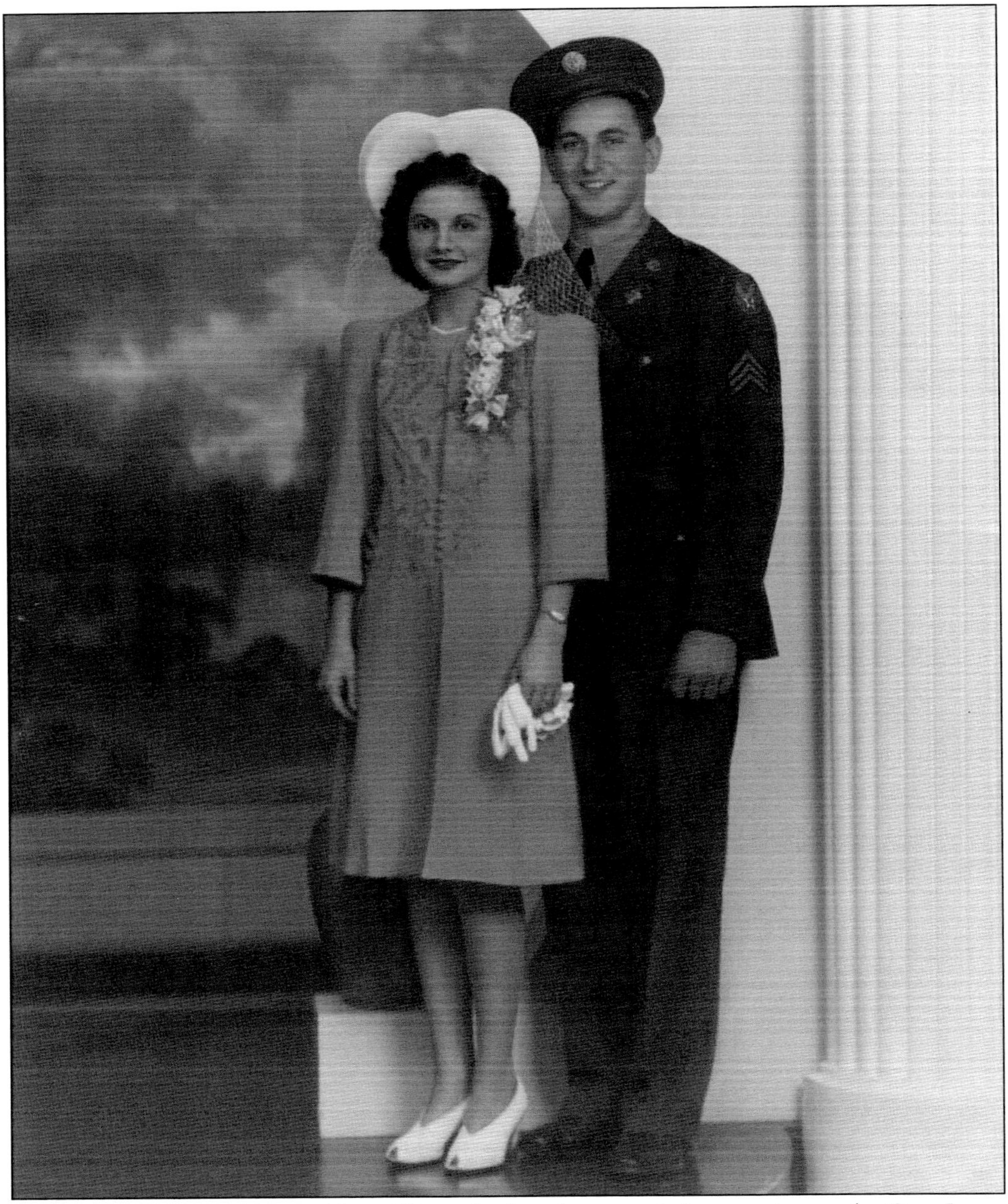

Evelyn, at age 21, and her girlfriend Doris, had made a pact before coming to the Casa Loma Ballroom on a cold February night in 1942 that they would have nothing to do with any guys in uniform. As Evelyn said, "They were up to no good." However, when Ivan Strahan, stationed at Jefferson Barracks, strolled over to the table, her plan fell apart and she gazed into her future husband's eyes for the first time. "It was love at first sight," Evelyn explained. A few months later, they married, as the photo above shows. To test the degree of significance of that event of 1942, I asked Evelyn if she remembered what band was playing that night. Without hesitation she answered, "Why, it was the Eddy Howard Band," convincing me that every detail of that night was stored away in her memory. (Photo from Terry Strahan.)

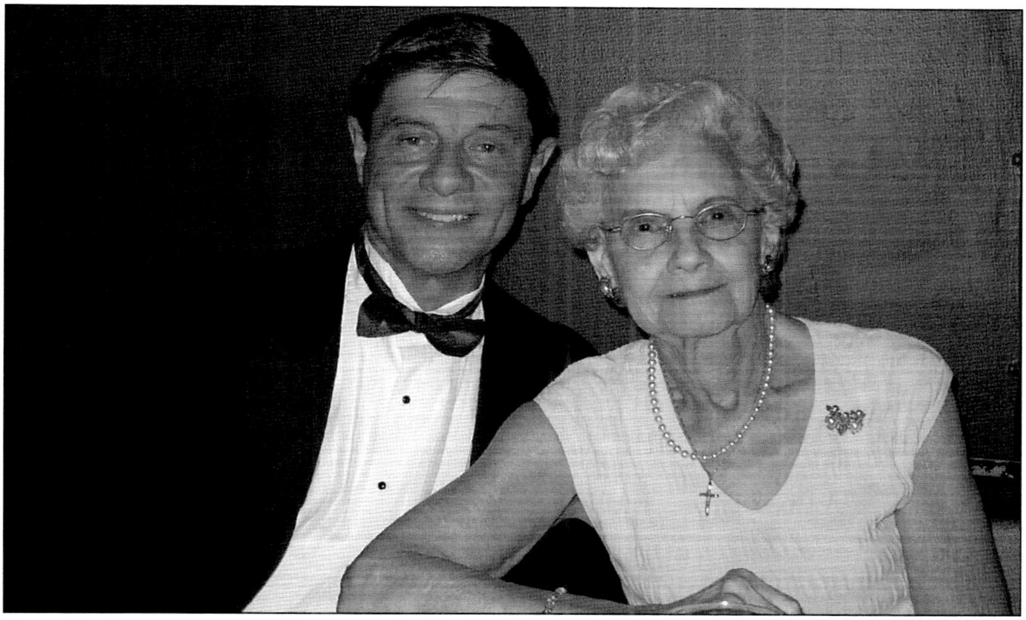

Terry Strahan, manager of the Casa Loma Ballroom, and his mother, Mrs. Evelyn Strahan, are seated near the booth at which Evelyn and Ivan first met over 62 years ago. And the family ties to the venerable Casa Loma Ballroom don't end there. Terry Strahan, besides being the current manager, was also a frequent visitor to the Casa Loma as a high school student back in 1964. That was during the days of the weekly filming of the *St. Louis Hop*, hosted by Russ Carter. (Photo by Dave Lossos, taken at a Pasta House Night at the Casa Loma Ballroom on August 27, 2004.)

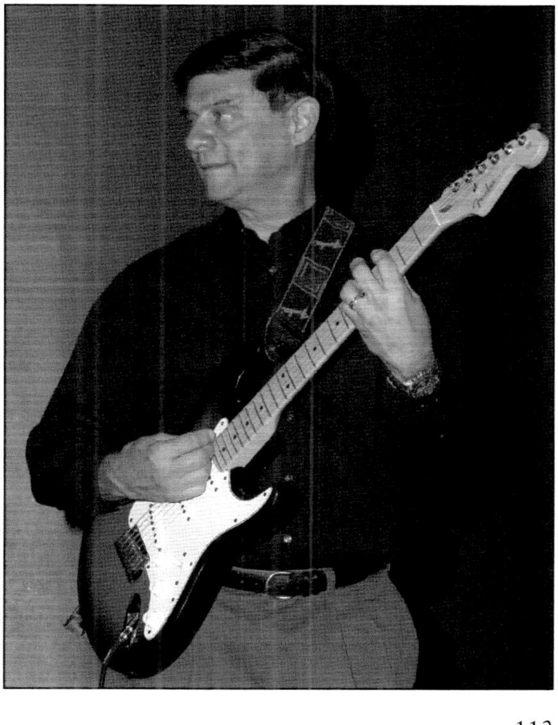

As if that wasn't enough, Terry Strahan has been known to perform a few numbers on the guitar with some of the bands who appear at the Casa Loma Ballroom. Seems only fitting, considering his Casa Loma heritage. (Photo by Larry Unger.)

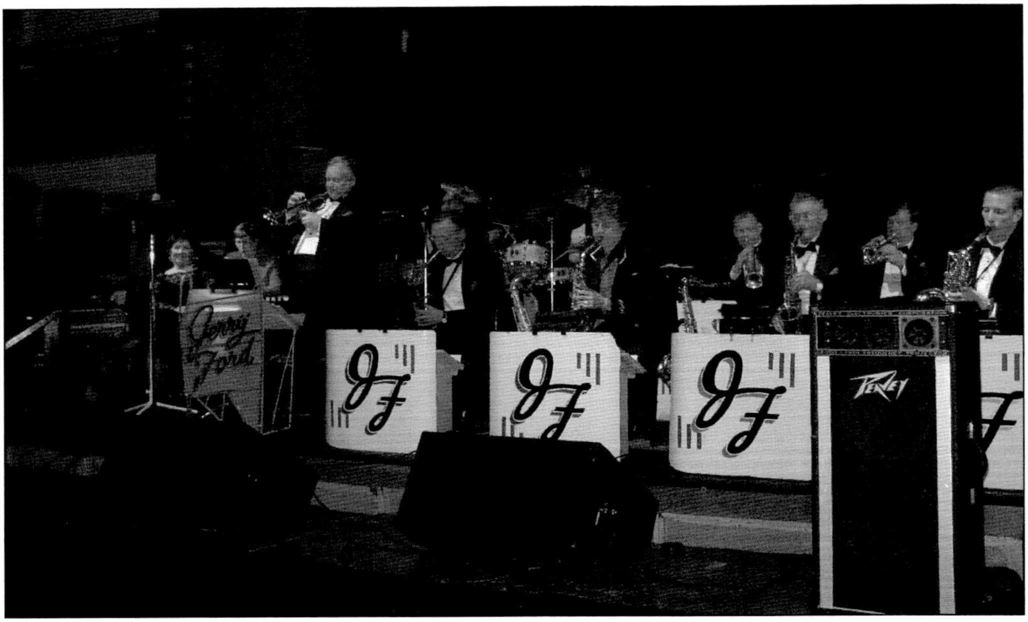

The Jerry Ford Orchestra performed onstage at the Casa Loma Ballroom on Friday, October 15, 2004. Based in Cape Girardeau, the group is always a favorite with those who enjoy big-band sound. (Photo by Dave Lossos.)

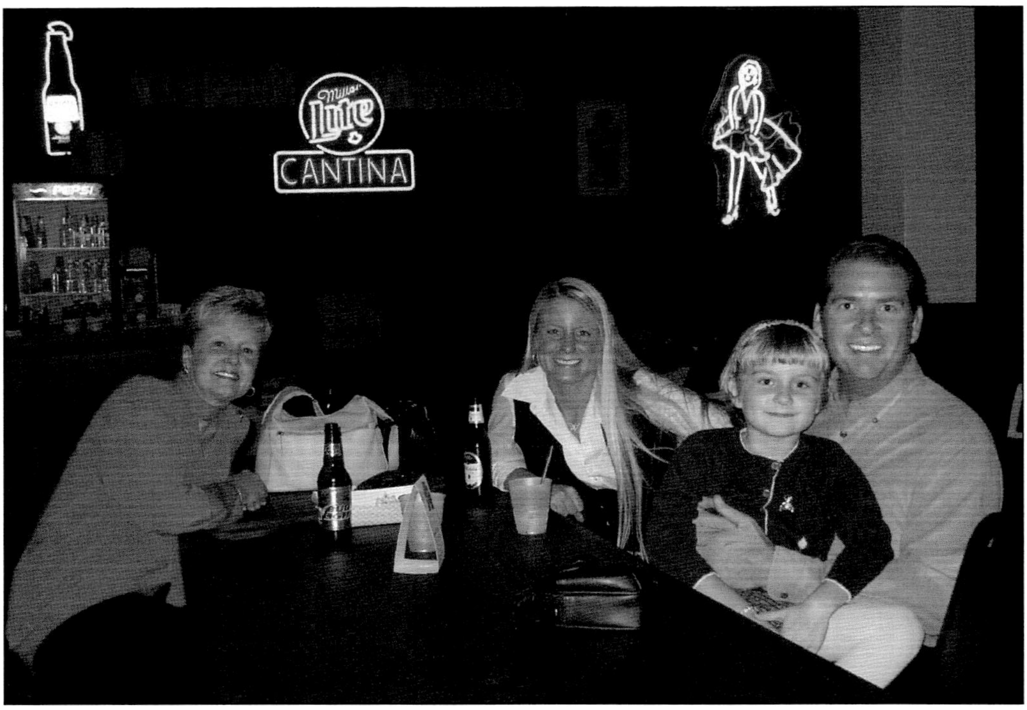

The Friday night swing and big bands are still a crowd pleaser for both the young and the young at heart. (Photo by Dave Lossos.)

The Gateway City Big Band poses outside the Casa Loma Ballroom in 2001 in preparation for their next CD release, *Live at the Casa Loma*. Pictured from left to right are Mike Bruce, Stan Minor, Jack Tartar, Victor Herbert, Phil Vonder Haar, Jerry Wood, Robert Waggoner, Don Clauson, Dan Anglim, Karen Kelly, Tom Cox, Jim Moore, Rick Sharp, John Laurenti, Kenn Kantola, and Jim Kalbfell. (Photo from Karen Kelly.)

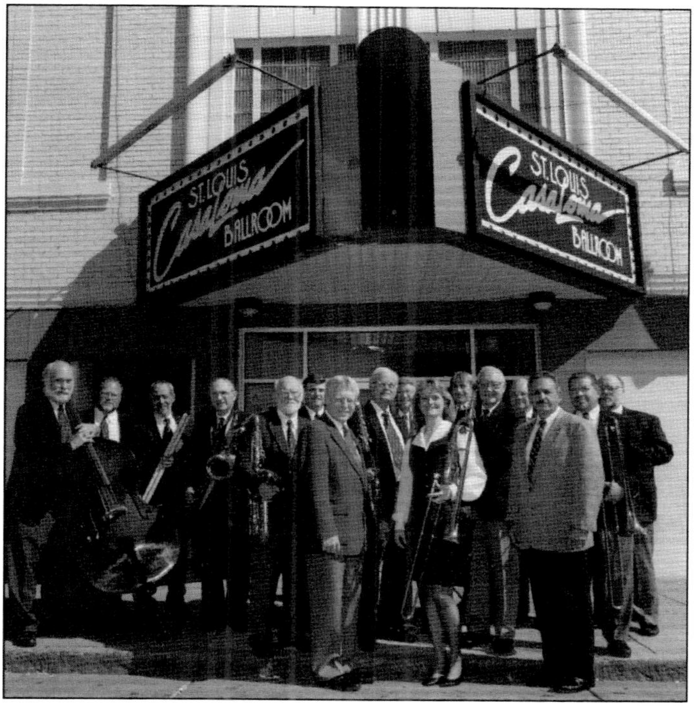

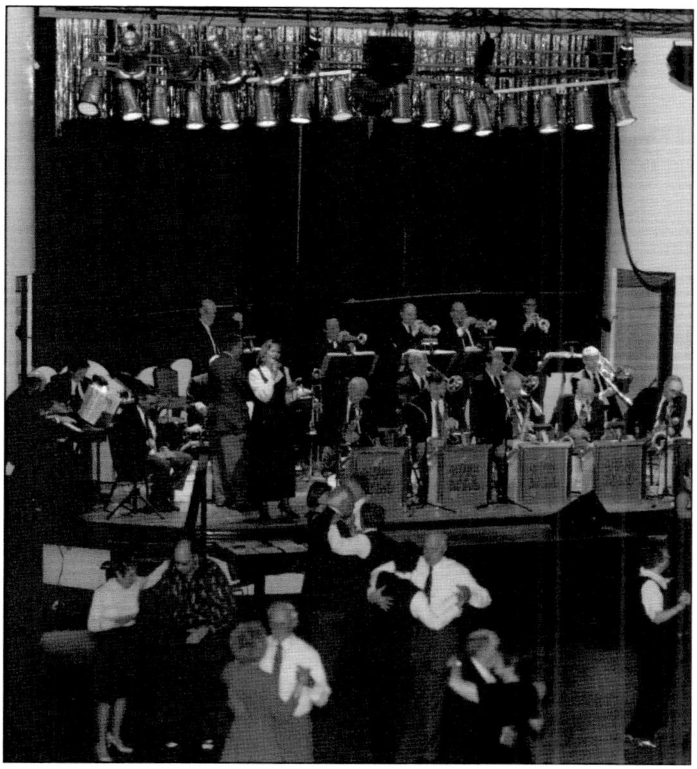

Dancers crowd the floor as the Gateway City Big Band plays the tunes they love. The band includes, from left to right, as follows: (front row) Henry Cummings, Jim Shiels, John Laurenti, Mike Bruce, Jack Tartar (hidden by director), Robert Waggoner, Karen Kelly; Herb Booth, Rick Sharp, Jim Kalbfell, and Bill Feldner; (middle row) Tom Cox, Kenn Kantola, and Dan Anglim; and (back row) Don Clauson, Jerry Wood, Jim Moore, Phil Vonder Haar, and Victor Herbert. (Photo from Karen Kelly.)

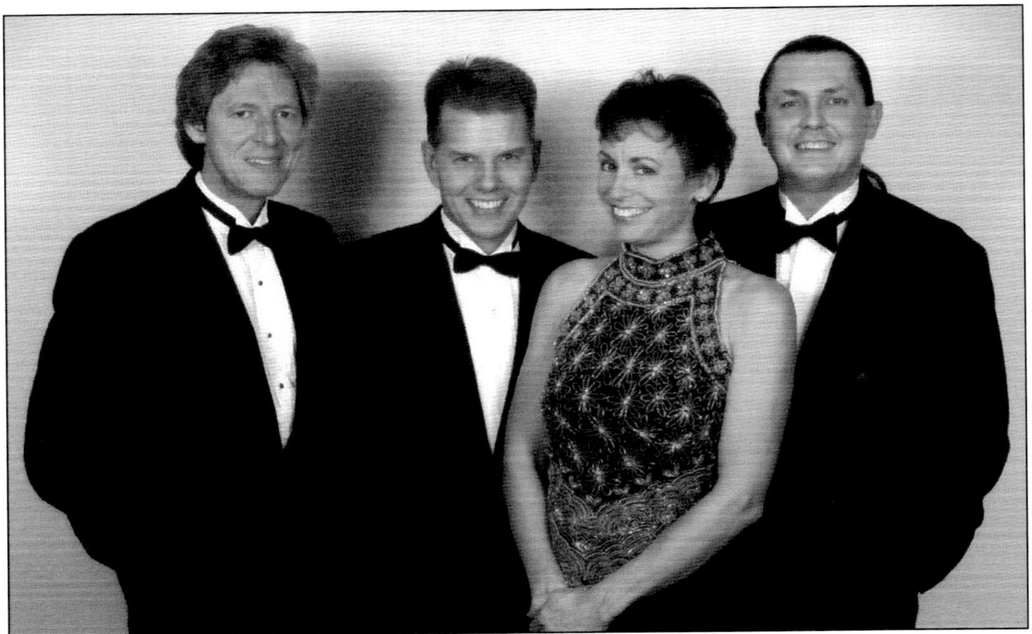

One of the most popular groups in St. Louis, Kittie Moller and Fanfare have been performing at the Casa Loma Ballroom since 1990. (Photo from Vincent P. Golomski.)

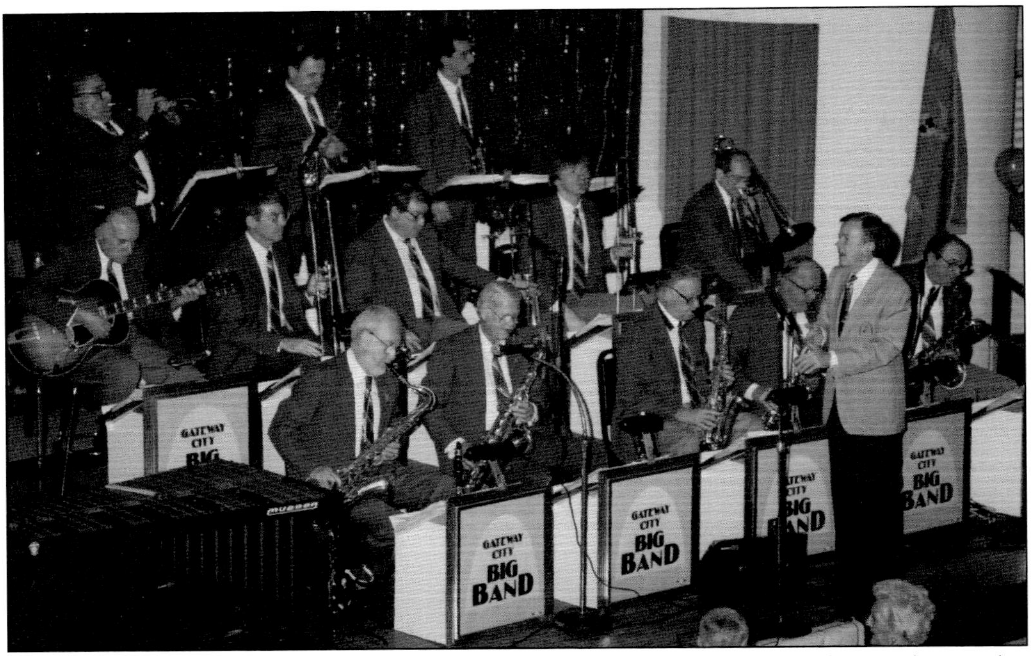

Jim Bolen directs the Gateway City Big Band at the Casa Loma Ballroom during this performance in 1991. Pictured from left to right are: (front row) Jim Knox, Don Clauson, Jim Moore, Will Dyer, and Victor Herbert; (middle row) Stan Shaw, Dan Anglim, Phil Eisner, Tom Cox, and Jim Mueller; (back row) Phil Balbi, Rick Sharp, and Mike Mench. (Photo from Karen Kelly.)

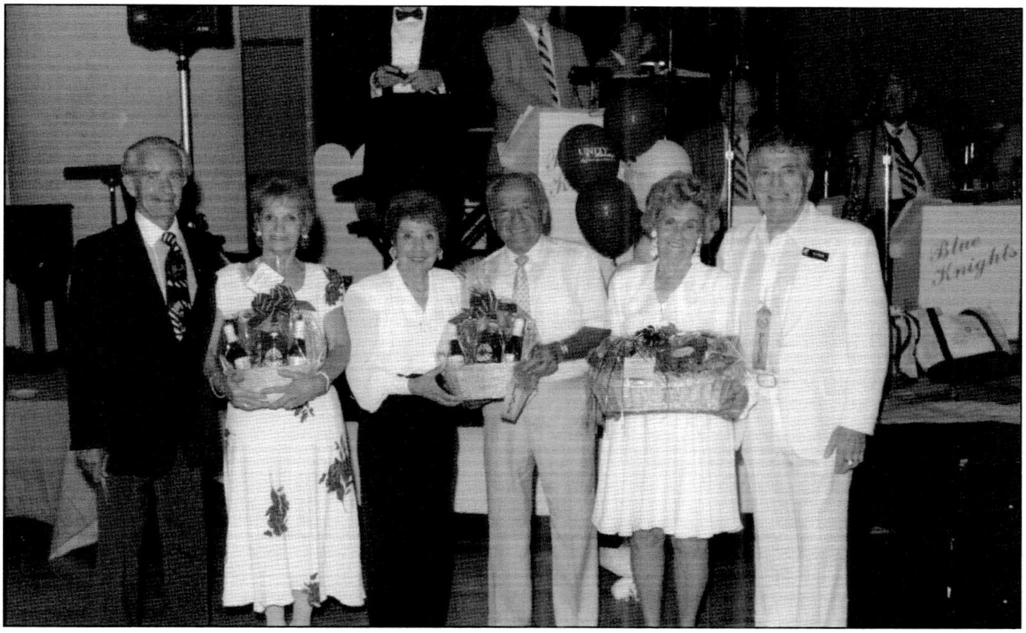

Winners of various dance contests are pictured here on May 3, 1996. Pictured are Frank and Joyce, Joe and Eva Renda, the winners of the swing contest, and Alfredo Ciolek and his dance partner Gladys. (Photo from Joe and Eva Renda.)

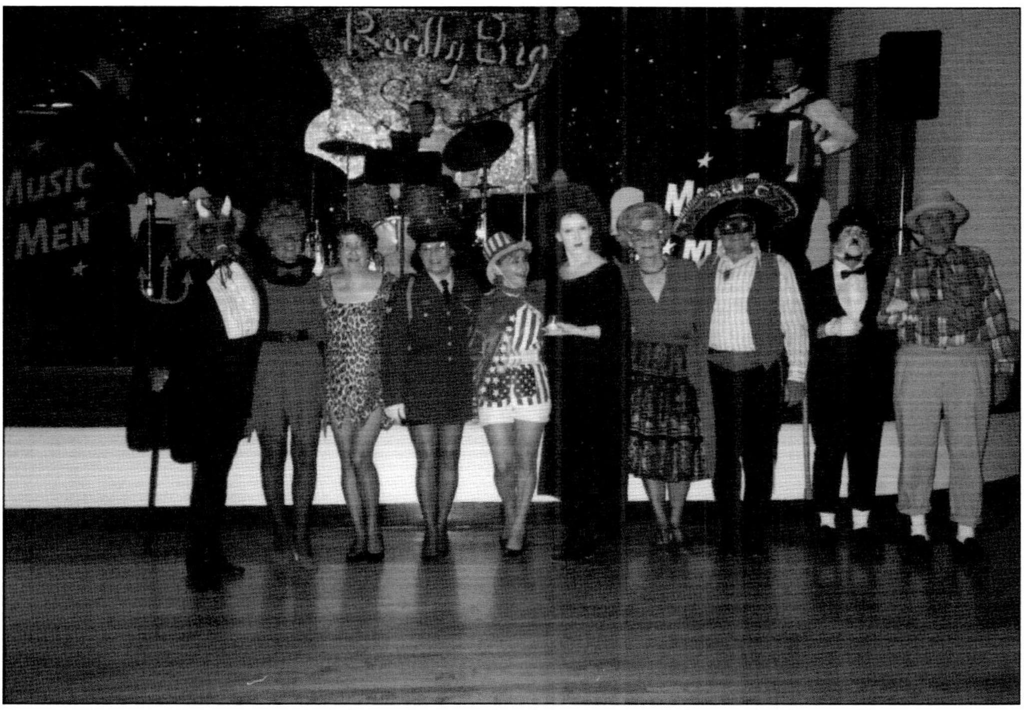

Annually, one of the most popular events at the Casa Loma Ballroom is the Halloween Dance. Here we see some of the party-goers from October 30, 1992. (Photo from Pat Brannon.)

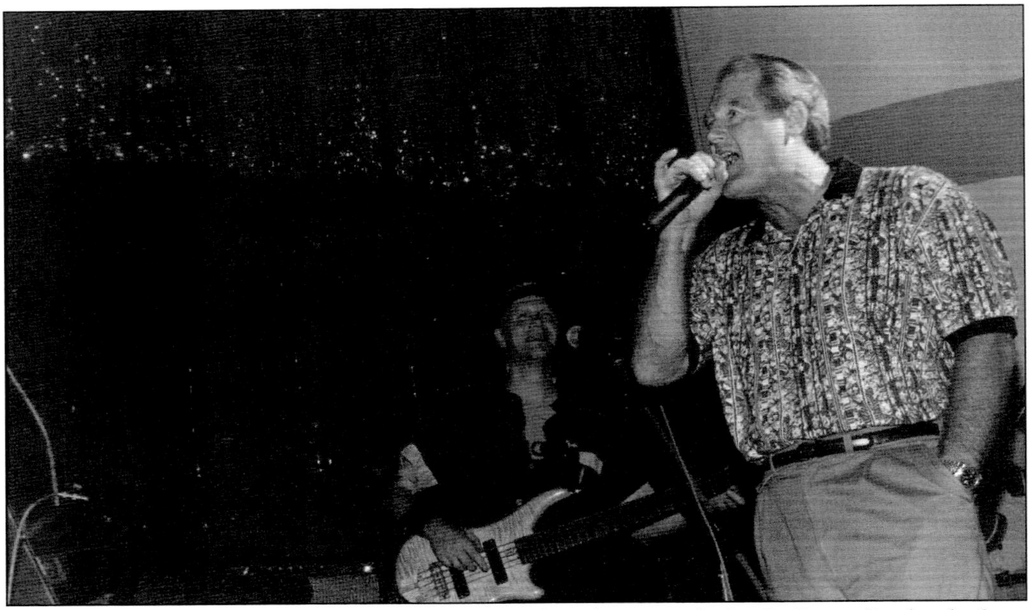

Football Hall of Famer Jackie Smith was a fixture for 15 years with the St. Louis Cardinals, from 1963 to 1977. At the time of his retirement, he ranked as the all-time receiver among tight ends with 480 receptions for 7,918 yards and 40 touchdowns. This photo shows another side of this popular St. Louis celebrity. (Photo from Pat Brannon.)

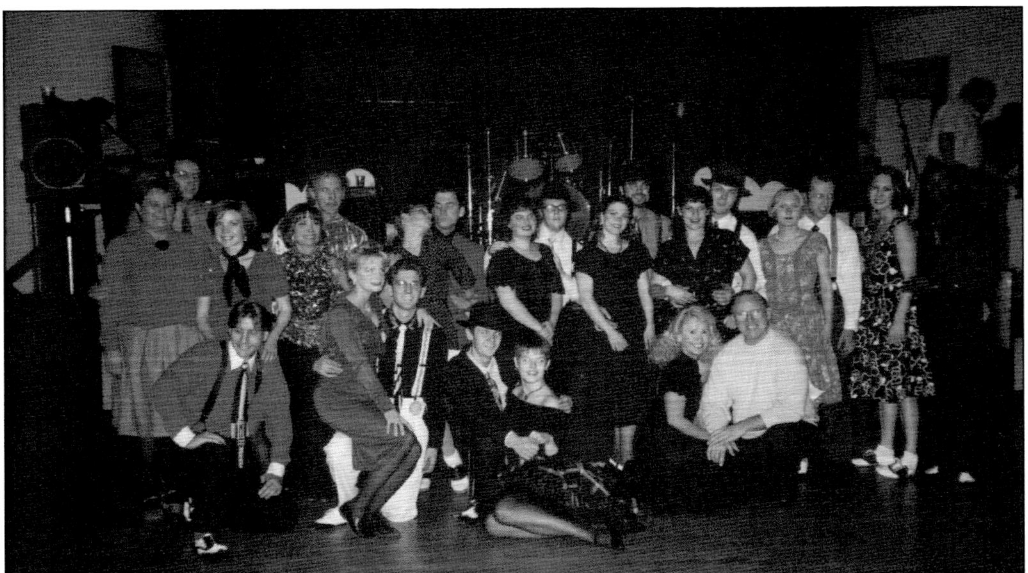

The St. Louis Imperial Dance Club was started in 1973. Its mission is to keep swing dancing alive in the St. Louis area. Throughout the years groups of dancers broke off from the St. Louis Imperial Dance Club and started their own clubs. Dancers wanted to be closer to home but they kept the Imperial club identity and are considered sister clubs. Shown here are members of the club that gathered at the Casa Loma Ballroom recently. (Photo from Pat Brannon.)

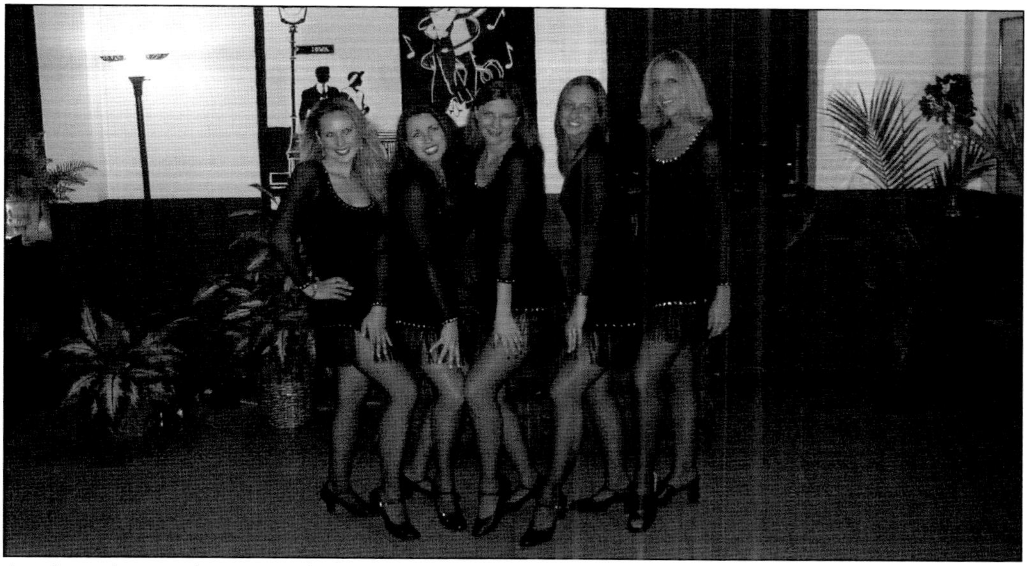

A relatively new feature at the Casa Loma Ballroom is the monthly Rock n' Roll Pasta Dinner Show and Dance catered by Pasta House Company. In addition to serving the patrons a four course meal, the Casa Loma's "Dancing Waitresses" perform dance routines between the various courses. Performing and serving this evening were Mindy Jacks, Lisa Jacks, Mandie Davis, Lora Schmitt, and Jennifer Brown. (Photo by Dave Lossos, taken at a Pasta House Night at the Casa Loma Ballroom on August 27, 2004.)

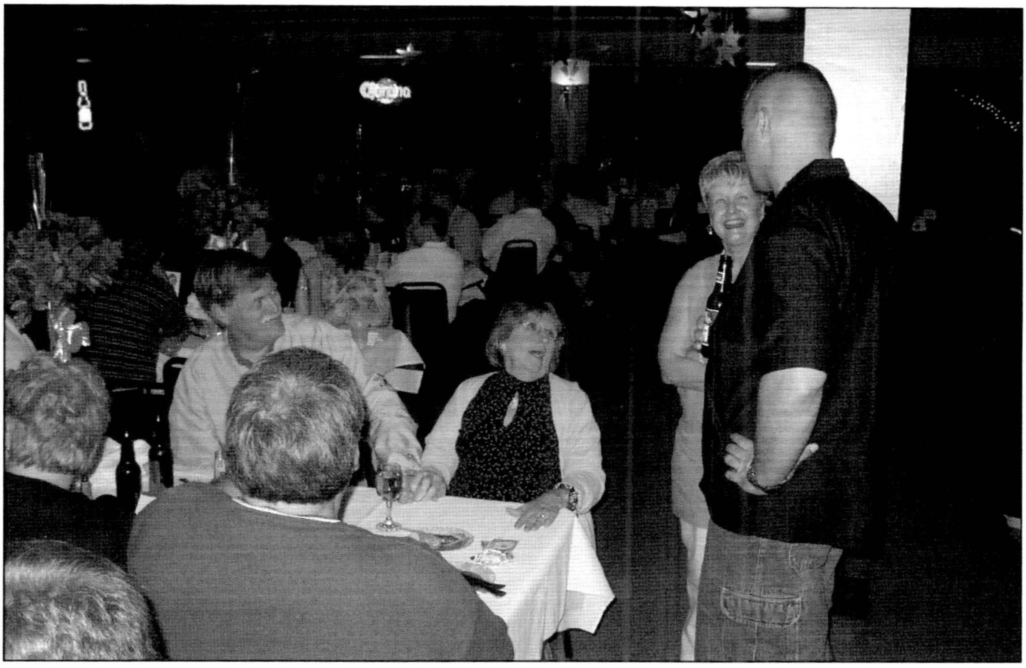

Good food, good entertainment, good friends, and good music make for a very enjoyable evening at the Casa Loma Pasta House Night. (Photo by Dave Lossos, taken at a Pasta House Night at the Casa Loma Ballroom on August 27, 2004.)

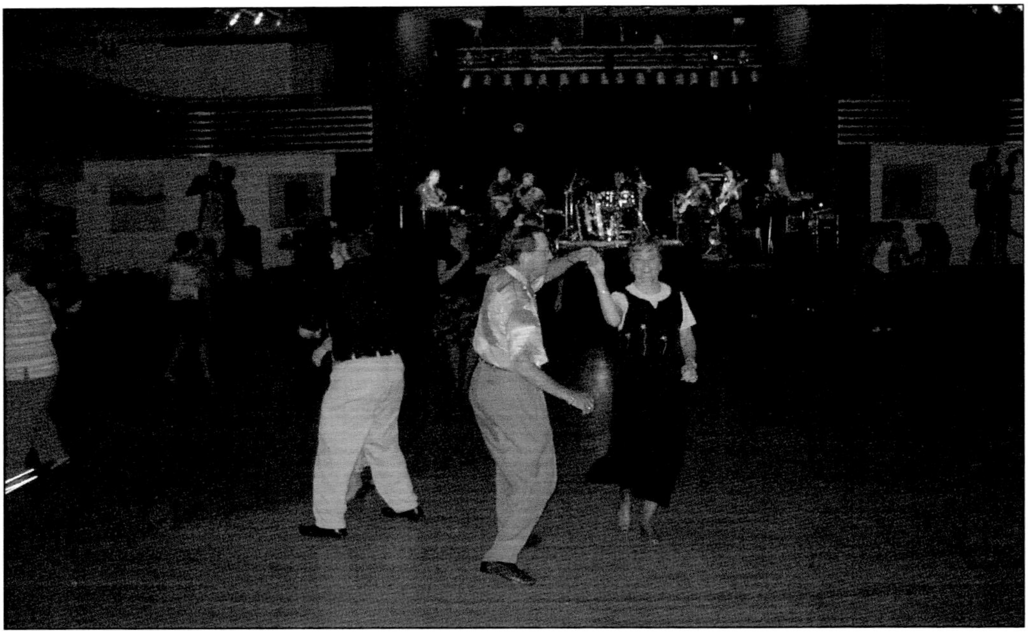

After dinner couples danced the night away on the huge dance floor. (Photo by Dave Lossos, taken at a Pasta House Night at the Casa Loma Ballroom on August 27, 2004.)

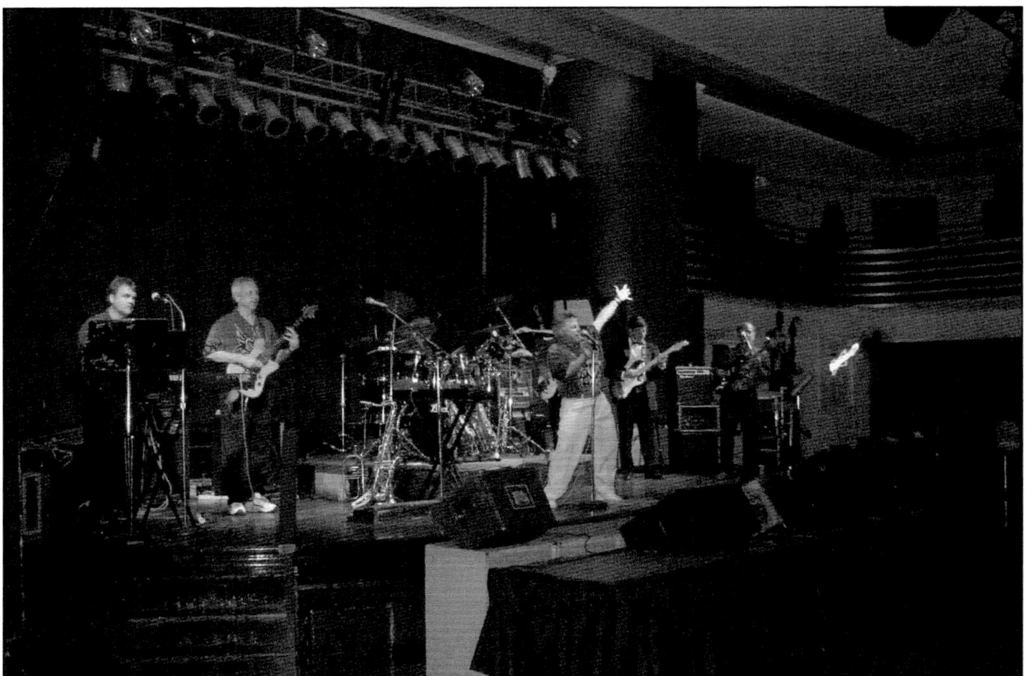

The Facts O' Life Band performed on the Casa Loma Ballroom stage. (Photo by Dave Lossos, taken at a Pasta House Night at the Casa Loma Ballroom on August 27, 2004.)

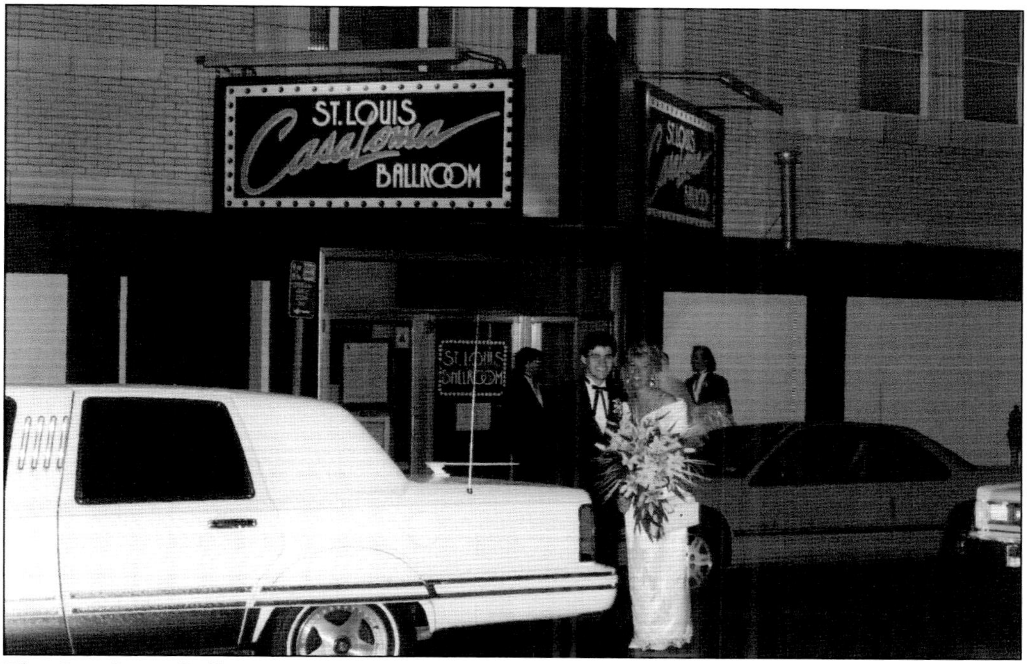

The Casa Loma Ballroom is an increasingly popular choice for wedding receptions. (Used with permission of Kent Miller Photography © 1998.)

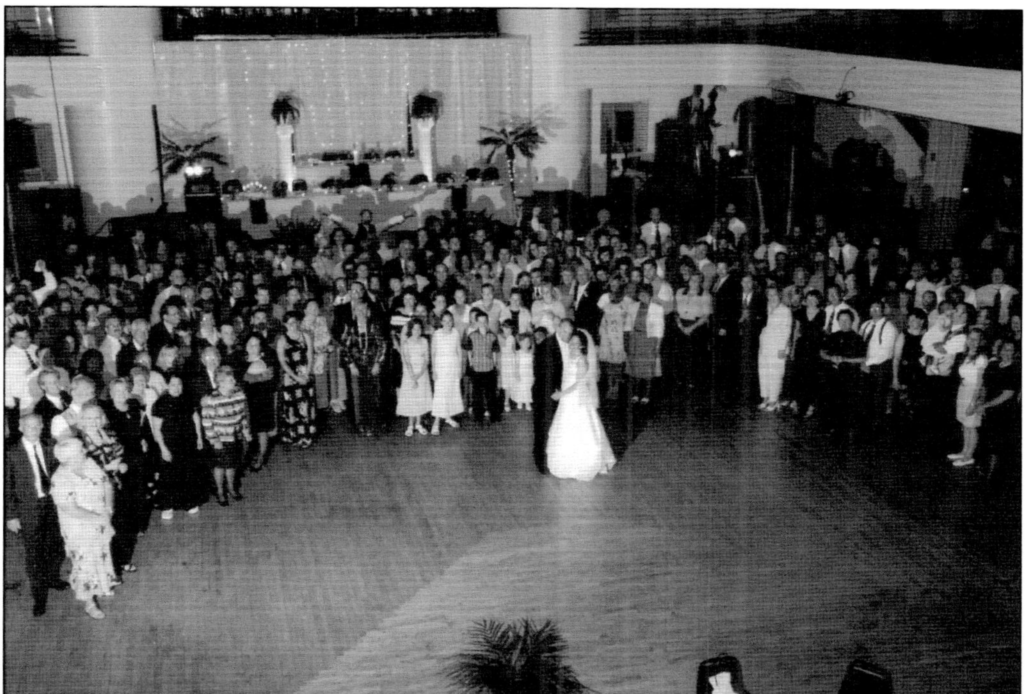

As you can see the largest of crowds can easily take to the floor of the Casa Loma Ballroom. (Photo from Pat Brannon.)

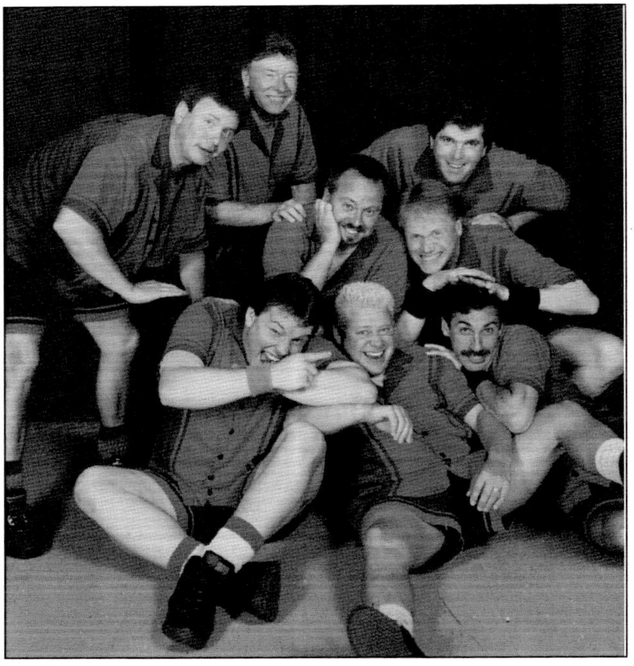

As their promo ad and website state "SH-BOOM is an 8-piece rock 'n' roll nostalgia band performing the greatest hits of the 50's, 60's, and 70's. Their highly entertaining and energetic delivery of the greatest rock music ever written, has kept the group on top for the past two decades." They have been performing at the Casa Loma Ballroom on a regular basis during that time. (Photo from Pat Brannon.)

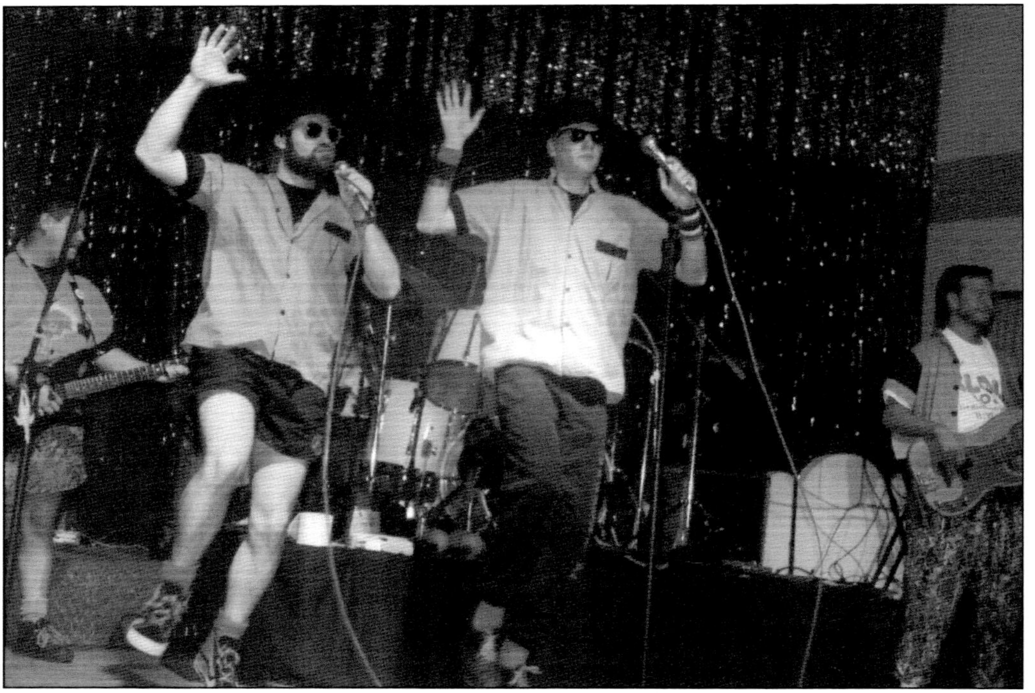

SH-BOOM is shown here performing on the Casa Loma Ballroom stage. Their unique wardrobe, zany antics, and musical presentations are always surefire crowd pleasers. (Photo from Pat Brannon.)

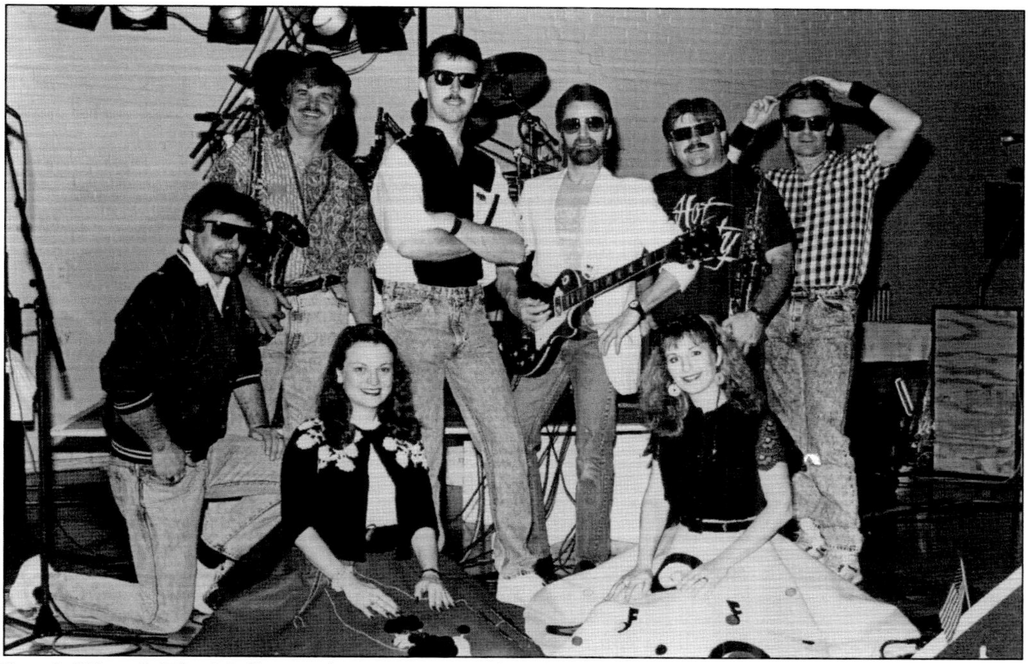

Butch Wax & The Hollywoods is a ten-piece band from St. Louis, Missouri. The band features two female singers and a horn section. They have been performing for nearly 20 years now. (Photo from Pat Brannon.)

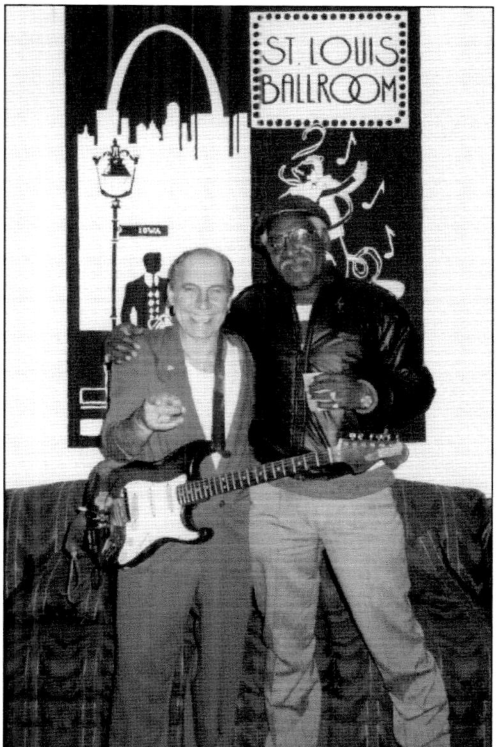

Casa Loma Ballroom veterans Jules Blattner and Marcel Strong pose in the lobby during one of their recent performances. (Photo from Pat Brannon.)

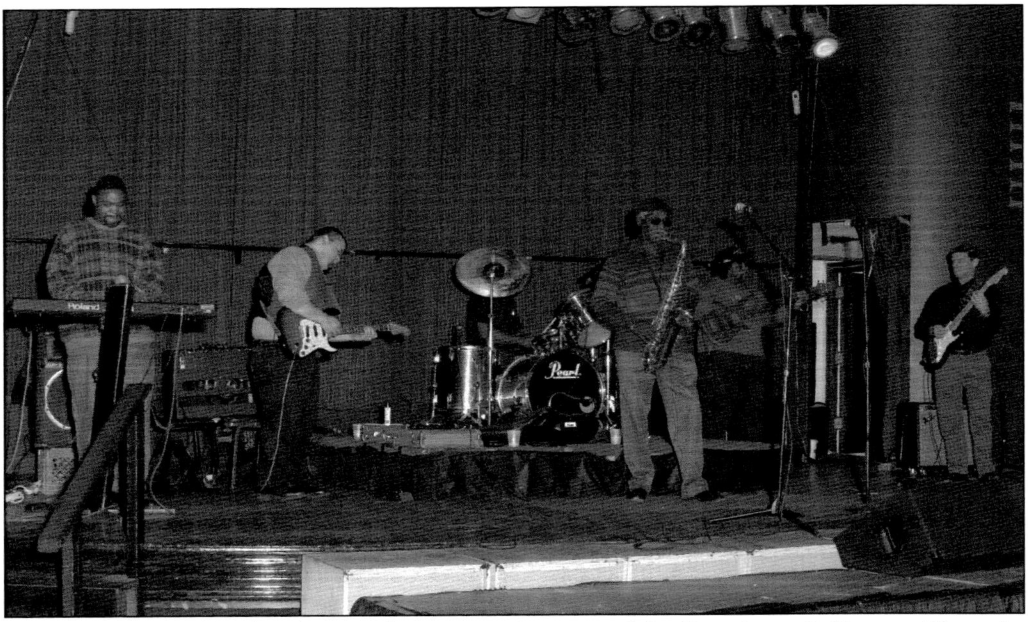

Marcel Strong and his band are performing on the stage of the Casa Loma Ballroom. (Photo by Larry Unger.)

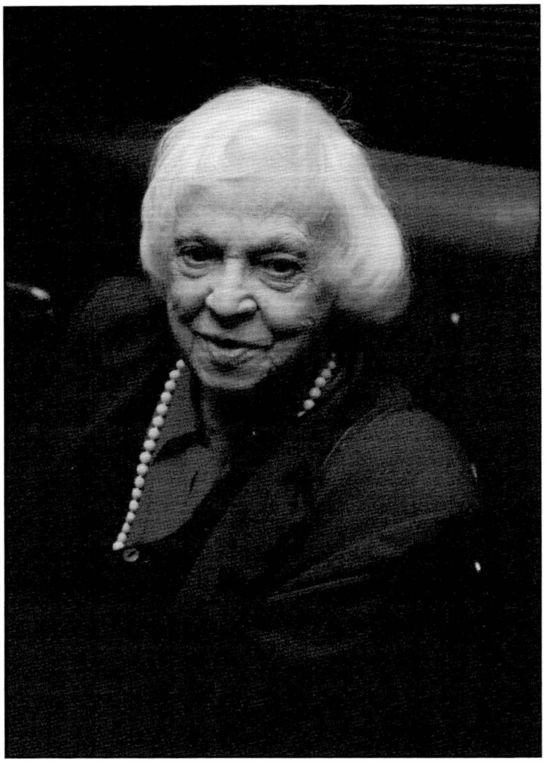

A familiar face to Casa Loma Ballroom patrons is that of Louise Brinkmann. She's been in the ticket box office for much of the time since 1967. (Photo from Terry Strahan.)

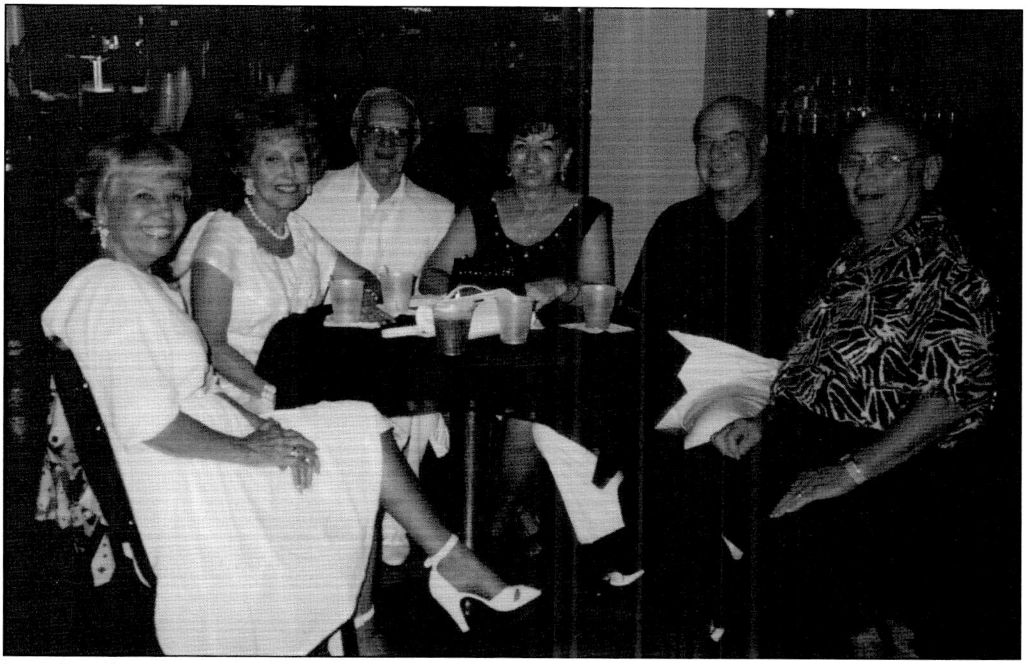

Regulars that you might see on any given Friday night are Roland and Madeline Lesie, and Rose and Al Bettale. The couple in the foreground is unidentified. (Photo from Pat Brannon.)

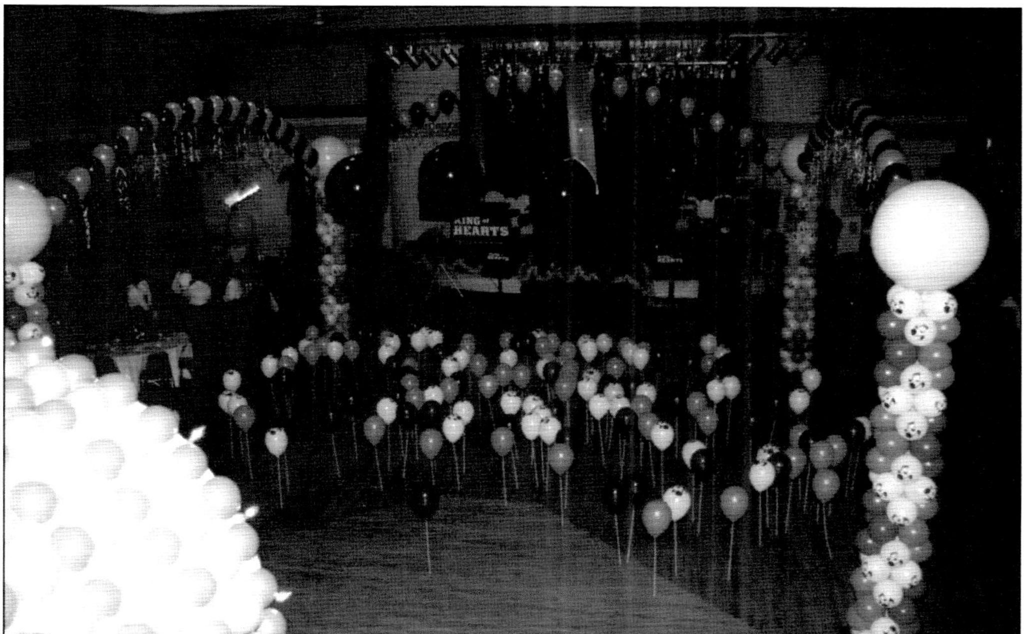

During a recent corporate event the Casa Loma Ballroom was turned into a balloon wonderland. The balloons on the dance floor "danced" alongside the patrons all night long. (Photo from Pat Brannon.)

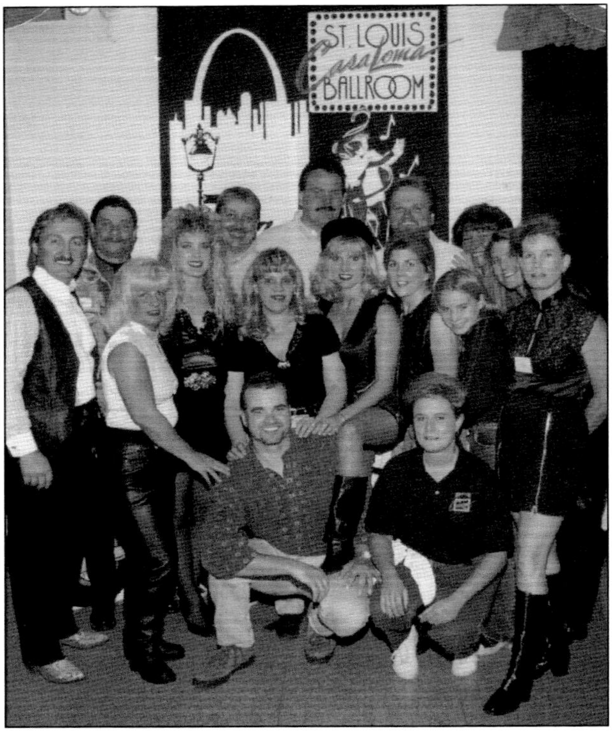

Some of the crew that made the Casa Loma Ballroom tick a few years back are pictured here: (kneeling) James and Collette; (second row) Anna Schlemmer, Theresa, Tammy, Teri Brannon, Lisa, Niece, and Debbie; (back row) Pat Brannon, Terry Strahan, Dave Brannon, Mike, Mel, Barb, and Trish. (Photo from Pat Brannon.)

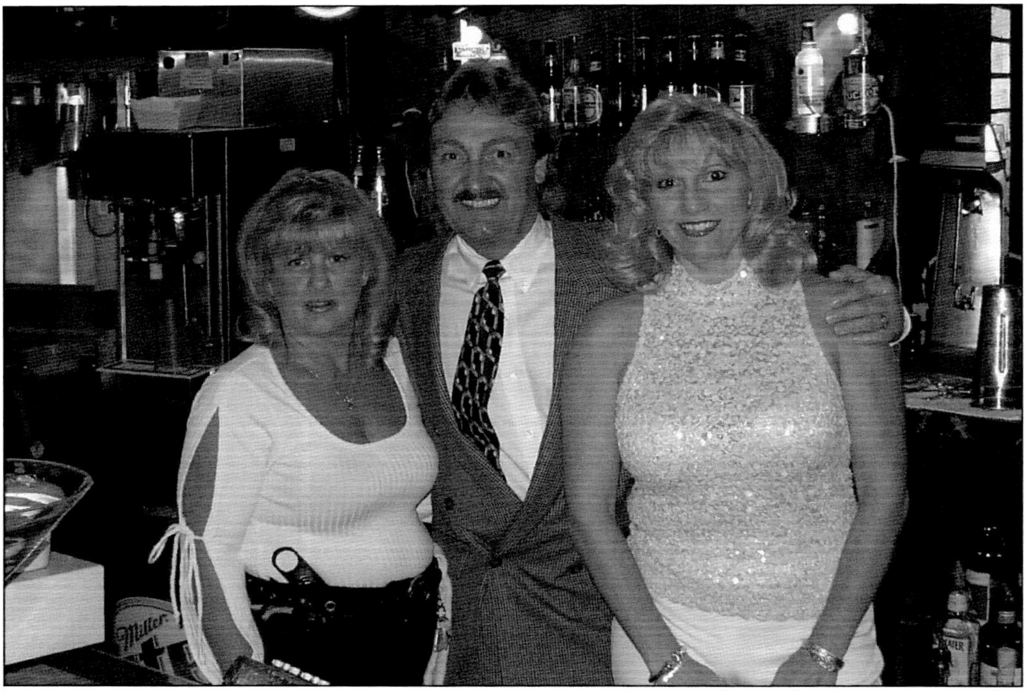

Today the Casa Loma Ballroom is owned and operated by Pat and Teri Brannon (on right). That's Anna Schlemmer on the left, the Casa Loma Bar Manager. (Photo by Dave Lossos.)

Acknowledgments

First I would like to single out two individuals who provided many of the remarkable photos that are used in this book. Dorothy Vincent graciously allowed me unfettered access to her marvelous collection of personally inscribed photographs of some of the many performers to appear at the Casa Loma Ballroom in the 30s, 40s, and 50s. What a joy it was to have such a treasure trove to choose from. A special thanks also goes to Carol Kawell Ellis, daughter of the original Casa Loma Ballroom proprietor. Carol invited me into her home and shared many items that she and her parents had collected over their years at the Casa Loma.

I owe Johnny (Ron Elz) Rabbitt a sincere thanks for not only the Foreword to this book, but for his enthusiastic endorsement of this project. I couldn't have asked for a better representative of St. Louis to be that actively involved in a book of this type.

Thanks to all those who contributed to this effort by supplying me with personal and extraordinary photos. This includes Melissa Peters, Jeanne Provaznik, Gerry and Marlene Strait, John and Marian Hargis, Al Williams, Dick and Bea Renna, Alfredo Ciolek, Virgil Vossmeyer, Gracia Carter, Pat Brannon, Becky Bruner, Nick Mucci, Dennis and Laura Reichert, Terry Strahan, Joe and Eva Renda, Larry Unger, Karen Kelly, Vince Golomski, Leona Sahaida/Ed Kotowski, and Kent Miller Photography.

A special thanks to Pat Brannon, the owner of the Casa Loma Ballroom, and his manager, Terry Strahan. In addition to all their assistance and the contribution of photos, they each infused in me their unbridled excitement during every phase of the book's development. They both made this a truly enjoyable endeavor.

And a final thanks to my wife Mary for her support and for helping me to edit this book

BIBLIOGRAPHY

(Arranged Chronologically)

St. Louis Post Dispatch—Fire story, Jan 20, 1940.
St. Louis Globe Democrat—Fire story, Jan 20, 1940.
St. Louis Post Dispatch—Arthur Murray free dance classes at Casa Loma, Dec. 11, 1949, photos.
St. Louis Globe Democrat—Entertainment—Plain Dance Music "Secret Weapon" of Popular Casa Loma, no by line, May 27, 1956, photo of Burian and Kawell.
St. Louis Post Dispatch—Community News—Casa Loma's Art Kawell Sells Ballroom. He Operated 32 Years by John R. Brophy, Aug 16, 1967, photos.
St. Louis Globe Democrat—Sunday Magazine—Time stands still at Casa Loma, by Andrew B. Wilson, Jan 17, 1971, photos
St. Louisan—Dancing in the Dark by John Terry, October, 1976, photos.
St. Louis Globe Democrat—Family, page 17A—The versatile accordionist by Bob Goddard, Dec. 2, 1976, photo. Article on Dick Renna.
South County Journal—The Casaloma Ballroom—Still a Slice of American by Lois Kendall, Apr. 4, 1979.
St. Louis—Arts & Leisure Dancin' by Kathleen Flood, April 1980, photos.
St. Louis Globe Democrat—Dance through time in ballrooms, bubbles by Ron Elz, Oct 16, 1984
St. Louis Globe Democrat—Casa Loma celebrates 50 years of swing by C. B. Adams. 1985. Photo of Ellen Reichert.
Meramec Journal—Puttin' On The Ritz by Patrick Martin, Nov 14, 1984
St. Louis Commerce—Where the waltz is still king by Janet Keller, Sept. 1985, photos
Ballroom Echoes by Lon A. Gault, 1989, Andrew Corbet Press
St. Louis Post Dispatch—Last Tango on Iowa by Ellen Futterman, July, 1990, photos.
St. Louis Post Dispatch—Front Page—Twist 'n' Shout by Tom Uhlenbrock, July 16, 1990, photos.
Riverfront Times—Dance Hall Days by Ron Ebest, July 18-24, 1990
St. Louis Post Dispatch—Entertainment—Last Dance: Ballroom's Memories Up For Bids by Joan Little, Aug 19, 1990, photos.
Riverfront Times—Shall We Dance? Oct 3-9, 1990
Senior Circuit—Big Bands Of St. Louis by Taffy Wilber, July 1998
South City Journals—15 Years of TV at the St. Louis Hop, hop, hop by Nancy K. Wenger, May 5, 2002
St. Louis Post Dispatch— Longtime host of popular television show "St. Louis Hop" dies by Lynn Venhaus, June 19, 2002
Riverfront Times—Dancing Fools by Ben Westhoff, Jan. 7, 2004
Southwest County Journal—And the band plays on at the Casa Loma Ballroom by Jim Fox, July 7, 2004

Index to *St. Louis Casa Loma Ballroom* is available online at
http://genealogyinstlouis.accessgenealogy.com/CasaLoma/